Netty in Action

NORMAN MAURER
MARVIN ALLEN WOLFTHAL

MANNING
SHELTER ISLAND

For online information and ordering of this and other Manning books, please visit www.manning.com. The publisher offers discounts on this book when ordered in quantity. For more information, please contact

Special Sales Department
Manning Publications Co.
20 Baldwin Road
PO Box 761
Shelter Island, NY 11964
Email: orders@manning.com

Manning Publications Co.
20 Baldwin Road
PO Box 761
Shelter Island, NY 11964

Development editors: Jeff Bleiel, Jennifer Stout
Technical development editor: Mark Elston
Copyeditor: Andy Carroll
Proofreader: Elizabeth Martin
Technical proofreaders: David Dossot, Neil Rutherford
Typesetter: Dennis Dalinnik
Cover designer: Marija Tudor

ISBN: 9781617291470

1 2 3 4 5 6 7 8 9 10 – EBM – 20 19 18 17 16 15

brief contents

contents

foreword

There was a day when people believed that web application servers would let us forget about how we write HTTP or RPC servers. Unfortunately, this daydream did not last long. The amount of load and the pace of the functional changes we are dealing with continue to increase beyond the extent that a traditional three-tier architecture can afford, and we are being forced to split our application into many pieces and distribute them into a large cluster of machines.

Running such a large distributed system leads to two interesting problems—the cost of operation and latency. How many machines could we save if we improved the performance of a single node by 30%, or by more than 100%? How could we achieve minimal latency when a query from a web browser triggers dozens of internal remote procedure calls across many different machines?

In *Netty in Action*, the first-ever book about the Netty project, Norman Maurer, one of the key contributors to Netty, gives you the definitive answers to such questions by showing you how to build a high-performance and low-latency network application in Netty. By the time you get to the end of this book, you'll be able to build every imaginable network application, from a lightweight HTTP server to a highly customized RPC server.

What's impressive about *Netty in Action* is not only that it is written by the key contributor who knows every single bit of Netty, but that it also contains case studies from several companies—Twitter, Facebook, and Firebase to name a few—that use Netty in their production systems. I'm confident that these case studies will inspire you by showing you how the companies that use them were able to unleash the power of their Netty-based applications.

You might be astonished to learn that Netty started as my personal project back in 2001 when I was an undergraduate student (http://t.motd.kr/ko/archives/1930), and that the project is still alive and kicking today, thanks to enthusiastic contributors like Norman, who spent many sleepless nights devoted to the project, (http://netty.io/community.html). I hope this book opens up another aspect of the project by inspiring its readers to contribute and continue to "open the future of network programming."

TRUSTIN LEE
FOUNDER OF NETTY

preface

Looking back, I still can't believe that I did it.

When I started to contribute to Netty in late 2011, I would never have imagined that I'd be writing a book about Netty and be one of the core developers of the Framework itself.

It all started when I got involved in 2009 with the Apache James project, a Java-based mail server developed under the Apache Software Foundation.

Apache James, like many applications, required a solid networking abstraction to build upon. While investigating the field of projects that provide networking abstractions, I stumbled upon Netty and immediately fell in love with it. As I became more familiar with Netty from a user's perspective, I started to turn my gaze on improvements and giving back to the community.

Despite my first contributions being of limited scope, it became obvious very quickly how beneficial making contributions and the related discussions with the community, especially with Trustin Lee, the founder of the project, were to my personal growth. This experience grabbed hold of me, and I enjoyed spending my free time becoming more engaged in the community. I found myself helping on mailing lists and joining discussions on the IRC channel. Working on Netty began as a hobby but it quickly evolved into a passion.

My passion for Netty eventually led to my employment at Red Hat. This was a dream come true, as Red Hat paid me to work on the project I had come to love. I eventually came to know Claus Ibsen who was working on Apache Camel at the time (and still does). Claus and I came to the realization that Netty had a solid user base and good JavaDocs, but it lacked a higher level of documentation. Claus is the author of *Camel in Action* (Manning Publications, 2010), and he turned me on to the idea of writing a similar book for Netty. I thought about the idea for a few weeks, and eventually I was sold. This is how *Netty in Action* got off the ground.

While writing *Netty in Action*, my involvement in the community continued to grow. I eventually became the second most active contributor (after Trustin Lee) with over 1,000 commits. I found myself speaking about Netty at conferences and technical meetups around the world. Eventually Netty opened another employment opportunity at Apple Inc. where I am currently employed as a Senior Software Engineer on the Cloud Infrastructure Engineering Team. I continue to work on Netty and make regular contributions back to the community, while helping to drive the project.

NORMAN MAURER
CLOUD INFRASTRUCTURE ENGINEERING, APPLE

My work as a Dell Services consultant at Harvard Pilgrim Health Care in Wellesley, MA, has focused primarily on creating reusable infrastructure components. Our goal is to expand the common code base in a way that not only benefits the software process in general, but also relieves application developers of responsibility for plumbing code that can be both pesky and mundane.

At one point it came to my attention that two related projects were working with a third-party claims-processing system that supported only direct TCP/IP communications. One of the projects needed to reimplement in Java a somewhat underdocumented legacy COBOL module built on the vendor's proprietary delimited format. This module was ultimately replaced by the other project, which would use a more recent XML-based interface to the same claims system (but still using straight sockets, no SOAP!).

This seemed to me an ideal opportunity to develop a common API, and an interesting one at that. I knew there would be stringent throughput and availability requirements and also that the design was still evolving. Clearly, the underlying networking code had to be completely decoupled from the business logic in order to support rapid cycles of iteration.

My research into high-performance networking frameworks for Java led me straight to Netty. (The hypothetical project you'll read about at the start of chapter 1 is pretty much taken from real life.) I soon became convinced that Netty's approach, using dynamically configurable encoders and decoders, was a perfect fit for our needs: both projects would employ the same API, deployed with the handlers needed for the specific data format in use. I became even more convinced when I discovered that the vendor's product was also based on Netty!

Just at that time I learned that the book *Netty in Action* I had been hoping for was actually in the works. I read the early drafts and soon contacted Norman with questions and a few suggestions. In the course of our conversations, we spoke often about the need to keep the end user's point of view in mind, and since I was currently involved in a live Netty project, I was happy to take on this role.

I hope that with this approach we've succeeded in meeting the needs of developers. If you have any suggestions on how we can make this book more useful, please contact us at https://forums.manning.com/forums/netty-in-action.

MARVIN ALLEN WOLFTHAL
DELL SERVICES

acknowledgments

The Manning team made the work on this book a joy, and they never complained when the joy went on a bit longer than anticipated. From Mike Stephens, who made it happen, and Jeff Bleiel, from whom we learned something new about collaboration, to Jennifer Stout, Andy Carroll, and Elizabeth Martin, who exhibited a level of calm patience that we can only envy, all have upheld standards of professionalism and quality that inspire authors to do their best.

Thanks to the people who helped to review this book, whether by reading the early release chapters and posting corrections in the Author Online forum, or by reviewing the manuscript at various stages during its development. You are part of it and should be proud. Without you, the book would not be the same. Special thanks to the following reviewers: Achim Friedland, Arash Bizhan Zadeh, Bruno Georges, Christian Bach, Daniel Beck, Declan Cox, Edward Ribeiro, Erik Onnen, Francis Marchi, Gregor Zurowski, Jian Jin, Jürgen Hoffmann, Maksym Prokhorenko, Nicola Grigoletti, Renato Felix, and Yestin Johnson. Also to our excellent technical proofreaders, David Dossot and Neil Rutherford.

We are very grateful to and would like to acknowledge Bruno de Carvalho, Sara Robinson, Greg Soltis, Erik Onnen, Andrew Cox, and Jeff Smick for contributing the case studies you will find in chapters 14 and 15.

Last but not least, thanks to all the people who support Netty and OpenSource in general; without you, the community, this project wouldn't have been possible. Through the community we have met new friends, talked at conferences all over the world, and grown both professionally and personally.

Norman Maurer

I'd like to thank my former coworker and friend Jürgen Hoffmann (aka Buddy). Jürgen helped me find my way into the OpenSource world and showed me what cool stuff can be built when you are brave enough to jump in. Without him there is a chance I would have never started programming and thus never found my true professional passion.

Another big thank you goes out to my friend Trustin Lee, founder of Netty, who helped and encouraged me to contribute to the Netty Project in the first place and who penned the foreword to our book. I'm honored to know you and to be able to call you a friend! I'm confident that by continuing to work together, Netty will stay awesome and be around for a long time!

Also I want to thank my coauthor Marvin Wolfthal. Despite Marvin joining the project late in its lifecycle, he helped to improve the overall structure and content by a considerable amount. Without him, the book would not have been possible in its current form. Which brings me to the Manning team itself, who were always helpful and gave the right guidance to make the idea of writing a book reality.

Thanks to my parents, Peter and Christa, for always supporting my visions and me.

Most importantly, thanks to my wife Jasmina and my kids Mia Soleil and Ben, for all the support they showed during the process of writing this book. Without you this book would not have been possible.

Marvin Wolfthal

First of all, I want to thank Norman Maurer, my coauthor, for both his fine work and his kindness. Though I came late to the project, I was made to feel as if I had been part of it from day one.

To my colleagues past and present at Dell Services and Harvard Pilgrim Health Care, I offer sincere thanks for their help and encouragement. They have created that rare environment where new ideas are not only expressed, but realized. To Deborah Norton, Larry Rapisarda, Dave Querusio, Vijay Bhatt, Craig Bogovich, and Sharath Krishna, special thanks for their support, and even more, their trust—I doubt many software developers have been granted the creative opportunities I have enjoyed in the past four years, including adding Netty to our toolkit.

But most of all, thanks to my beloved wife, Katherine, who never lets me forget the things that really matter.

about this book

Netty is a Java framework for the rapid development of high-performance network applications. It encapsulates the complexities of network programming and makes the most recent advances in networking and web technologies accessible to a broader range of developers than ever before.

Netty is more than a collection of interfaces and classes; it also defines an architectural model and a rich set of design patterns. But until now, the lack of a comprehensive and systematic user's guide has been an obstacle to getting started with Netty, a situation *Netty in Action* aims to remedy. Beyond explaining the details of the framework components and APIs, this book will show how Netty can help you to write more efficient, reusable, and maintainable code.

Who should read this book?

This book assumes you are comfortable with intermediate Java topics such as generics and multithreading. Experience with advanced network programming is not required, but familiarity with the basic Java networking APIs will prove very helpful.

Netty uses Apache Maven as its build management tool. If you have not used Maven, the appendix will provide the information you need to run the book's sample code. You'll also be able to reuse the sample Maven configurations as starting points for your own Netty-based projects.

Roadmap

Netty in Action has four parts and an appendix.

Part 1: Netty concepts and architecture

Part 1 is a detailed guide to the framework, covering its design, components, and programming interfaces.

Chapter 1 begins with a brief overview of the blocking and non-blocking network APIs and the corresponding JDK interfaces. We introduce Netty as a toolkit for building highly scalable, asynchronous and event-driven networking applications. We take a first look at the basic building blocks of the framework: channels, callbacks, futures, events, and handlers.

Chapter 2 explains how to configure your system for building and running with the book's sample code. We test it out with a simple application, a server that echoes the messages it receives from connected clients. We introduce bootstrapping—assembling and configuring all the components of an application at runtime.

Chapter 3 begins with a discussion of the technical and architectural aspects of Netty. The core components of the framework are introduced: `Channel`, `EventLoop`, `ChannelHandler`, and `ChannelPipeline`. The chapter concludes with an explanation of the differences between bootstrapping servers and clients.

Chapter 4 discusses network transports and contrasts the use of blocking and non-blocking transports with the JDK APIs and with Netty. We study the interface hierarchy underlying Netty's transport API and the transport types they support.

Chapter 5 is devoted to the framework's data handling API—`ByteBuf`, Netty's byte container. We describe its advantages over the JDK's `ByteBuffer`, and the ways in which the memory used by a `ByteBuf` can be allocated and accessed. We show how to manage memory resources using reference counting.

Chapter 6 focuses on the core components `ChannelHandler` and `ChannelPipeline`, which are responsible for dispatching application processing logic and moving data and events through the network layer. Additional topics include the role of `ChannelHandlerContext` in implementing advanced use cases and the sharing of `ChannelHandlers` among multiple `ChannelPipelines`. The chapter concludes with an illustration of handling exceptions triggered by inbound and outbound events.

Chapter 7 provides a general overview of threading models and covers Netty's threading model in detail. We examine `interface EventLoop`, which is the principal component of Netty's concurrency API, and explain its relationship with threads and `Channels`. This information is essential for understanding how Netty implements asynchronous, event-driven networking. We show how to perform task scheduling using `EventLoop`.

Chapter 8 explores bootstrapping in depth, starting with the `Bootstrap` class hierarchy. We revisit the basic use cases as well as some special ones, such as bootstrapping a client connection within a server application, bootstrapping datagram channels, and adding multiple channels during the bootstrapping phase. The chapter concludes with a discussion of how to shut down an application gracefully and release all resources in an orderly fashion.

Chapter 9 is about unit testing `ChannelHandlers`, for which Netty provides a special `Channel` implementation, `EmbeddedChannel`. The examples show how to use this class with JUnit to test both inbound and outbound handler implementations.

Part 2: Codecs

Data conversion is one of the most common operations in network programming. Part 2 describes the rich set of tools Netty provides to simplify this task.

Chapter 10 begins by explaining decoders and encoders, which transform sequences of bytes from one format to another. A ubiquitous example is converting an unstructured byte stream to and from a protocol-specific layout. A codec, then, is a component that combines both an encoder and a decoder in order to handle conversions in both directions. We provide several examples to show how easy it is to create custom decoders and encoders with Netty's codec framework classes.

Chapter 11 examines the codecs and `ChannelHandlers` Netty provides for a variety of use cases. These classes include ready-to-use codecs for protocols such as SSL/TLS, HTTP/HTTPS, WebSocket, and SPDY, and decoders that can be extended to handle almost any delimited, variable length or fixed-length protocol. The chapter concludes with a look at framework components for writing large volumes of data and for serialization.

Part 3: Network protocols

Part 3 elaborates on several network protocols that have been touched on briefly earlier in the book. We'll see once again how Netty makes it easy to adopt complex APIs in your applications without having to be concerned with their internal complexities.

Chapter 12 shows how to use the WebSocket protocol to implement bidirectional communications between a web server and client. The example application is a chat room server that allows all connected users to communicate with one another in real time.

Chapter 13 illustrates Netty's support for connectionless protocols with a server and client that utilize the broadcast capabilities of the User Datagram Protocol (UDP). As in the previous examples, we employ a set of protocol-specific support classes: `DatagramPacket` and `NioDatagramChannel`.

Part 4: Case studies

Part 4 presents five case studies submitted by well-known companies that have used Netty to implement mission-critical systems. These examples illustrate not only real-world usages of the framework components we have discussed throughout the book, but also the application of Netty's design and architectural principles to building highly scalable and extensible applications.

Chapter 14 has case studies submitted by Droplr, Firebase, and Urban Airship.

Chapter 15 has case studies submitted by Facebook and Twitter.

Appendix: Introduction to Maven

The primary goal of the appendix is to provide a basic introduction to Apache Maven so that you can compile and run the book's sample code listings and extend them to create your own projects as you begin to work with Netty.

The following topics are presented:

- The primary goals and uses of Maven
- Installing and configuring Maven
- Basic Maven concepts: the POM file, artifacts, coordinates, dependencies, plugins, and repositories
- Example Maven configurations, POM inheritance, and aggregation
- Maven's command-line syntax

Code conventions and downloads

This book provides copious examples that show how you can make use of each of the topics covered. Source code in listings or in text appears in a `fixed-width font like this` to separate it from ordinary text. In addition, class and method names, object properties, and other code-related terms and content in text are presented using `fixed-width font`.

Occasionally, code is italicized, as in *`reference`*`.dump()`. In this case *`reference`* should not be entered literally but replaced with the content that is required.

The book's source code is available from the publisher's website at www.manning.com/books/netty-in-action and at GitHub: https://github.com/normanmaurer/netty-in-action. It is structured as a multimodule Maven project, with a top-level POM and modules corresponding to the book's chapters.

About the authors

Norman Maurer is one of the core developers of Netty, a member of the Apache Software Foundation, and a contributor to many OpenSource Projects over the past years. He's a Senior Software Engineer for Apple, where he works on Netty and other network-related projects as part of the iCloud Team.

Marvin Wolfthal has been active in many areas of software development as a developer, architect, lecturer, and author. He has been working with Java since its earliest days and assisted Sun Microsystems in developing its first programs dedicated to promoting distributed object technologies. As part of these efforts he wrote the first cross-language programming courses using C++, Java, and CORBA for Sun Education. Since then his primary focus has been middleware design and development, primarily for the financial services industry. Currently a consultant with Dell Services, he is engaged in extending methodologies that have emerged from the Java world to other areas of enterprise computing; for example, applying the practices of Continuous Integration to database development. Marvin is also a pianist and composer whose work is published by Universal Edition, Vienna. He and his wife Katherine live in Weston, MA, with their three feline companions Fritz, Willy, and Robbie.

Author Online

Purchase of *Netty in Action* includes free access to a private web forum run by Manning Publications where you can make comments about the book, ask technical questions, and receive help from the authors and from other users. To access the forum and subscribe to it, point your web browser to www.manning.com/books/netty-in-action. This page provides information on how to get on the forum once you are registered, what kind of help is available, and the rules of conduct on the forum. It also provides links to the source code for the examples in the book, errata, and other downloads.

Manning's commitment to our readers is to provide a venue where a meaningful dialog between individual readers and between readers and the authors can take place. It is not a commitment to any specific amount of participation on the part of the authors, whose contribution to the AO remains voluntary (and unpaid). We suggest you try asking the authors some challenging questions lest their interest stray!

The Author Online forum and the archives of previous discussions will be accessible from the publisher's website as long as the book is in print.

about the cover illustration

The figure on the cover of *Netty in Action* is captioned "A Resident of the Luxembourg Quarter." The illustration is taken from a nineteenth-century collection of works by many artists, edited by Louis Curmer and published in Paris in 1841. The title of the collection is *Les Français peints par eux-mêmes,* which translates as *The French People Painted by Themselves.* Each illustration is finely drawn and colored by hand and the rich variety of drawings in the collection reminds us vividly of how culturally apart the world's regions, towns, villages, and neighborhoods were just 200 years ago. Isolated from each other, people spoke different dialects and languages. In the streets or in the countryside, it was easy to identify where they lived and what their trade or station in life was just by their dress.

Dress codes have changed since then and the diversity by region, so rich at the time, has faded away. It is now hard to tell apart the inhabitants of different continents, let alone different towns or regions. Perhaps we have traded cultural diversity for a more varied personal life—certainly for a more varied and fast-paced technological life.

At a time when it is hard to tell one computer book from another, Manning celebrates the inventiveness and initiative of the computer business with book covers based on the rich diversity of regional life of two centuries ago, brought back to life by pictures from collections such as this one.

Part 1

Netty concepts and architecture

Netty is an advanced framework for creating high-performance networking applications. In part 1 we'll explore its capabilities in depth and demonstrate three main points:

- You don't have to be a networking expert to build applications with Netty.
- Using Netty is much easier than using the underlying Java APIs directly.
- Netty promotes good design practices, such as keeping your application logic decoupled from the network layer.

In chapter 1, we'll begin with a summary of the evolution of Java networking. After we've reviewed the basic concepts of asynchronous communications and event-driven processing we'll take a first look at Netty's core components. You'll be ready to build your first Netty application in chapter 2! In chapter 3 you'll begin your detailed exploration of Netty, from its core network protocols (chapter 4) and data-handling layers (chapters 5–6) to its concurrency model (chapter 7).

We'll conclude part 1 by putting all the pieces together, and you'll see how to configure the components of a Netty-based application to work together at runtime (chapter 8) and finally, how Netty helps you to test your applications (chapter 9).

1 Netty—asynchronous and event-driven

This chapter covers

- Networking in Java
- Introducing Netty
- Netty's core components

Suppose you're just starting on a new mission-critical application for a large, important company. In the first meeting you learn that the system must scale up to 150,000 concurrent users with no loss of performance. All eyes are on you. What do you say?

If you can say with confidence, "Sure, no problem," then hats off to you. But most of us would probably take a more cautious position, like: "Sounds doable." Then, as soon as we could get to a computer, we'd search for "high performance Java networking."

If you run this search today, among the first results you'll see this:

> ***Netty: Home***
>
> netty.io/
>
> Netty is an asynchronous event-driven **network** application framework for rapid development of maintainable **high performance** protocol servers & clients.

If you discovered Netty this way, as many have, your next steps were probably to browse the site, download the code, peruse the Javadocs and a few blogs, and start hacking. If you already had solid network programming experience, you probably made good progress; otherwise, perhaps not.

Why? High-performance systems like the one in our example require more than first-class coding skills; they demand expertise in several complex areas: networking, multithreading, and concurrency. Netty captures this domain knowledge in a form that can be used even by networking neophytes. But up to now, the lack of a comprehensive guide has made the learning process far more difficult than need be—hence this book.

Our primary goal in writing it has been to make Netty accessible to the broadest possible range of developers. This includes many who have innovative content or services to offer but neither the time nor inclination to become networking specialists. If this applies to you, we believe you'll be pleasantly surprised at how quickly you'll be ready to create your first Netty application. At the other end of the spectrum, we aim to support advanced practitioners who are seeking tools for creating their own network protocols.

Netty does indeed provide an extremely rich networking toolkit, and we'll spend most of our time exploring its capabilities. But Netty is ultimately a *framework,* and its architectural approach and design principles are every bit as important as its technical content. Accordingly, we'll be talking about points such as

- Separation of concerns (decoupling business and network logic)
- Modularity and reusability
- Testability as a first-order requirement

In this first chapter, we'll begin with background on high-performance networking, particularly its implementation in the Java Development Kit (JDK). With this context in place, we'll introduce Netty, its core concepts, and building blocks. By the end of the chapter, you'll be ready to tackle your first Netty-based client and server.

1.1 Networking in Java

Developers who started out in the early days of networking spent a lot of time learning the intricacies of the C language socket libraries and dealing with their quirks on different operating systems. The earliest versions of Java (1995–2002) introduced enough of an object-oriented façade to hide some of the thornier details, but creating a complex client/server protocol still required a lot of boilerplate code (and a fair amount of peeking under the hood to get it all working smoothly).

Those first Java APIs (`java.net`) supported only the so-called blocking functions provided by the native system socket libraries. The following listing shows an unadorned example of server code using these calls.

Listing 1.1 Blocking I/O example

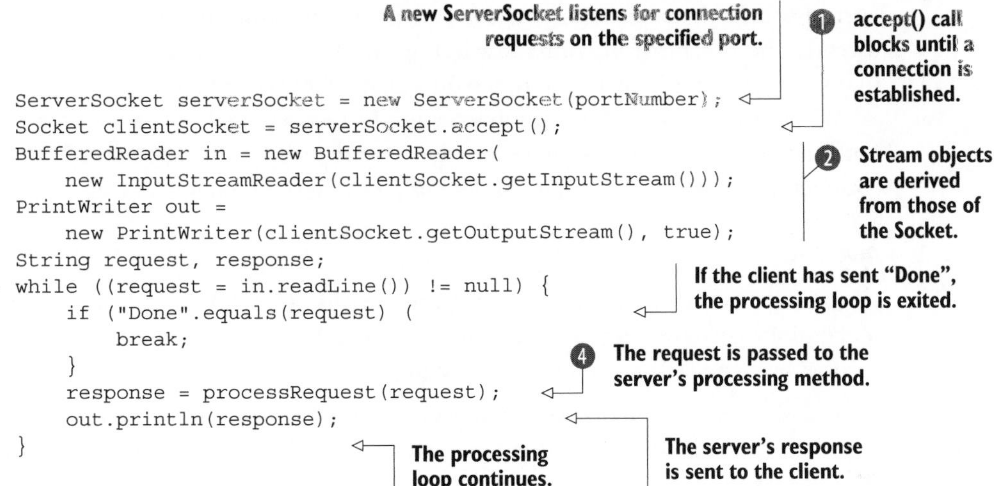
A new ServerSocket listens for connection requests on the specified port.
1 accept() call blocks until a connection is established.
2 Stream objects are derived from those of the Socket.
3 Processing loop begins.
If the client has sent "Done", the processing loop is exited.
4 The request is passed to the server's processing method.
The server's response is sent to the client.
The processing loop continues.

```
ServerSocket serverSocket = new ServerSocket(portNumber);
Socket clientSocket = serverSocket.accept();
BufferedReader in = new BufferedReader(
    new InputStreamReader(clientSocket.getInputStream()));
PrintWriter out =
    new PrintWriter(clientSocket.getOutputStream(), true);
String request, response;
while ((request = in.readLine()) != null) {
    if ("Done".equals(request) (
        break;
    }
    response = processRequest(request);
    out.println(response);
}
```

The previous listing implements one of the basic `Socket` API patterns. Here are the most important points:

- `accept()` blocks until a connection is established on the `ServerSocket` ❶, then returns a new `Socket` for communication between the client and the server. The `ServerSocket` then resumes listening for incoming connections.
- A `BufferedReader` and a `PrintWriter` are derived from the `Socket`'s input and output streams ❷. The former reads text from a character input stream, the latter prints formatted representations of objects to a text output stream.
- `readLine()` blocks until a string terminated by a linefeed or carriage return is read in ❸.
- The client's request is processed ❹.

This code will handle only one connection at a time. To manage multiple, concurrent clients, you need to allocate a new `Thread` for each new client `Socket`, as shown in figure 1.1.

Let's consider the implications of such an approach. First, at any point many threads could be dormant, just waiting for input or output data to appear on the line. This is

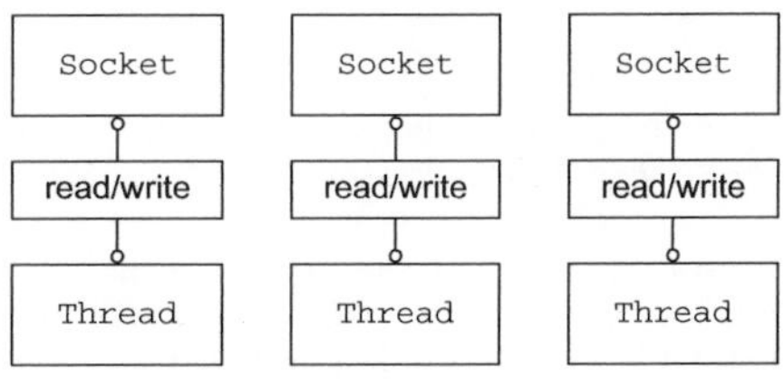
Socket
Socket
Socket
read/write
read/write
read/write
Thread
Thread
Thread

Figure 1.1 Multiple connections using blocking I/O

likely to be a waste of resources. Second, each thread requires an allocation of stack memory whose default size ranges from 64 KB to 1 MB, depending on the OS. Third, even if a Java virtual machine (JVM) can physically support a very large number of threads, the overhead of context-switching will begin to be troublesome long before that limit is reached, say by the time you reach 10,000 connections.

While this approach to concurrency might be acceptable for a small-to-moderate number of clients, the resources needed to support 100,000 or more simultaneous connections make it far from ideal. Fortunately, there is an alternative.

1.1.1 Java NIO

In addition to the blocking system calls underlying the code in listing 1.1, the native socket libraries have long included *non-blocking* calls, which provide considerably more control over the utilization of network resources.

- Using `setsockopt()` you can configure `sockets` so that read/write calls will return immediately if there is no data; that is, if a blocking call would have blocked.[1]
- You can register a set of non-blocking sockets using the system's event notification API[2] to determine whether any of them have data ready for reading or writing.

Java support for non-blocking I/O was introduced in 2002, with the JDK 1.4 package `java.nio`.

> **New or non-blocking?**
> NIO was originally an acronym for New Input/Output, but the Java API has been around long enough that it is no longer new. Most users now think of NIO as signifying non-blocking I/O, whereas blocking I/O is OIO or old input/output. You may also encounter references to plain I/O.

1.1.2 Selectors

Figure 1.2 shows a non-blocking design that virtually eliminates the drawbacks described in the previous section.

The class `java.nio.channels.Selector` is the linchpin of Java's non-blocking I/O implementation. It uses the event notification API to indicate which, among a set of non-blocking `sockets`, are ready for I/O. Because any read or write operation can be

---

1 W. Richard Stevens, "4.3BSD returned EWOULDBLOCK if an operation on a non-blocking descriptor could not complete without blocking," *Advanced Programming in the UNIX Environment* (Addison-Wesley, 1992), p. 364.

2 Also referred to as I/O multiplexing, this interface has evolved over the years from the original `select()` and `poll()` calls to more performant implementations. See Sangjin Han's "Scalable Event Multiplexing: epoll vs. kqueue" article, www.eecs.berkeley.edu/~sangjin/2012/12/21/epoll-vs-kqueue.html.

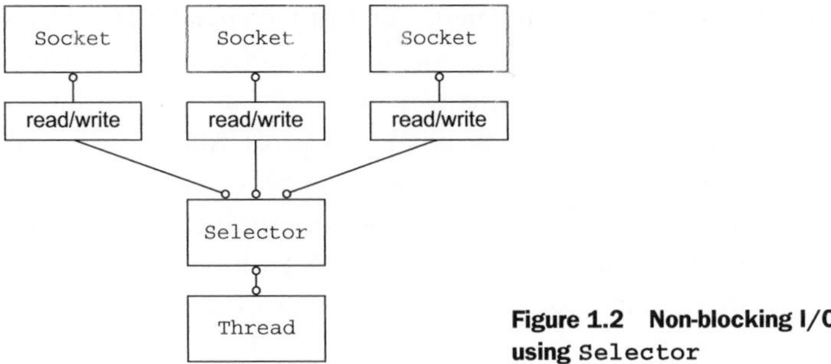

Figure 1.2 Non-blocking I/O using `Selector`

checked at any time for its completion status, a *single* thread, as shown in figure 1.2, can handle *multiple* concurrent connections.

Overall, this model provides much better resource management than the blocking I/O model:

- Many connections can be handled with fewer threads, and thus with far less overhead due to memory management and context-switching.
- Threads can be retargeted to other tasks when there is no I/O to handle.

Although many applications have been built using the Java NIO API directly, doing so correctly and safely is far from trivial. In particular, processing and dispatching I/O reliably and efficiently under heavy load is a cumbersome and error-prone task best left to a high-performance networking expert—Netty.

1.2 Introducing Netty

Not so long ago the scenario we presented at the outset—supporting thousands upon thousands of concurrent clients—would have been judged impossible. Today, as system users we take this capability for granted, and as developers we expect the bar to move even higher. We know there will always be demands for greater throughput and scalability—to be delivered at lower cost.

Don't underestimate the importance of that last point. We've learned from long and painful experience that the direct use of low-level APIs exposes complexity and introduces a critical dependency on skills that tend to be in short supply. Hence, a fundamental concept of object orientation: hide the complexity of underlying implementations behind simpler abstractions.

This principle has stimulated the development of numerous frameworks that encapsulate solutions to common programming tasks, many of them germane to distributed systems development. It's probably safe to assert that all professional Java developers are familiar with at least one of these.[3] For many of us they have

[3] Spring is probably the best known and is actually an entire ecosystem of application frameworks addressing object creation, batch processing, database programming, and so on.

become indispensable, enabling us to meet both our technical requirements and our schedules.

In the networking domain, Netty is the preeminent framework for Java.[4] Harnessing the power of Java's advanced APIs behind an easy-to-use API, Netty leaves you free to focus on what really interests you—the unique value of your application.

Before we begin our first close look at Netty, please examine the key features summarized in table 1.1. Some are technical, and others are more architectural or philosophical. We'll revisit them more than once in the course of this book.

Table 1.1 Netty feature summary

Category	Netty features
Design	Unified API for multiple transport types, both blocking and non-blocking. Simple but powerful threading model. True connectionless datagram socket support. Chaining of logic components to support reuse.
Ease of use	Extensive Javadoc and large example set. No required dependencies beyond JDK 1.6+. (Some optional features may require Java 1.7+ and/or additional dependencies.)
Performance	Better throughput and lower latency than core Java APIs. Reduced resource consumption thanks to pooling and reuse. Minimal memory copying.
Robustness	No `OutOfMemoryError` due to slow, fast, or overloaded connection. Eliminates unfair read/write ratio typical of NIO applications in high-speed networks.
Security	Complete SSL/TLS and StartTLS support. Usable in restricted environments such as Applet or OSGI.
Community-driven	Release early and often.

1.2.1 Who uses Netty?

Netty has a vibrant and growing user community that includes large companies such as Apple, Twitter, Facebook, Google, Square, and Instagram, as well as popular open source projects such as Infinispan, HornetQ, Vert.x, Apache Cassandra, and Elasticsearch, all of which have employed its powerful network abstractions in their core code.[5] Among startups, Firebase and Urban Airship are using Netty, the former for long-lived HTTP connections and the latter for all kinds of push notifications.

Whenever you use Twitter, you are using Finagle,[6] their Netty-based framework for inter-system communication. Facebook uses Netty in Nifty, their Apache Thrift service.

---

[4] Netty was awarded the Duke's Choice Award in 2011. See www.java.net/dukeschoice/2011.

[5] For a full list of known adopters see http://netty.io/wiki/adopters.html.

[6] For information on Finagle see https://twitter.github.io/finagle/.

Scalability and performance are critical concerns for both companies, and both are regular contributors to Netty.[7]

In turn, Netty has benefited from these projects, enhancing both its scope and flexibility through implementations of protocols such as FTP, SMTP, HTTP, and WebSocket, as well as others, both binary and text-based.

1.2.2 Asynchronous and event-driven

We'll be using the word asynchronous a great deal, so this is a good time to clarify the context. Asynchronous, that is, *un-synchronized*, events are certainly familiar. Consider email: you may or may not get a response to a message you have sent, or you may receive an unexpected message even while sending one. Asynchronous events can also have an *ordered* relationship. You generally get an answer to a question only *after* you have asked it, and you may be able to do something else while you are waiting for it.

In everyday life, asynchrony just happens, so you may not think about it much. But getting a computer program to work the same way presents some very special problems. In essence, a system that is both asynchronous *and* event-driven exhibits a particular and, to us, extremely valuable kind of behavior: it can respond to events occurring at any time and in any order.

This capability is critical for achieving the highest levels of *scalability*, defined as "the ability of a system, network, or process to handle a growing amount of work in a capable manner or its ability to be enlarged to accommodate that growth."[8]

What is the connection between asynchrony and scalability?

- Non-blocking network calls free us from having to wait for the completion of an operation. Fully asynchronous I/O builds on this feature and carries it a step further: an asynchronous method returns immediately and notifies the user when it is complete, directly or at a later time.
- Selectors allow us to monitor many connections for events with many fewer threads.

Putting these elements together, with non-blocking I/O we can handle very large numbers of events much more rapidly and economically than would be possible with blocking I/O. From the point of view of networking, this is key to the kind of systems we want to build, and as you'll see, it is also key to Netty's design from the ground up.

In the next section we'll take a first look at Netty's core components. For now, think of them as domain objects rather than concrete Java classes. Over time, we'll see how they collaborate to provide notification about events that occur on the network and make them available for processing.

---

[7] Chapters 15 and 16 present case studies describing how some of the companies mentioned here use Netty to solve real-world problems.

[8] André B. Bondi, "Characteristics of scalability and their impact on performance," *Proceedings of the second international workshop on Software and performance—WOSP '00* (2000), p. 195.

1.3 Netty's core components

In this section we'll discuss Netty's primary building blocks:

- `Channels`
- Callbacks
- `Futures`
- Events and handlers

These building blocks represent different types of constructs: resources, logic, and notifications. Your applications will use them to access the network and the data that flows through it.

For each component, we'll provide a basic definition and, where appropriate, a simple code example that illustrates its use.

1.3.1 Channels

A `Channel` is a basic construct of Java NIO. It represents

> an open connection to an entity such as a hardware device, a file, a network socket, or a program component that is capable of performing one or more distinct I/O operations, for example reading or writing.[9]

For now, think of a `Channel` as a vehicle for incoming (inbound) and outgoing (outbound) data. As such, it can be open or closed, connected or disconnected.

1.3.2 Callbacks

A *callback* is simply a method, a reference to which has been provided to another method. This enables the latter to call the former at an appropriate time. Callbacks are used in a broad range of programming situations and represent one of the most common ways to notify an interested party that an operation has completed.

Netty uses callbacks internally when handling events; when a callback is triggered the event can be handled by an implementation of `interface ChannelHandler`. The next listing shows an example: when a new connection has been established the `ChannelHandler` callback `channelActive()` will be called and will print a message.

Listing 1.2 `ChannelHandler` triggered by a callback

```
public class ConnectHandler extends ChannelInboundHandlerAdapter {
    @Override
    public void channelActive(ChannelHandlerContext ctx)
        throws Exception {
        System.out.println(
            "Client " + ctx.channel().remoteAddress() + " connected");
    }
}
```

channelActive(ChannelHandlerContext) is called when a new connection is established.

[9] Java Platform, Standard Edition 8 API Specification, java.nio.channels, Interface Channel, http://docs.oracle.com/javase/8/docs/api/java/nio/channels/package-summary.html.

1.3.3 Futures

A Future provides another way to notify an application when an operation has completed. This object acts as a placeholder for the result of an asynchronous operation; it will complete at some point in the future and provide access to the result.

The JDK ships with `interface java.util.concurrent.Future`, but the provided implementations allow you only to check manually whether the operation has completed or to block until it does. This is quite cumbersome, so Netty provides its own implementation, `ChannelFuture`, for use when an asynchronous operation is executed.

`ChannelFuture` provides additional methods that allow us to register one or more `ChannelFutureListener` instances. The listener's callback method, `operationComplete()`, is called when the operation has completed. The listener can then determine whether the operation completed successfully or with an error. If the latter, we can retrieve the `Throwable` that was produced. In short, the notification mechanism provided by the `ChannelFutureListener` eliminates the need for manually checking operation completion.

Each of Netty's outbound I/O operations returns a `ChannelFuture`; that is, none of them block. As we said earlier, Netty is asynchronous and event-driven from the ground up.

Listing 1.3 shows that a `ChannelFuture` is returned as part of an I/O operation. Here, `connect()` will return directly without blocking and the call will complete in the background. When this will happen may depend on several factors, but this concern is abstracted away from the code. Because the thread is not blocked waiting for the operation to complete, it can do other work in the meantime, thus using resources more efficiently.

Listing 1.3 Asynchronous connect

```
Channel channel = ...;
// Does not block
ChannelFuture future = channel.connect(
    new InetSocketAddress("192.168.0.1", 25));
```

Asynchronous connection to a remote peer

Listing 1.4 shows how to utilize the `ChannelFutureListener`. First you connect to a remote peer. Then you register a new `ChannelFutureListener` with the `ChannelFuture` returned by the `connect()` call. When the listener is notified that the connection is established, you check the status ❶. If the operation is successful, you write data to the `Channel`. Otherwise you retrieve the `Throwable` from the `ChannelFuture`.

Listing 1.4 Callback in action

```
Channel channel = ...;
// Does not block
ChannelFuture future = channel.connect(
    new InetSocketAddress("192.168.0.1", 25));
future.addListener(new ChannelFutureListener() {
```

Connects asynchronously to a remote peer.

Registers a ChannelFutureListener to be notified once the operation completes.

```
    @Override
    public void operationComplete(ChannelFuture future) {
        if (future.isSuccess()){
            ByteBuf buffer = Unpooled.copiedBuffer(
                "Hello",Charset.defaultCharset());
            ChannelFuture wf = future.channel()
                .writeAndFlush(buffer);
            ....
        } else {
            Throwable cause = future.cause();
            cause.printStackTrace();
        }
    }
});
```

Checks the status of the operation. ❶

If the operation is successful, creates a ByteBuf to hold the data.

Sends the data asynchronously to the remote peer. Returns a ChannelFuture.

If an error occurred, accesses the Throwable that describes the cause.

Note that error handling is entirely up to you, subject, of course, to any constraints imposed by the specific error at hand. For example, in case of a connection failure, you could try to reconnect or establish a connection to another remote peer.

If you're thinking that a `ChannelFutureListener` is a more elaborate version of a callback, you're correct. In fact, callbacks and `Futures` are complementary mechanisms; in combination they make up one of the key building blocks of Netty itself.

1.3.4 Events and handlers

Netty uses distinct events to notify us about changes of state or the status of operations. This allows us to trigger the appropriate action based on the event that has occurred. Such actions might include

- Logging
- Data transformation
- Flow-control
- Application logic

Netty is a networking framework, so events are categorized by their relevance to inbound or outbound data flow. Events that may be triggered by inbound data or an associated change of state include

- Active or inactive connections
- Data reads
- User events
- Error events

An outbound event is the result of an operation that will trigger an action in the future, which may be

- Opening or closing a connection to a remote peer
- Writing or flushing data to a socket

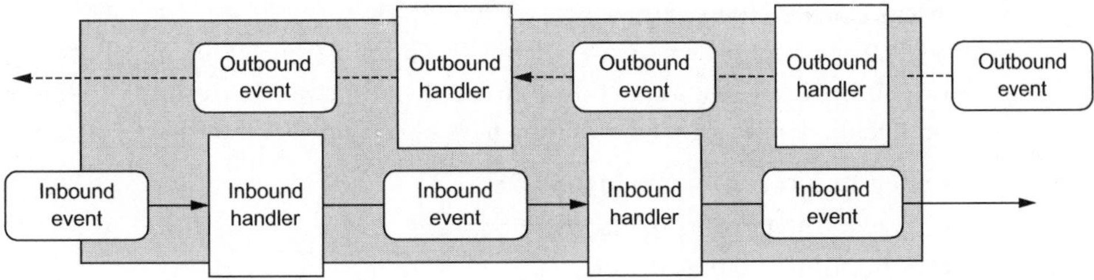

Figure 1.3 Inbound and outbound events flowing through a chain of `ChannelHandlers`

Every event can be dispatched to a user-implemented method of a handler class. This is a good example of an event-driven paradigm translating directly into application building blocks. Figure 1.3 shows how an event can be handled by a chain of such event handlers.

Netty's `ChannelHandler` provides the basic abstraction for handlers like the ones shown in figure 1.3. We'll have a lot more to say about `ChannelHandler` in due course, but for now you can think of each handler instance as a kind of callback to be executed in response to a specific event.

Netty provides an extensive set of predefined handlers that you can use out of the box, including handlers for protocols such as HTTP and SSL/TLS. Internally, `ChannelHandlers` use events and futures themselves, making them consumers of the same abstractions your applications will employ.

1.3.5 Putting it all together

In this chapter you've been introduced to Netty's approach to high-performance networking and to some of the primary components of its implementation. Let's assemble a big-picture view of what we've discussed.

FUTURES, CALLBACKS, AND HANDLERS

Netty's asynchronous programming model is built on the concepts of `Futures` and callbacks, with the dispatching of events to handler methods happening at a deeper level. Taken together, these elements provide a processing environment that allows the logic of your application to evolve independently of any concerns with network operations. This is a key goal of Netty's design approach.

Intercepting operations and transforming inbound or outbound data on the fly requires only that you provide callbacks or utilize the `Futures` that are returned by operations. This makes chaining operations easy and efficient and promotes the writing of reusable, generic code.

SELECTORS, EVENTS, AND EVENT LOOPS

Netty abstracts the `Selector` away from the application by firing events, eliminating all the handwritten dispatch code that would otherwise be required. Under the covers, an `EventLoop` is assigned to each `Channel` to handle all of the events, including

- Registration of interesting events
- Dispatching events to `ChannelHandlers`
- Scheduling further actions

The `EventLoop` itself is driven by only one thread that handles all of the I/O events for one `Channel` and does not change during the lifetime of the `EventLoop`. This simple and powerful design eliminates any concern you might have about synchronization in your `ChannelHandlers`, so you can focus on providing the right logic to be executed when there is interesting data to process. As we'll see when we explore Netty's threading model in detail, the API is simple and compact.

1.4 Summary

In this chapter, we looked at the background of the Netty framework, including the evolution of the Java networking API, the distinctions between blocking and non-blocking network operations, and the advantages of asynchronous I/O for high-volume, high-performance networking.

We then moved on to an overview of Netty's features, design, and benefits. These include the mechanisms underlying Netty's asynchronous model, including callbacks, `Futures`, and their use in combination. We also touched on how events are generated and how they can be intercepted and handled.

Going forward, we'll explore in much greater depth how this rich collection of tools can be utilized to meet the specific needs of your applications.

In the next chapter, we'll delve into the basics of Netty's API and programming model, and you'll write your first client and server.

2 Your first Netty application

This chapter covers

- Setting up the development environment
- Writing an Echo server and client
- Building and testing the applications

In this chapter we'll show you how to build a Netty-based client and server. The applications are simple—the client sends messages to the server, and the server echoes them back—but the exercise is important for two reasons.

First, it will provide a test bed for setting up and verifying your development tools and environment, which is essential if you plan to work with the book's sample code in preparation for your own development efforts.

Second, you'll acquire hands-on experience with a key aspect of Netty, touched on in the previous chapter: building application logic with `ChannelHandlers`. This will prepare you for the in-depth study of the Netty API we'll begin in chapter 3.

2.1 Setting up the development environment

To compile and run the book's examples, the only tools you need are the JDK and Apache Maven, both freely available for download.

We'll also assume that you're going to want to tinker with the example code and soon start writing your own. Although you *can* get by with a plain text editor, we strongly recommend the use of an integrated development environment (IDE) for Java.

2.1.1 Obtaining and installing the Java Development Kit

Your OS may already have a JDK installed. To find out, type the following on the command line:

```
javac -version
```

If you get back `javac 1.7...` or `1.8...` you're all set and can skip this step.[1]

Otherwise, get version 8 of the JDK from http://java.com/en/download/manual.jsp. Be careful to download the JDK and not the Java Runtime Environment (JRE), which can run Java applications but not compile them. An installer executable is provided for each platform. Should you need installation instructions, you'll find them on the same site.

It's a good idea to do the following:

- Set the environment variable `JAVA_HOME` to the location of your JDK installation. (On Windows, the default will be something like C:\Program Files\Java\jdk1.8.0_60.)
- Add `%JAVA_HOME%\bin` (`${JAVA_HOME}/bin` on Linux) to your execution path.

2.1.2 Downloading and installing an IDE

The following are the most widely used Java IDEs, all freely available:

- Eclipse—www.eclipse.org
- NetBeans—www.netbeans.org
- Intellij Idea Community Edition—www.jetbrains.com

All three have full support for Apache Maven, the build tool we'll use. NetBeans and Intellij are distributed as installer executables. Eclipse is usually distributed as a zip archive, although there are a number of customized versions that have self-installers.

2.1.3 Downloading and installing Apache Maven

Even if you're already familiar with Maven, we recommend that you at least skim this section.

Maven is a widely used build-management tool developed by the Apache Software Foundation (ASF). The Netty project uses it, as do this book's examples. You don't need to be a Maven expert to build and run the examples, but if you want to expand on them, we recommend reading the Maven introduction in the appendix.

---

[1] A restricted feature set of Netty will run with JDK 1.6 but JDK 7 or higher is required for compilation, as well as for running the latest version of Maven.

> **Do you need to install Maven?**
> Eclipse and NetBeans come with an embedded Maven installation that will work fine for our purposes out of the box. If you'll be working in an environment that has its own Maven repository, your administrator probably has a Maven installation package preconfigured to work with it.

At the time of this book's publication, the latest Maven version was 3.3.3. You can download the appropriate tar.gz or zip file for your system from http://maven.apache.org/download.cgi. Installation is simple: extract the contents of the archive to any folder of your choice (we'll call this `<install_dir>`). This will create the directory <install_dir>\apache-maven-3.3.3.

As with the Java environment,

- Set the environment variable `M2_HOME` to point to <install_dir>\apache-maven-3.3.3.
- Add `%M2_HOME%\bin` (or `${M2_HOME}/bin` on Linux) to your execution path.

This will enable you to run Maven by executing `mvn.bat` (or `mvn`) on the command line.

2.1.4 *Configuring the toolset*

If you have set the `JAVA_HOME` and `M2_HOME` system variables as recommended, you may find that when you start your IDE it has already discovered the locations of your Java and Maven installations. If you need to perform manual configuration, all the IDE versions we've listed have menu items for setting these variables under Preferences or Settings. Please consult the documentation for details.

This completes the setup of your development environment. In the next sections we'll present the details of the first Netty applications you'll build, and we'll get deeper into the framework APIs. After that you'll use the tools you've just set up to build and run the Echo server and client.

2.2 *Netty client/server overview*

Figure 2.1 presents a high-level view of the Echo client and server you'll be writing. While your main focus may be writing web-based applications to be accessed by browsers, you'll definitely gain a more complete understanding of the Netty API by implementing both the client and server.

Although we've spoken of the client, the figure shows multiple clients connected simultaneously to the server. The number of clients that can be supported is limited, in theory, only by the system resources available (and any constraints that might be imposed by the JDK version in use).

The interaction between an Echo client and the server is very simple; after the client establishes a connection, it sends one or more messages to the server, which in turn

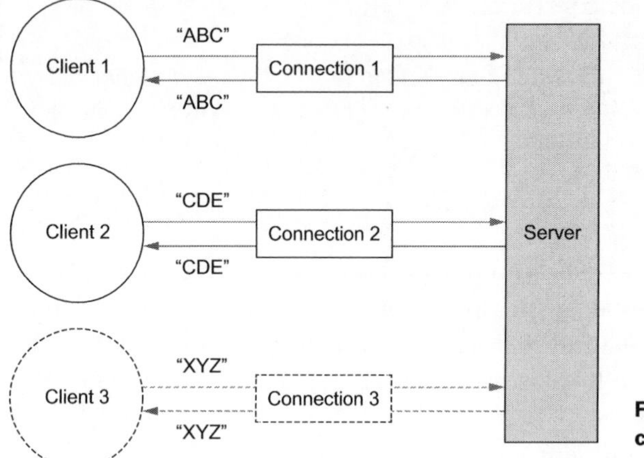

Figure 2.1 Echo client and server

echoes each message to the client. While this may not seem terribly useful by itself, it exemplifies the request-response interaction that's typical of client/server systems.

We'll begin this project by examining the server-side code.

2.3 Writing the Echo server

All Netty servers require the following:

- *At least one* `ChannelHandler`—This component implements the server's processing of data received from the client—its business logic.
- *Bootstrapping*—This is the startup code that configures the server. At a minimum, it binds the server to the port on which it will listen for connection requests.

In the remainder of this section we'll describe the logic and bootstrapping code for the Echo server.

2.3.1 ChannelHandlers and business logic

In chapter 1 we introduced `Futures` and callbacks and illustrated their use in an event-driven design. We also discussed `ChannelHandler`, the parent of a family of interfaces whose implementations receive and react to event notifications. In Netty applications, all data-processing logic is contained in implementations of these core abstractions.

Because your Echo server will respond to incoming messages, it will need to implement `interface ChannelInboundHandler`, which defines methods for acting on *inbound* events. This simple application will require only a few of these methods, so it will be sufficient to subclass `ChannelInboundHandlerAdapter`, which provides a default implementation of `ChannelInboundHandler`.

The following methods interest us:

- `channelRead()`—Called for each incoming message
- `channelReadComplete()`—Notifies the handler that the last call made to `channelRead()` was the last message in the current batch
- `exceptionCaught()`—Called if an exception is thrown during the read operation

The Echo server's `ChannelHandler` implementation is `EchoServerHandler`, shown in the following listing.

Listing 2.1 `EchoServerHandler`

```
@Sharable
public class EchoServerHandler extends ChannelInboundHandlerAdapter {

    @Override
    public void channelRead(ChannelHandlerContext ctx, Object msg) {
        ByteBuf in = (ByteBuf) msg;
        System.out.println(
            "Server received: " + in.toString(CharsetUtil.UTF_8));
        ctx.write(in);
    }

    @Override
    public void channelReadComplete(ChannelHandlerContext ctx) {
        ctx.writeAndFlush(Unpooled.EMPTY_BUFFER)
            .addListener(ChannelFutureListener.CLOSE);
    }

    @Override
    public void exceptionCaught(ChannelHandlerContext ctx,
        Throwable cause) {
        cause.printStackTrace();
        ctx.close();
    }
}
```

Indicates that a ChannelHandler can be safely shared by multiple channels

Logs the message to the console

Writes the received message to the sender without flushing the outbound messages

Flushes pending messages to the remote peer and closes the channel

Prints the exception stack trace

Closes the channel

`ChannelInboundHandlerAdapter` has a straightforward API, and each of its methods can be overridden to hook into the event lifecycle at the appropriate point. Because you need to handle all received data, you override `channelRead()`. In this server you simply echo the data to the remote peer.

Overriding `exceptionCaught()` allows you to react to any `Throwable` subtypes—here you log the exception and close the connection. A more elaborate application might try to recover from the exception, but in this case simply closing the connection signals to the remote peer that an error has occurred.

What happens if an exception isn't caught?

Every `Channel` has an associated `ChannelPipeline`, which holds a chain of `ChannelHandler` instances. By default, a handler will forward the invocation of a handler method to the next one in the chain. Therefore, if `exceptionCaught()` is not implemented somewhere along the chain, exceptions received will travel to the end of the `ChannelPipeline` and will be logged. For this reason, your application should supply at least one `ChannelHandler` that implements `exceptionCaught()`. (Section 6.4 discusses exception handling in detail.)

In addition to `ChannelInboundHandlerAdapter`, there are many `ChannelHandler` subtypes and implementations to learn about, and we'll cover these in detail in chapters 6 and 7. For now, please keep these key points in mind:

- `ChannelHandlers` are invoked for different types of events.
- Applications implement or extend `ChannelHandlers` to hook into the event lifecycle and provide custom application logic.
- Architecturally, `ChannelHandlers` help to keep your business logic decoupled from networking code. This simplifies development as the code evolves in response to changing requirements.

2.3.2 Bootstrapping the server

Having discussed the core business logic implemented by `EchoServerHandler`, we can now examine the bootstrapping of the server itself, which involves the following:

- Bind to the port on which the server will listen for and accept incoming connection requests
- Configure `Channels` to notify an `EchoServerHandler` instance about inbound messages

Transports

In this section you'll encounter the term *transport*. In the standard, multilayered view of networking protocols, the transport layer is the one that provides services for end-to-end or host-to-host communications.

Internet communications are based on the TCP transport. *NIO transport* refers to a transport that's mostly identical to TCP except for server-side performance enhancements provided by the Java NIO implementation.

Transports will be discussed in detail in chapter 4.

The following listing shows the complete code for the EchoServer class.

Listing 2.2 EchoServer class

```
public class EchoServer {
    private final int port;

    public EchoServer(int port) {
        this.port = port;
    }

    public static void main(String[] args) throws Exception {
        if (args.length != 1) {
            System.err.println(
                "Usage: " + EchoServer.class.getSimpleName() +
                " <port>");
        }
        int port = Integer.parseInt(args[0]);
        new EchoServer(port).start();
    }

    public void start() throws Exceptio3n {
        final EchoServerHandler serverHandler = new EchoServerHandler();
        EventLoopGroup group = new NioEventLoopGroup();
        try {
            ServerBootstrap b = new ServerBootstrap();
            b.group(group)
                .channel(NioServerSocketChannel.class)
                .localAddress(new InetSocketAddress(port))
                .childHandler(new ChannelInitializer<SocketChannel>(){
                @Override
                public void initChannel(SocketChannel ch)
                    throws Exception {
                        ch.pipeline().addLast(serverHandler);
                    }
                });
            ChannelFuture f = b.bind().sync();
            f.channel().closeFuture().sync();
        } finally {
            group.shutdownGracefully().sync();
        }
    }
}
```

Sets the port value (throws a NumberFormatException if the port argument is malformed)

Calls the server's start() method

❶ Creates the EventLoopGroup

❷ Creates the ServerBootstrap

❸ Specifies the use of an NIO transport Channel

❹ Sets the socket address using the specified port

❺ Adds an EchoServerHandler to the Channel's ChannelPipeline

EchoServerHandler is @Sharable so we can always use the same one.

❻ Binds the server asynchronously; sync() waits for the bind to complete.

❼ Gets the CloseFuture of the Channel and blocks the current thread until it's complete

❽ Shuts down the EventLoopGroup, releasing all resources

In ❷ you create a ServerBootstrap instance. Because you're using the NIO transport, you specify the NioEventLoopGroup ❶ to accept and handle new connections and the NioServerSocketChannel ❸ as the channel type. After this you set the local address to an InetSocketAddress with the selected port ❹. The server will bind to this address to listen for new connection requests.

In ❺ you make use of a special class, `ChannelInitializer`. This is key. When a new connection is accepted, a new child `Channel` will be created, and the `ChannelInitializer` will add an instance of your `EchoServerHandler` to the `Channel`'s `ChannelPipeline`. As we explained earlier, this handler will receive notifications about inbound messages.

Although NIO is scalable, its proper configuration, especially as regards multithreading, is not trivial. Netty's design encapsulates most of the complexity, and we'll discuss the relevant abstractions (`EventLoopGroup`, `SocketChannel`, and `ChannelInitializer`) in more detail in chapter 3.

Next you bind the server ❻ and wait until the bind completes. (The call to `sync()` causes the current `Thread` to block until then.) At ❼, the application will wait until the server's `Channel` closes (because you call `sync()` on the `Channel`'s `CloseFuture`). You can then shut down the `EventLoopGroup` and release all resources, including all created threads ❽.

NIO is used in this example because it's currently the most widely used transport, thanks to its scalability and thoroughgoing asynchrony. But a different transport implementation could be used as well. If you wished to use the OIO transport in your server, you'd specify `OioServerSocketChannel` and `OioEventLoopGroup`. We'll explore transports in greater detail in chapter 4.

In the meantime, let's review the important steps in the server implementation you just completed. These are the primary code components of the server:

- The `EchoServerHandler` implements the business logic.
- The `main()` method bootstraps the server.

The following steps are required in bootstrapping:

- Create a `ServerBootstrap` instance to bootstrap and bind the server.
- Create and assign an `NioEventLoopGroup` instance to handle event processing, such as accepting new connections and reading/writing data.
- Specify the local `InetSocketAddress` to which the server binds.
- Initialize each new `Channel` with an `EchoServerHandler` instance.
- Call `ServerBootstrap.bind()` to bind the server.

At this point the server is initialized and ready to be used. In the next section we'll examine the code for the client application.

2.4 Writing an Echo client

The Echo client will

1. Connect to the server
2. Send one or more messages
3. For each message, wait for and receive the same message back from the server
4. Close the connection

Writing the client involves the same two main code areas you saw in the server: business logic and bootstrapping.

2.4.1 *Implementing the client logic with ChannelHandlers*

Like the server, the client will have a `ChannelInboundHandler` to process the data. In this case, you'll extend the class `SimpleChannelInboundHandler` to handle all the needed tasks, as shown in listing 2.3. This requires overriding the following methods:

- `channelActive()`—Called after the connection to the server is established
- `channelRead0()`—Called when a message is received from the server
- `exceptionCaught()`—Called if an exception is raised during processing

Listing 2.3 `ChannelHandler` for the client

```
@Sharable
public class EchoClientHandler extends
    SimpleChannelInboundHandler<ByteBuf> {
    @Override
    public void channelActive(ChannelHandlerContext ctx) {
        ctx.writeAndFlush(Unpooled.copiedBuffer("Netty rocks!",
        CharsetUtil.UTF_8);
    }

    @Override
    public void channelRead0(ChannelHandlerContext ctx, ByteBuf in) {
        System.out.println(
            "Client received: " + in.toString(CharsetUtil.UTF_8));
    }

    @Override
    public void exceptionCaught(ChannelHandlerContext ctx,
        Throwable cause) {
        cause.printStrackTrace();
        ctx.close();
      }
}
```

Marks this class as one whose instances can be shared among channels

When notified that the channel is active, sends a message

Logs a dump of the received message

On exception, logs the error and closes channel

First you override `channelActive()`, invoked when a connection has been established. This ensures that something is written to the server as soon as possible, which in this case is a byte buffer that encodes the string `"Netty rocks!"`.

Next you override the method `channelRead0()`. This method is called whenever data is received. Note that the message sent by the server may be received in chunks. That is, if the server sends 5 bytes, there's no guarantee that all 5 bytes will be received at once. Even for such a small amount of data, the `channelRead0()` method could be called twice, first with a `ByteBuf` (Netty's `byte` container) holding 3 bytes, and second with a `ByteBuf` holding 2 bytes. As a stream-oriented protocol, TCP guarantees that the bytes will be received in the order in which they were sent by the server.

The third method you override is `exceptionCaught()`. Just as in `EchoServerHandler` (listing 2.2), `Throwable` is logged and the channel is closed, in this case terminating the connection to the server.

> **SimpleChannelInboundHandler vs. ChannelInboundHandler**
>
> You may be wondering why we used `SimpleChannelInboundHandler` in the client instead of the `ChannelInboundHandlerAdapter` used in the `EchoServerHandler`. This has to do with the interaction of two factors: how the business logic processes messages and how Netty manages resources.
>
> In the client, when `channelRead0()` completes, you have the incoming message and you're done with it. When the method returns, `SimpleChannelInboundHandler` takes care of releasing the memory reference to the `ByteBuf` that holds the message.
>
> In `EchoServerHandler` you still have to echo the incoming message to the sender, and the `write()` operation, which is asynchronous, may not complete until after `channelRead()` returns (shown in listing 2.1). For this reason `EchoServerHandler` extends `ChannelInboundHandlerAdapter`, which doesn't release the message at this point.
>
> The message is released in `channelReadComplete()` in the `EchoServerHandler` when `writeAndFlush()` is called (listing 2.1).
>
> Chapters 5 and 6 will cover message resource management in detail.

2.4.2 Bootstrapping the client

As you'll see in the next listing, bootstrapping a client is similar to bootstrapping a server, with the difference that instead of binding to a listening port the client uses host and port parameters to connect to a remote address, here that of the Echo server.

Listing 2.4 Main class for the client

```
public class EchoClient {
    private final String host;
    private final int port;

    public EchoClient(String host, int port) {
        this.host = host;
        this.port = port;
    }

    public void start() throws Exception {
        EventLoopGroup group = new NioEventLoopGroup();
        try {
            Bootstrap b = new Bootstrap();
            b.group(group)
                .channel(NioSocketChannel.class)
                .remoteAddress(new InetSocketAddress(host, port))
                .handler(new ChannelInitializer<SocketChannel>() {
```

Creates Bootstrap

Specifies EventLoopGroup to handle client events; NIO implementation is needed.

Channel type is the one for NIO transport.

Sets the server's InetSocketAddress

Adds an EchoClientHandler to the pipeline when a Channel is created

```
                @Override
                public void initChannel(SocketChannel ch)
                    throws Exception {
                    ch.pipeline().addLast(
                        new EchoClientHandler());
                }
            });
            ChannelFuture f = b.connect().sync();
            f.channel().closeFuture().sync();
        } finally {
            group.shutdownGracefully().sync();
        }
    }

    public static void main(String[] args) throws Exception {
        if (args.length != 2) {
            System.err.println(
                "Usage: " + EchoClient.class.getSimpleName() +
                " <host> <port>");
            return;
        }

        String host = args[0];
        int port = Integer.parseInt(args[1]);
        new EchoClient(host, port).start();
    }
}
```

Connects to the remote peer; waits until the connect completes

Blocks until the Channel closes

Shuts down the thread pools and the release of all resources

As before, the NIO transport is used. Note that you could use different transports in the client and server; for example, NIO transport on the server side and OIO transport on the client side. In chapter 4 we'll examine the factors and scenarios that would lead you to select a specific transport for a specific use case.

Let's review the important points introduced in this section:

- A `Bootstrap` instance is created to initialize the client.
- An `NioEventLoopGroup` instance is assigned to handle the event processing, which includes creating new connections and processing inbound and outbound data.
- An `InetSocketAddress` is created for the connection to the server.
- An `EchoClientHandler` will be installed in the pipeline when the connection is established.
- After everything is set up, `Bootstrap.connect()` is called to connect to the remote peer.

Having finished the client, you can proceed to build the system and test it out.

2.5 Building and running the Echo server and client

In this section we'll cover all the steps needed to compile and run the Echo server and client.

> **The Echo client/server Maven project**
>
> This book's appendix uses the configuration of the Echo client/server project to explain in detail how multimodule Maven projects are organized. This isn't required reading for building and running the applications, but it's recommended for gaining a better understanding of the book's examples and of the Netty project itself.

2.5.1 Running the build

To build the Echo client and server, go to the chapter2 directory under the code samples root directory and execute the following command:

```
mvn clean package
```

This should produce something very much like the output shown in listing 2.5 (we've edited out a few nonessential steps in the build).

Listing 2.5 Building the Echo client and server

```
[INFO] Scanning for projects...
[INFO] -------------------------------------------------------------------
[INFO] Reactor Build Order:
[INFO]
[INFO] Chapter 2. Your First Netty Application - Echo App
[INFO] Chapter 2. Echo Client
[INFO] Chapter 2. Echo Server
[INFO]
[INFO] -------------------------------------------------------------------
[INFO] Building Chapter 2. Your First Netty Application - 2.0-SNAPSHOT
[INFO] -------------------------------------------------------------------
[INFO]
[INFO] --- maven-clean-plugin:2.6.1:clean (default-clean) @ chapter2 ---
[INFO]
[INFO] -------------------------------------------------------------------
[INFO] Building Chapter 2. Echo Client 2.0-SNAPSHOT
[INFO] -------------------------------------------------------------------
[INFO]
[INFO] --- maven-clean-plugin:2.6.1:clean (default-clean)
    @ echo-client ---
[INFO]
[INFO] --- maven-resources-plugin:2.6:resources (default-resources)
    @ echo-client ---
[INFO] Using 'UTF-8' encoding to copy filtered resources.
[INFO] Copying 1 resource
[INFO]
[INFO] --- maven-compiler-plugin:3.3:compile (default-compile)
    @ echo-client ---
```

```
[INFO] Changes detected - recompiling the module!
[INFO] Compiling 2 source files to
    \netty-in-action\chapter2\Client\target\classes
[INFO]
[INFO] --- maven-resources-plugin:2.6:testResources (default-testResources)
    @ echo-client ---
[INFO] Using 'UTF-8' encoding to copy filtered resources.
[INFO] skip non existing resourceDirectory
    \netty-in-action\chapter2\Client\src\test\resources
[INFO]
[INFO] --- maven-compiler-plugin:3.3:testCompile (default-testCompile)
    @ echo-client ---
[INFO] No sources to compile
[INFO]
[INFO] --- maven-surefire-plugin:2.18.1:test (default-test)
    @ echo-client ---
[INFO] No tests to run.
[INFO]
[INFO] --- maven-jar-plugin:2.6:jar (default-jar) @ echo-client ---
[INFO] Building jar:
    \netty-in-action\chapter2\Client\target\echo-client-2.0-SNAPSHOT.jar
[INFO]
[INFO] ------------------------------------------------------------------------
[INFO] Building Chapter 2. Echo Server 2.0-SNAPSHOT
[INFO] ------------------------------------------------------------------------
[INFO]
[INFO] --- maven-clean-plugin:2.6.1:clean (default-clean)
    @ echo-server ---
[INFO]
[INFO] --- maven-resources-plugin:2.6:resources (default-resources)
    @ echo-server ---
[INFO] Using 'UTF-8' encoding to copy filtered resources.
[INFO] Copying 1 resource
[INFO]
[INFO] --- maven-compiler-plugin:3.3:compile (default-compile)
    @ echo-server ---
[INFO] Changes detected - recompiling the module!
[INFO] Compiling 2 source files to
    \netty-in-action\chapter2\Server\target\classes
[INFO]
[INFO] --- maven-resources-plugin:2.6:testResources (default-testResources)
    @ echo-server ---
[INFO] Using 'UTF-8' encoding to copy filtered resources.
[INFO] skip non existing resourceDirectory
    \netty-in-action\chapter2\Server\src\test\resources
[INFO]
[INFO] --- maven-compiler-plugin:3.3:testCompile (default-testCompile)
    @ echo-server ---
[INFO] No sources to compile
[INFO]
[INFO] --- maven-surefire-plugin:2.18.1:test (default-test)
    @ echo-server ---
[INFO] No tests to run.
[INFO]
[INFO] --- maven-jar-plugin:2.6:jar (default-jar) @ echo-server ---
```

```
[INFO] Building jar:
    \netty-in-action\chapter2\Server\target\echo-server-2.0-SNAPSHOT.jar
[INFO] ------------------------------------------------------------------------
[INFO] Reactor Summary:
[INFO]
[INFO] Chapter 2. Your First Netty Application ... SUCCESS [  0.134 s]
[INFO] Chapter 2. Echo Client .................... SUCCESS [  1.509 s]
[INFO] Chapter 2. Echo Ser........................ SUCCESS [  0.139 s]
[INFO] ------------------------------------------------------------------------
[INFO] BUILD SUCCESS
[INFO] ------------------------------------------------------------------------
[INFO] Total time: 1.886 s
[INFO] Finished at: 2015-11-18T17:14:10-05:00
[INFO] Final Memory: 18M/216M
[INFO] ------------------------------------------------------------------------
```

Here are the main steps recorded in the preceding build log:

- Maven determines the build order: first the parent pom.xml, and then the modules (subprojects).
- If the Netty artifacts aren't found in the user's local repository, Maven will download them from the public Maven repositories (not shown here).
- The `clean` and `compile` phases of the build lifecycle are run.
- The `maven-jar-plugin` is executed.

The Maven Reactor Summary shows that all projects have been successfully built. A listing of the target directories in the two subprojects should now resemble the following listing.

Listing 2.6 Build artifacts

```
Directory of nia\chapter2\Client\target
03/16/2015  09:45 PM    <DIR>          classes
03/16/2015  09:45 PM             5,614 echo-client-1.0-SNAPSHOT.jar
03/16/2015  09:45 PM    <DIR>          generated-sources
03/16/2015  09:45 PM    <DIR>          maven-archiver
03/16/2015  09:45 PM    <DIR>          maven-status

Directory of nia\chapter2\Server/target
03/16/2015  09:45 PM    <DIR>          classes
03/16/2015  09:45 PM             5,629 echo-server-1.0-SNAPSHOT.jar
03/16/2015  09:45 PM    <DIR>          generated-sources
03/16/2015  09:45 PM    <DIR>          maven-archiver
03/16/2015  09:45 PM    <DIR>          maven-status
```

2.5.2 Running the Echo server and client

To run the application components, you could use the Java command directly. But in the POM file, the `exec-maven-plugin` is configured to do this for you (see the appendix for details).

Open two console windows side by side, one logged into the chapter2\Server directory and the other into chapter2\Client.

In the server's console, execute this command:

```
mvn exec:java
```

You should see something like the following:

```
[INFO] Scanning for projects...
[INFO]
[INFO] ----------------------------------------------------------------------
[INFO] Building Echo Server 1.0-SNAPSHOT
[INFO] ----------------------------------------------------------------------
[INFO]
[INFO] >>> exec-maven-plugin:1.2.1:java (default-cli) >
    validate @ echo-server >>>
[INFO]
[INFO] <<< exec-maven-plugin:1.2.1:java (default-cli) <
    validate @ echo-server <<<
[INFO]
[INFO] --- exec-maven-plugin:1.2.1:java (default-cli) @ echo-server ---
    nia.chapter2.echoserver.EchoServer
    started and listening for connections on /0:0:0:0:0:0:0:0:9999
```

The server has been started and is ready to accept connections. Now execute the same command in the client's console:

```
mvn exec:java
```

You should see the following:

```
[INFO] Scanning for projects...
[INFO]
[INFO] -------------------------------------------------------------------
[INFO] Building Echo Client 1.0-SNAPSHOT
[INFO] -------------------------------------------------------------------
[INFO]
[INFO] >>> exec-maven-plugin:1.2.1:java (default-cli) >
    validate @ echo-client >>>
[INFO]
[INFO] <<< exec-maven-plugin:1.2.1:java (default-cli) <
    validate @ echo-client <<<
[INFO]
[INFO] --- exec-maven-plugin:1.2.1:java (default-cli) @ echo-client ---
    Client received: Netty rocks!
[INFO] -------------------------------------------------------------------
[INFO] BUILD SUCCESS
[INFO] -------------------------------------------------------------------
[INFO] Total time: 2.833 s
[INFO] Finished at: 2015-03-16T22:03:54-04:00
[INFO] Final Memory: 10M/309M
[INFO] -------------------------------------------------------------------
```

And in the server console you should see this:

```
Server received: Netty rocks!
```

You'll see this log statement in the server's console every time you run the client.

Here's what happens:

1. As soon as the client is connected, it sends its message: `Netty rocks!`
2. The server reports the received message and echoes it to the client.
3. The client reports the returned message and exits.

What you've seen is the expected behavior; now let's see how failures are handled. The server should still be running, so type Ctrl-C in the server console to stop the process. Once it has terminated, start the client again with

```
mvn exec:java
```

This shows the output you should see from the client when it's unable to connect to the server.

Listing 2.7 Exception handling in the Echo client

```
[INFO] Scanning for projects...
[INFO]
[INFO] -------------------------------------------------------------------
[INFO] Building Echo Client 1.0-SNAPSHOT
[INFO] -------------------------------------------------------------------
[INFO]
[INFO] >>> exec-maven-plugin:1.2.1:java (default-cli) >
    validate @ echo-client >>>
[INFO]
[INFO] <<< exec-maven-plugin:1.2.1:java (default-cli) <
    validate @ echo-client <<<
[INFO]
[INFO] --- exec-maven-plugin:1.2.1:java (default-cli) @ echo-client ---
[WARNING]
java.lang.reflect.InvocationTargetException
        at sun.reflect.NativeMethodAccessorImpl.invoke0(Native Method)
    . . .
    Caused by: java.net.ConnectException: Connection refused:
    no further information: localhost/127.0.0.1:9999
        at sun.nio.ch.SocketChannelImpl.checkConnect(Native Method)
        at sun.nio.ch.SocketChannelImpl
        .finishConnect(SocketChannelImpl.java:739)
        at io.netty.channel.socket.nio.NioSocketChannel
        .doFinishConnect(NioSocketChannel.java:208)
        at io.netty.channel.nio
        .AbstractNioChannel$AbstractNioUnsafe
        .finishConnect(AbstractNioChannel.java:281)
        at io.netty.channel.nio.NioEventLoop
        .processSelectedKey(NioEventLoop.java:528)
        at io.netty.channel.nio.NioEventLoop.
        processSelectedKeysOptimized(NioEventLoop.java:468)
        at io.netty.channel.nio.NioEventLoop
        .processSelectedKeys(NioEventLoop.java:382)
        at io.netty.channel.nio.NioEventLoop
```

```
        .run(NioEventLoop.java:354)
        at io.netty.util.concurrent.SingleThreadEventExecutor$2
        .run(SingleThreadEventExecutor.java:116)
        at io.netty.util.concurrent.DefaultThreadFactory
        $DefaultRunnableDecorator.run(DefaultThreadFactory.java:137)
    . . .
[INFO] ------------------------------------------------------------------------
[INFO] BUILD FAILURE
[INFO] ------------------------------------------------------------------------
[INFO] Total time: 3.801 s
[INFO] Finished at: 2015-03-16T22:11:16-04:00
[INFO] Final Memory: 10M/309M
[INFO] ------------------------------------------------------------------------
[ERROR] Failed to execute goal org.codehaus.mojo:
    exec-maven-plugin:1.2.1:java (default-cli) on project echo-client:
        An exception occured while executing the Java class. null:
        InvocationTargetException: Connection refused:
        no further information: localhost/127.0.0.1:9999 -> [Help 1]
```

What happened? The client tried to connect to the server, which it expected to find running at `localhost:9999`. This failed (as expected) because the server had been stopped previously, causing a `java.net.ConnectException` in the client. This exception triggered the `exceptionCaught()` method of the `EchoClientHandler`, which prints out the stack trace and closes the channel (see listing 2.3.)

2.6 Summary

In this chapter you set up your development environment and built and ran your first Netty client and server. Although this is a simple application, it will scale to several thousand concurrent connections—many more messages per second than a plain vanilla socket-based Java application would be able to handle.

In the following chapters, you'll see many more examples of how Netty simplifies scalability and concurrency. We'll also go deeper into Netty's support for the architectural principle of separation of concerns. By providing the right abstractions for decoupling business logic from networking logic, Netty makes it easy to keep pace with rapidly evolving requirements without jeopardizing system stability.

In the next chapter, we'll provide an overview of Netty's architecture. This will give you the context for the in-depth and comprehensive study of Netty's internals that will follow in subsequent chapters.

3 Netty components and design

This chapter covers

- Technical and architectural aspects of Netty
- `Channel`, `EventLoop`, and `ChannelFuture`
- `ChannelHandler` and `ChannelPipeline`
- Bootstrapping

In chapter 1 we presented a summary of the history and technical foundations of high-performance network programming in Java. This provided the background for an overview of Netty's core concepts and building blocks.

In chapter 2 we expanded the scope of our discussion to application development. By building a simple client and server you learned about bootstrapping and gained hands-on experience with the all-important `ChannelHandler` API. Along the way, you also verified that your development tools were functioning properly.

As we build on this material in the rest of the book, we'll explore Netty from two distinct but closely related points of view: as a class library and as a framework. Both are essential to writing efficient, reusable, and maintainable code with Netty.

From a high-level perspective, Netty addresses two corresponding areas of concern, which we might label broadly as *technical* and *architectural*. First, its asynchronous and event-driven implementation, built on Java NIO, guarantees maximum application performance and scalability under heavy load. Second, Netty embodies a set of design patterns that decouple application logic from the network layer, simplifying development while maximizing the testability, modularity, and reusability of code.

As we study Netty's individual components in greater detail, we'll pay close attention to how they collaborate to support these architectural best practices. By following the same principles, we can reap all the benefits Netty can provide. With this goal in mind, in this chapter we'll review the main concepts and components we've introduced up to now.

3.1 Channel, EventLoop, and ChannelFuture

The following sections will add detail to our discussion of the `Channel`, `EventLoop`, and `ChannelFuture` classes which, taken together, can be thought of as representing Netty's networking abstraction:

- `Channel`—`Sockets`
- `EventLoop`—Control flow, multithreading, concurrency
- `ChannelFuture`—Asynchronous notification

3.1.1 Interface Channel

Basic I/O operations (`bind()`, `connect()`, `read()`, and `write()`) depend on primitives supplied by the underlying network transport. In Java-based networking, the fundamental construct is `class Socket`. Netty's `Channel` interface provides an API that greatly reduces the complexity of working directly with `Sockets`. Additionally, `Channel` is the root of an extensive class hierarchy having many predefined, specialized implementations, of which the following is a short list:

- `EmbeddedChannel`
- `LocalServerChannel`
- `NioDatagramChannel`
- `NioSctpChannel`
- `NioSocketChannel`

3.1.2 Interface EventLoop

The `EventLoop` defines Netty's core abstraction for handling events that occur during the lifetime of a connection. We'll discuss `EventLoop` in detail in chapter 7 in the context of Netty's thread-handling model. For now, figure 3.1 illustrates at a high level the relationships among `Channels`, `EventLoops`, `Threads`, and `EventLoopGroups`.

These relationships are:

- An `EventLoopGroup` contains one or more `EventLoops`.
- An `EventLoop` is bound to a single `Thread` for its lifetime.
- All I/O events processed by an `EventLoop` are handled on its dedicated `Thread`.
- A `Channel` is registered for its lifetime with a single `EventLoop`.
- A single `EventLoop` may be assigned to one or more `Channels`.

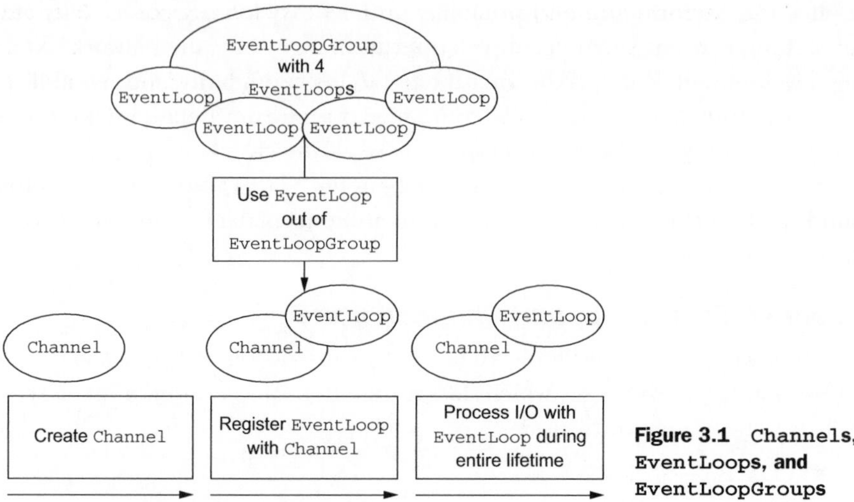

Figure 3.1 `Channels`, `EventLoops`, and `EventLoopGroups`

Note that this design, in which the I/O for a given `Channel` is executed by the same `Thread`, virtually eliminates the need for synchronization.

3.1.3 Interface ChannelFuture

As we've explained, all I/O operations in Netty are asynchronous. Because an operation may not return immediately, we need a way to determine its result at a later time. For this purpose, Netty provides `ChannelFuture`, whose `addListener()` method registers a `ChannelFutureListener` to be notified when an operation has completed (whether or not successfully).

> **MORE ON CHANNELFUTURE** Think of a `ChannelFuture` as a placeholder for the result of an operation that's to be executed in the future. *When* exactly it will be executed may depend on several factors and thus be impossible to predict with precision, but it is certain that it *will* be executed. Furthermore, all operations belonging to the same `Channel` are guaranteed to be executed in the order in which they were invoked.

We'll discuss `EventLoop` and `EventLoopGroup` in depth in chapter 7.

3.2 ChannelHandler and ChannelPipeline

Now we'll take a more detailed look at the components that manage the flow of data and execute an application's processing logic.

3.2.1 Interface ChannelHandler

From the application developer's standpoint, the primary component of Netty is the `ChannelHandler`, which serves as the container for all application logic that applies to handling inbound and outbound data. This is possible because `ChannelHandler` methods are triggered by network events (where the term "event" is used very broadly). In fact, a `ChannelHandler` can be dedicated to almost any kind of action, such as converting data from one format to another or handling exceptions thrown during processing.

As an example, `ChannelInboundHandler` is a subinterface you'll implement frequently. This type receives inbound events and data to be handled by your application's business logic. You can also flush data from a `ChannelInboundHandler` when you're sending a response to a connected client. The business logic of your application will often reside in one or more `ChannelInboundHandlers`.

3.2.2 Interface ChannelPipeline

A `ChannelPipeline` provides a container for a chain of `ChannelHandlers` and defines an API for propagating the flow of inbound and outbound events along the chain. When a `Channel` is created, it is automatically assigned its own `ChannelPipeline`.

`ChannelHandlers` are installed in the `ChannelPipeline` as follows:

- A `ChannelInitializer` implementation is registered with a `ServerBootstrap`.
- When `ChannelInitializer.initChannel()` is called, the `ChannelInitializer` installs a custom set of `ChannelHandlers` in the pipeline.
- The `ChannelInitializer` removes itself from the `ChannelPipeline`.

Let's go a bit deeper into the symbiotic relationship between `ChannelPipeline` and `ChannelHandler` to examine what happens to data when you send or receive it.

`ChannelHandler` has been designed specifically to support a broad range of uses, and you can think of it as a generic container for any code that processes events (including data) coming and going through the `ChannelPipeline`. This is illustrated in figure 3.2, which shows the derivation of `ChannelInboundHandler` and `ChannelOutboundHandler` from `ChannelHandler`.

The movement of an event through the pipeline is the work of the `ChannelHandlers` that have been installed during the initialization, or bootstrapping phase of the application. These objects receive events, execute the processing logic for which they have been implemented, and pass the data to the next handler in the chain. The order in which they are executed is determined by the order in which they were added. For all practical purposes, it's this ordered arrangement of `ChannelHandlers` that we refer to as the `ChannelPipeline`.

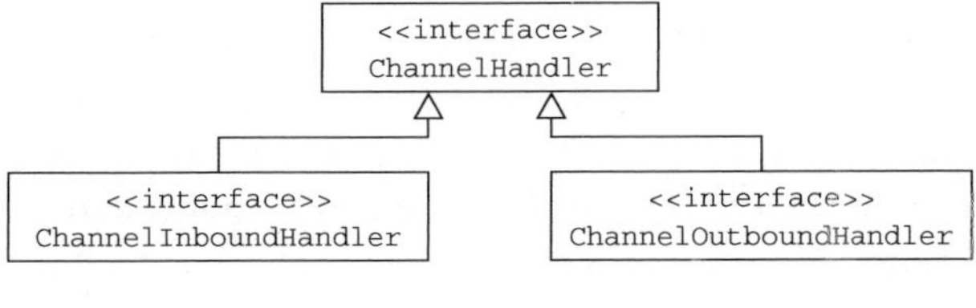

Figure 3.2 `ChannelHandler` class hierarchy

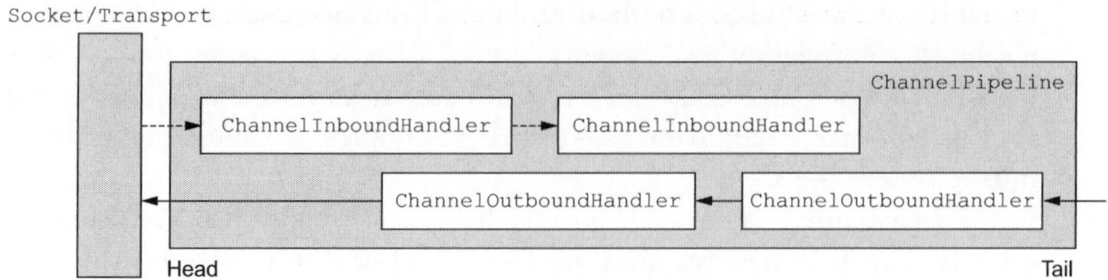

Figure 3.3 `ChannelPipeline` **with inbound and outbound** `ChannelHandlers`

Figure 3.3 illustrates the distinction between inbound and outbound data flow in a Netty application. From the point of view of a client application, events are said to be *outbound* if the movement is from the client to the server and *inbound* in the opposite case.

Figure 3.3 also shows that both inbound and outbound handlers can be installed in the same pipeline. If a message or any other inbound event is read, it will start from the head of the pipeline and be passed to the first `ChannelInboundHandler`. This handler may or may not actually modify the data, depending on its specific function, after which the data will be passed to the next `ChannelInboundHandler` in the chain. Finally, the data will reach the tail of the pipeline, at which point all processing is terminated.

The outbound movement of data (that is, data being *written*) is identical in concept. In this case, data flows from the tail through the chain of `ChannelOutboundHandlers` until it reaches the head. Beyond this point, outbound data will reach the network transport, shown here as a `Socket`. Typically, this will trigger a write operation.

> **More on inbound and outbound handlers**
>
> An event can be forwarded to the next handler in the current chain by using the `ChannelHandlerContext` that's supplied as an argument to each method. Because you'll sometimes ignore uninteresting events, Netty provides the abstract base classes `ChannelInboundHandlerAdapter` and `ChannelOutboundHandlerAdapter`. Each provides method implementations that simply pass the event to the next handler by calling the corresponding method on the `ChannelHandlerContext`. You can then extend the class by overriding the methods that interest you.

Given that outbound and inbound operations are distinct, you might wonder what happens when the two categories of handlers are mixed in the same `ChannelPipeline`. Although both inbound and outbound handlers extend `ChannelHandler`, Netty distinguishes implementations of `ChannelInboundHandler` and `ChannelOutboundHandler` and ensures that data is passed only between handlers of the same directional type.

When a `ChannelHandler` is added to a `ChannelPipeline`, it's assigned a `ChannelHandlerContext`, which represents the binding between a `ChannelHandler` and the

ChannelPipeline. Although this object can be used to obtain the underlying Channel, it's mostly utilized to write outbound data.

There are two ways of sending messages in Netty. You can write directly to the Channel or write to a ChannelHandlerContext object associated with a ChannelHandler. The former approach causes the message to start from the tail of the ChannelPipeline, the latter causes the message to start from the *next* handler in the ChannelPipeline.

3.2.3 A closer look at ChannelHandlers

As we said earlier, there are many different types of ChannelHandlers, and the functionality of each is largely determined by its superclass. Netty provides a number of default handler implementations in the form of adapter classes, which are intended to simplify the development of an application's processing logic. You've seen that each ChannelHandler in a pipeline is responsible for forwarding events to the next handler in the chain. These adapter classes (and their subclasses) do this automatically, so you can override only the methods and events you want to specialize.

Why adapters?

There are a few adapter classes that reduce the effort of writing custom ChannelHandlers to a bare minimum, because they provide default implementations of all the methods defined in the corresponding interface.

These are the adapters you'll call most often when creating your custom handlers:

- ChannelHandlerAdapter
- ChannelInboundHandlerAdapter
- ChannelOutboundHandlerAdapter
- ChannelDuplexHandlerAdapter

Next we'll examine three ChannelHandler subtypes: encoders, decoders, and SimpleChannelInboundHandler<T>, a subclass of ChannelInboundHandlerAdapter.

3.2.4 Encoders and decoders

When you send or receive a message with Netty, a data conversion takes place. An inbound message will be *decoded*; that is, converted from bytes to another format, typically a Java object. If the message is outbound, the reverse will happen: it will be *encoded* to bytes from its current format. The reason for both conversions is simple: network data is always a series of bytes.

Various types of abstract classes are provided for encoders and decoders, corresponding to specific needs. For example, your application may use an intermediate format that doesn't require the message to be converted to bytes immediately. You'll still need an encoder, but it will derive from a different superclass. To determine the appropriate one, you can apply a simple naming convention.

In general, base classes will have a name resembling `ByteToMessageDecoder` or `MessageToByteEncoder`. In the case of a specialized type, you may find something like `ProtobufEncoder` and `ProtobufDecoder`, provided to support Google's protocol buffers.

Strictly speaking, other handlers could do what encoders and decoders do. But just as there are adapter classes to simplify the creation of channel handlers, all of the encoder/decoder adapter classes provided by Netty implement either `ChannelInboundHandler` or `ChannelOutboundHandler`.

You'll find that for inbound data the `channelRead` method/event is overridden. This method is called for each message that's read from the inbound `Channel`. It will then call the `decode()` method of the provided decoder and forward the decoded bytes to the next `ChannelInboundHandler` in the pipeline.

The pattern for outbound messages is the reverse: an encoder converts the message to bytes and forwards them to the next `ChannelOutboundHandler`.

3.2.5 Abstract class SimpleChannelInboundHandler

Most frequently your application will employ a handler that receives a decoded message and applies business logic to the data. To create such a `ChannelHandler`, you need only extend the base class `SimpleChannelInboundHandler<T>`, where `T` is the Java type of the message you want to process. In this handler you'll override one or more methods of the base class and obtain a reference to the `ChannelHandlerContext`, which is passed as an input argument to all the handler methods.

The most important method in a handler of this type is `channelRead0(ChannelHandlerContext,T)`. The implementation is entirely up to you, except for the requirement that the current I/O thread not be blocked. We'll have much more to say on this topic later.

3.3 Bootstrapping

Netty's bootstrap classes provide containers for the configuration of an application's network layer, which involves either binding a process to a given port or connecting one process to another one running on a specified host at a specified port.

In general, we refer to the former use case as bootstrapping a server and the latter as bootstrapping a client. This terminology is simple and convenient, but it slightly obscures the important fact that the terms "server" and "client" denote different network *behaviors*; namely, listening for incoming connections versus establishing connections with one or more processes.

> **CONNECTION-ORIENTED PROTOCOLS** Please keep in mind that strictly speaking the term "connection" applies only to connection-oriented protocols such as TCP, which guarantee ordered delivery of messages between the connected endpoints.

Accordingly, there are two types of bootstraps: one intended for clients (called simply `Bootstrap`), and the other for servers (`ServerBootstrap`). Regardless of which protocol your application uses or the type of data processing it performs, the only thing that determines which bootstrap class it uses is its function as a client or server. Table 3.1 compares the two types of bootstraps.

Table 3.1 Comparison of `Bootstrap` classes

Category	`Bootstrap`	`ServerBootstrap`
Networking function	Connects to a remote host and port	Binds to a local port
Number of `EventLoopGroups`	1	2

The first difference between the two types of bootstraps has been discussed: a `ServerBootstrap` binds to a port, because servers must listen for connections, while a `Bootstrap` is used by client applications that want to connect to a remote peer.

The second difference is perhaps more significant. Bootstrapping a client requires only a single `EventLoopGroup`, but a `ServerBootstrap` requires two (which can be the same instance). Why?

A server needs two distinct sets of `Channels`. The first set will contain a single `ServerChannel` representing the server's own listening socket, bound to a local port. The second set will contain all of the `Channels` that have been created to handle incoming client connections—one for each connection the server has accepted. Figure 3.4 illustrates this model, and shows why two distinct `EventLoopGroups` are required.

The `EventLoopGroup` associated with the `ServerChannel` assigns an `EventLoop` that is responsible for creating `Channels` for incoming connection requests. Once a

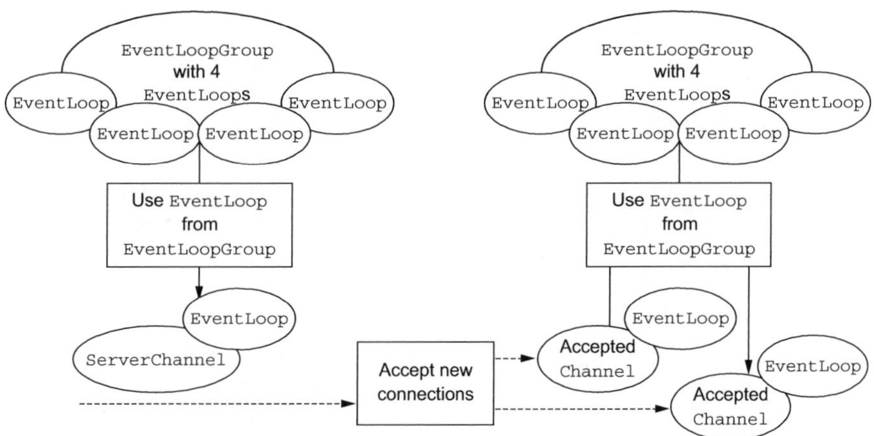

Figure 3.4 Server with two `EventLoopGroups`

connection has been accepted, the second EventLoopGroup assigns an EventLoop to its Channel.

3.4 Summary

In this chapter we discussed the importance of understanding Netty from both technical and architectural standpoints. We revisited in greater detail some of the concepts and components previously introduced, especially ChannelHandler, ChannelPipeline, and bootstrapping.

In particular, we discussed the hierarchy of ChannelHandlers and introduced encoders and decoders, describing their complementary functions in converting data to and from network byte format.

Many of the following chapters are devoted to in-depth study of these components, and the overview presented here should help you keep the big picture in focus.

The next chapter will explore the network transports provided by Netty and how to choose the one best suited to your application.

Transports

4

> ***This chapter covers***
> - OIO—blocking transport
> - NIO—asynchronous transport
> - Local transport—asynchronous communications within a JVM
> - Embedded transport—testing your `ChannelHandler`s

The data that flows through a network always has the same type: bytes. How these bytes are moved around depends mostly on what we refer to as the network transport, a concept that helps us to abstract away the underlying mechanics of data transfer. Users don't care about the details; they just want to be certain that their bytes are reliably sent and received.

If you have experience with network programming in Java, you may have discovered at some point that you needed to support a great many more concurrent connections than expected. If you then tried to switch from a blocking to a non-blocking transport, you might have encountered problems because the two network APIs are quite different.

Netty, however, layers a common API over all its transport implementations, making such a conversion far simpler than you can achieve using the JDK directly.

The resulting code will be uncontaminated by implementation details, and you won't need to perform extensive refactoring of your entire code base. In short, you can spend your time doing something productive.

In this chapter, we'll study this common API, contrasting it with the JDK to demonstrate its far greater ease of use. We'll explain the transport implementations that come bundled with Netty and the use cases appropriate to each. With this information in hand, you should find it straightforward to choose the best option for your application.

The only prerequisite for this chapter is knowledge of the Java programming language. Experience with network frameworks or network programming is a plus, but not a requirement.

We'll start by seeing how transports work in a real-world situation.

4.1 Case study: transport migration

We'll begin our study of transports with an application that simply accepts a connection, writes "Hi!" to the client, and closes the connection.

4.1.1 Using OIO and NIO without Netty

We'll present blocking (OIO) and asynchronous (NIO) versions of the application that use only the JDK APIs. The next listing shows the blocking implementation. If you've ever experienced the joy of network programming with the JDK, this code will evoke pleasant memories.

Listing 4.1 Blocking networking without Netty

```
public class PlainOioServer {
    public void serve(int port) throws IOException {
        final ServerSocket socket = new ServerSocket(port);      <-- Binds the server to the specified port
        try {
            for (;;) {
                final Socket clientSocket = socket.accept();     <-- Accepts a connection
                System.out.println(
                    "Accepted connection from " + clientSocket);
                new Thread(new Runnable() {                      <-- Creates a new thread to handle the connection
                    @Override
                    public void run() {
                        OutputStream out;
                        try {
                            out = clientSocket.getOutputStream();
                            out.write("Hi!\r\n".getBytes(        <-- Writes message to the connected client
                                Charset.forName("UTF-8")));
                            out.flush();
                            clientSocket.close();                <-- Closes the connection
                        }
                        catch (IOException e) {
                            e.printStackTrace();
                        }
```

```
                    finally {
                        try {
                            clientSocket.close();
                        }
                        catch (IOException ex) {
                            // ignore on close
                        }
                    }
                }
            }).start();                         Starts the thread
        }
    }
    catch (IOException e) {
        e.printStackTrace();
    }
  }
}
```

This code handles a moderate number of simultaneous clients adequately. But as the application becomes popular, you notice that it isn't scaling very well to tens of thousands of concurrent incoming connections. You decide to convert to asynchronous networking, but soon discover that the asynchronous API is completely different, so now you have to rewrite your application.

The non-blocking version is shown in the following listing.

Listing 4.2 Asynchronous networking without Netty

```
public class PlainNioServer {
    public void serve(int port) throws IOException {
        ServerSocketChannel serverChannel = ServerSocketChannel.open();
        serverChannel.configureBlocking(false);
        ServerSocket ssocket = serverChannel.socket();
        InetSocketAddress address = new InetSocketAddress(port);
        ssocket.bind(address);                  Binds the server to the selected port
        Selector selector = Selector.open();    Opens the Selector for handling channels
        serverChannel.register(selector, SelectionKey.OP_ACCEPT);   Registers the ServerSocket with the Selector to accept connections
        final ByteBuffer msg = ByteBuffer.wrap("Hi!\r\n".getBytes());
        for (;;) {
            try {
                selector.select();              Waits for new events to process; blocks until the next incoming event
            } catch (IOException ex) {
                ex.printStackTrace();
                // handle exception
                break;
            }
            Set<SelectionKey> readyKeys = selector.selectedKeys();   Obtains all SelectionKey instances that received events
            Iterator<SelectionKey> iterator = readyKeys.iterator();
            while (iterator.hasNext()) {
                SelectionKey key = iterator.next();
                iterator.remove();
                try {
                    if (key.isAcceptable()) {   Checks if the event is a new connection ready to be accepted
```

```
                ServerSocketChannel server =
                    (ServerSocketChannel)key.channel();
            SocketChannel client = server.accept();
            client.configureBlocking(false);
            client.register(selector, SelectionKey.OP_WRITE |
                SelectionKey.OP_READ, msg.duplicate());
            System.out.println(
                "Accepted connection from " + client);
            }
            if (key.isWritable()) {
                SocketChannel client =
                    (SocketChannel)key.channel();
                ByteBuffer buffer =
                    (ByteBuffer)key.attachment();
                while (buffer.hasRemaining()) {
                    if (client.write(buffer) == 0) {
                        break;
                    }
                }
                client.close();
            }
        } catch (IOException ex) {
            key.cancel();
            try {
                key.channel().close();
            } catch (IOException cex) {
                // ignore on close
            }
        }
        }
      }
    }
}
```

Accepts client and registers it with the selector

Checks if the socket is ready for writing data

Writes data to the connected client

Closes the connection

As you can see, although this code does the very same thing as the preceding version, it is quite different. If reimplementing this simple application for non-blocking I/O requires a complete rewrite, consider the level of effort that would be required to port something truly complex.

With this in mind, let's see how the application looks when implemented using Netty.

4.1.2 Using OIO and NIO with Netty

We'll start by writing another blocking version of the application, this time using the Netty framework, as shown in the following listing.

Listing 4.3 Blocking networking with Netty

```
public class NettyOioServer {
    public void server(int port) throws Exception {
        final ByteBuf buf = Unpooled.unreleasableBuffer(
            Unpooled.copiedBuffer("Hi!\r\n", Charset.forName("UTF-8")));
        EventLoopGroup group = new OioEventLoopGroup();
```

```
        try {
            ServerBootstrap b = new ServerBootstrap();
            b.group(group)
                .channel(OioServerSocketChannel.class)
                .localAddress(new InetSocketAddress(port))
                .childHandler(new ChannelInitializer<SocketChannel>() {
                    @Override
                    public void initChannel(SocketChannel ch)
                        throws Exception {
                        ch.pipeline().addLast(
                            new ChannelInboundHandlerAdapter() {
                                @Override
                                public void channelActive(
                                    ChannelHandlerContext ctx)
                                        throws Exception {
                                    ctx.writeAndFlush(buf.duplicate())
                                        .addListener(
                                            ChannelFutureListener.CLOSE);
                                }
                            });
                    }
                });
            ChannelFuture f = b.bind().sync();
            f.channel().closeFuture().sync();
        } finally {
            group.shutdownGracefully().sync();
        }
    }
}
```

Annotations: Creates a ServerBootstrap. Uses OioEventLoopGroup to allow blocking mode (old I/O). Specifies ChannelInitializer that will be called for each accepted connection. Adds a ChannelInboundHandlerAdapter to intercept and handle events. Writes message to client and adds ChannelFutureListener to close connection once message is written. Binds server to accept connections. Releases all resources.

Next we'll implement the same logic with non-blocking I/O using Netty.

4.1.3 Non-blocking Netty version

The next listing is virtually identical to listing 4.3 except for the two highlighted lines. This is all that's required to switch from blocking (OIO) to non-blocking (NIO) transport.

Listing 4.4 Asynchronous networking with Netty

```
public class NettyNioServer {
    public void server(int port) throws Exception {
        final ByteBuf buf = Unpooled.copiedBuffer("Hi!\r\n",
            Charset.forName("UTF-8"));
        EventLoopGroup group = new NioEventLoopGroup();
        try {
            ServerBootstrap b = new ServerBootstrap();
            b.group(group).channel(NioServerSocketChannel.class)
                .localAddress(new InetSocketAddress(port))
                .childHandler(new ChannelInitializer<SocketChannel>() {
                    @Override
                    public void initChannel(SocketChannel ch)
                        throws Exception{
                        ch.pipeline().addLast(
                            new ChannelInboundHandlerAdapter() {
```

Annotations: Uses NioEventLoopGroup for non-blocking mode. Creates ServerBootstrap. Specifies ChannelInitializer to be called for each accepted connection. Adds ChannelInboundHandlerAdapter to receive events and process them.

```
                @Override
                public void channelActive(
                    ChannelHandlerContext ctx) throws Exception {
                        ctx.writeAndFlush(buf.duplicate())
                            .addListener(
                                ChannelFutureListener.CLOSE);
                }
            });
        }
    });
    ChannelFuture f = b.bind().sync();
    f.channel().closeFuture().sync();
} finally {
    group.shutdownGracefully().sync();
}
}
}
```

Writes message to client and adds ChannelFutureListener to close the connection once the message is written

Binds server to accept connections

Releases all resources

Because Netty exposes the same API for every transport implementation, whichever you choose, your code remains virtually unaffected. In all cases the implementation is defined in terms of the interfaces `Channel`, `ChannelPipeline`, and `ChannelHandler`.

Having seen some of the benefits of using Netty-based transports, let's take a closer look at the transport API itself.

4.2 Transport API

At the heart of the transport API is interface `Channel`, which is used for all I/O operations. The `Channel` class hierarchy is shown in figure 4.1.

The figure shows that a `Channel` has a `ChannelPipeline` and a `ChannelConfig` assigned to it. The `ChannelConfig` holds all of the configuration settings for the `Channel` and supports hot changes. Because a specific transport may have unique settings, it may implement a subtype of `ChannelConfig`. (Please refer to the Javadocs for the `ChannelConfig` implementations.)

Since `Channel`s are unique, declaring `Channel` as a subinterface of `java.lang.Comparable` is intended to guarantee ordering. Thus, the implementation of `compareTo()` in `AbstractChannel` throws an `Error` if two distinct `Channel` instances return the same hash code.

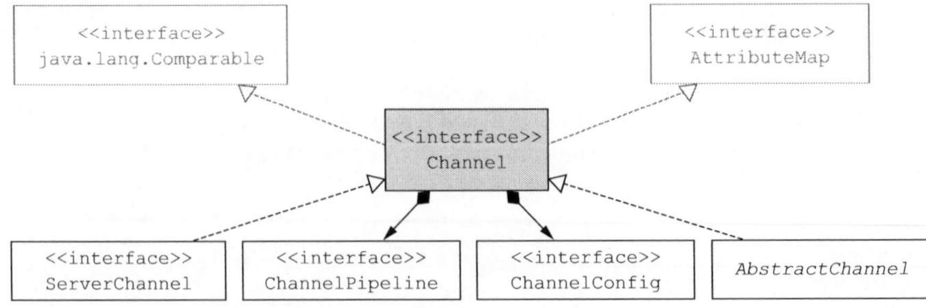

Figure 4.1 Channel interface hierarchy

The ChannelPipeline holds all of the ChannelHandler instances that will be applied to inbound and outbound data and events. These ChannelHandlers implement the application's logic for handling state changes and for data processing.

Typical uses for ChannelHandlers include:

- Transforming data from one format to another
- Providing notification of exceptions
- Providing notification of a Channel becoming active or inactive
- Providing notification when a Channel is registered with or deregistered from an EventLoop
- Providing notification about user-defined events

INTERCEPTING FILTER The ChannelPipeline implements a common design pattern, Intercepting Filter. UNIX pipes are another familiar example: commands are chained together, with the output of one command connecting to the input of the next in line.

You can also modify a ChannelPipeline on the fly by adding or removing ChannelHandler instances as needed. This capability of Netty can be exploited to build highly flexible applications. For example, you could support the STARTTLS[1] protocol on demand simply by adding an appropriate ChannelHandler (SslHandler) to the ChannelPipeline whenever the protocol is requested.

In addition to accessing the assigned ChannelPipeline and ChannelConfig, you can make use of Channel methods, the most important of which are listed in table 4.1.

Table 4.1 Channel methods

Method name	Description
eventLoop	Returns the EventLoop that is assigned to the Channel.
pipeline	Returns the ChannelPipeline that is assigned to the Channel.
isActive	Returns true if the Channel is active. The meaning of active may depend on the underlying transport. For example, a Socket transport is active once connected to the remote peer, whereas a Datagram transport would be active once it's open.
localAddress	Returns the local SocketAddress.
remoteAddress	Returns the remote SocketAddress.
write	Writes data to the remote peer. This data is passed to the ChannelPipeline and queued until it's flushed.
flush	Flushes the previously written data to the underlying transport, such as a Socket.
writeAndFlush	A convenience method for calling write() followed by flush().

1 See STARTTLS, http://en.wikipedia.org/wiki/STARTTLS.

Later on we'll discuss the uses of all these features in detail. For now, keep in mind that the broad range of functionality offered by Netty relies on a small number of interfaces. This means that you can make significant modifications to application logic without wholesale refactoring of your code base.

Consider the common task of writing data and flushing it to the remote peer. The following listing illustrates the use of `Channel.writeAndFlush()` for this purpose.

Listing 4.5 Writing to a `Channel`

```
Channel channel = ...
ByteBuf buf = Unpooled.copiedBuffer("your data", CharsetUtil.UTF_8);
ChannelFuture cf = channel.writeAndFlush(buf);
cf.addListener(new ChannelFutureListener() {
    @Override
    public void operationComplete(ChannelFuture future) {
        if (future.isSuccess()) {
            System.out.println("Write successful");
        } else {
            System.err.println("Write error");
            future.cause().printStacktrace();
        }
    }
});
```

Annotations:
- Creates ByteBuf that holds the data to write
- Writes the data and flushes it
- Adds ChannelFutureListener to receive notification after write completes
- Write operation completes without error
- Logs an error

Netty's `Channel` implementations are thread-safe, so you can store a reference to a `Channel` and use it whenever you need to write something to the remote peer, even when many threads are in use. The following listing shows a simple example of writing with multiple threads. Note that the messages are guaranteed to be sent in order.

Listing 4.6 Using a `Channel` from many threads

```
final Channel channel = ...
final ByteBuf buf = Unpooled.copiedBuffer("your data",
    CharsetUtil.UTF_8).retain();
Runnable writer = new Runnable() {
    @Override
    public void run() {
        channel.write(buf.duplicate());
    }
};
Executor executor = Executors.newCachedThreadPool();

// write in one thread
executor.execute(writer);

// write in another thread
executor.execute(writer);
...
```

- Creates a ByteBuf that holds data to write
- Creates Runnable, which writes data to channel
- Obtains reference to the thread pool Executor
- Hands over write task to executor for execution in one thread
- Hands over another write task for execution in another thread

4.3 Included transports

Netty comes bundled with several transports that are ready for use. Because not all of them support every protocol, you have to select a transport that is compatible with the protocols employed by your application. In this section we'll discuss these relationships.

Table 4.2 lists all of the transports provided by Netty.

Table 4.2 Netty-provided transports

Name	Package	Description
NIO	`io.netty.channel.socket.nio`	Uses the `java.nio.channels` package as a foundation—a selector-based approach.
Epoll	`io.netty.channel.epoll`	Uses JNI for `epoll()` and non-blocking IO. This transport supports features available only on Linux, such as `SO_REUSEPORT`, and is faster than the NIO transport as well as fully non-blocking.
OIO	`io.netty.channel.socket.oio`	Uses the `java.net` package as a foundation—uses blocking streams.
Local	`io.netty.channel.local`	A local transport that can be used to communicate in the VM via pipes.
Embedded	`io.netty.channel.embedded`	An embedded transport, which allows using `ChannelHandlers` without a true network-based transport. This can be quite useful for testing your `ChannelHandler` implementations.

We'll discuss these transports in greater detail in the next sections.

4.3.1 NIO—non-blocking I/O

NIO provides a fully asynchronous implementation of all I/O operations. It makes use of the selector-based API that has been available since the NIO subsystem was introduced in JDK 1.4.

The basic concept behind the selector is to serve as a registry where you request to be notified when the state of a `Channel` changes. The possible state changes are

- A new `Channel` was accepted and is ready.
- A `Channel` connection was completed.
- A `Channel` has data that is ready for reading.
- A `Channel` is available for writing data.

After the application reacts to the change of state, the selector is reset and the process repeats, running on a thread that checks for changes and responds to them accordingly.

The constants shown in table 4.3 represent the bit patterns defined by `class java.nio.channels.SelectionKey`. These patterns are combined to specify the set of state changes about which the application is requesting notification.

Table 4.3 Selection operation bit-set

Name	Description
OP_ACCEPT	Requests notification when a new connection is accepted, and a Channel is created.
OP_CONNECT	Requests notification when a connection is established.
OP_READ	Requests notification when data is ready to be read from the Channel.
OP_WRITE	Requests notification when it is possible to write more data to the Channel. This handles cases when the socket buffer is completely filled, which usually happens when data is transmitted more rapidly than the remote peer can handle.

These internal details of NIO are hidden by the user-level API common to all of Netty's transport implementations. Figure 4.2 shows the process flow.

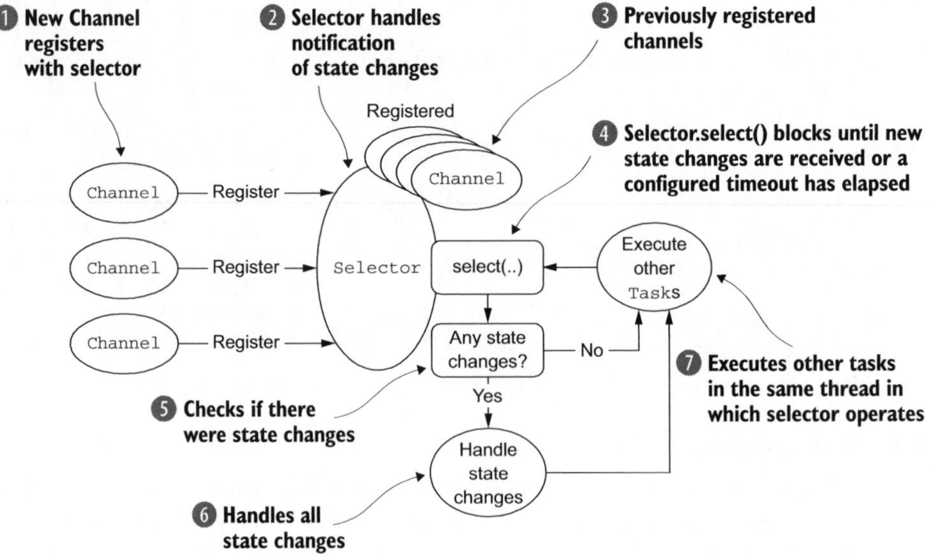

Figure 4.2 Selecting and processing state changes

Zero-copy

Zero-copy is a feature currently available only with NIO and Epoll transport. It allows you to quickly and efficiently move data from a file system to the network without copying from kernel space to user space, which can significantly improve performance in protocols such as FTP or HTTP. This feature is not supported by all OSes. Specifically it is not usable with file systems that implement data encryption or compression—only the raw content of a file can be transferred. Conversely, transferring files that have already been encrypted isn't a problem.

4.3.2 Epoll—native non-blocking transport for Linux

As we explained earlier, Netty's NIO transport is based on the common abstraction for asynchronous/non-blocking networking provided by Java. Although this ensures that Netty's non-blocking API will be usable on any platform, it also entails limitations, because the JDK has to make compromises in order to deliver the same capabilities on all systems.

The growing importance of Linux as a platform for high-performance networking has led to the development of a number of advanced features, including *epoll*, a highly scalable I/O event-notification feature. This API, available since version 2.5.44 (2002) of the Linux kernel, provides better performance than the older POSIX `select` and `poll` system calls[2] and is now the *de facto* standard for non-blocking networking on Linux. The Linux JDK NIO API uses these epoll calls.

Netty provides an NIO API for Linux that uses epoll in a way that's more consistent with its own design and less costly in the way it uses interrupts.[3] Consider utilizing this version if your applications are intended for Linux; you'll find that performance under heavy load is superior to that of the JDK's NIO implementation.

The semantics of this transport are identical to those shown in figure 4.2, and its use is straightforward. For an example, refer to listing 4.4. To substitute epoll for NIO in that listing, replace `NioEventLoopGroup` with `EpollEventLoopGroup` and `NioServerSocketChannel.class` with `EpollServerSocketChannel.class`.

4.3.3 OIO—old blocking I/O

Netty's OIO transport implementation represents a compromise: it is accessed via the common transport API, but because it's built on the blocking implementation of `java.net`, it's not asynchronous. Yet it's very well-suited to certain uses.

For example, you might need to port legacy code that uses libraries that make blocking calls (such as JDBC[4]) and it may not be practical to convert the logic to non-blocking. Instead, you could use Netty's OIO transport in the short term, and port your code later to one of the pure asynchronous transports. Let's see how it works.

In the `java.net` API, you usually have one thread that accepts new connections arriving at the listening `ServerSocket`. A new socket is created for the interaction with the peer, and a new thread is allocated to handle the traffic. This is required because any I/O operation on a specific socket can block at any time. Handling multiple sockets with a single thread can easily lead to a blocking operation on one socket tying up all the others as well.

---

[2] See epoll(4) in the Linux manual pages, http://linux.die.net/man/4/epoll.

[3] The JDK implementation is level-triggered, whereas Netty's is edge-triggered. See the explanation on the epoll Wikipedia page for details, http://en.wikipedia.org/wiki/Epoll - Triggering_modes.

[4] JDBC documentation is available at www.oracle.com/technetwork/java/javase/jdbc/index.html.

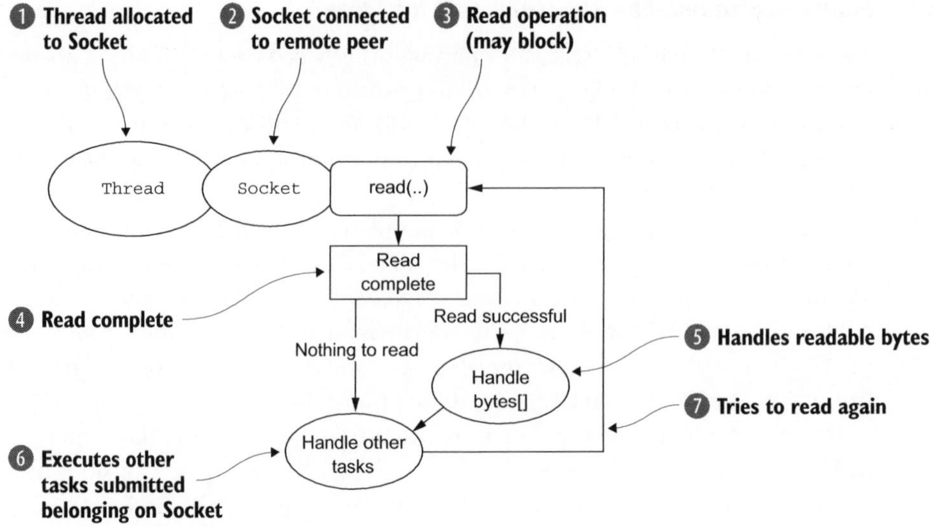

Figure 4.3 OIO processing logic

Given this, you may wonder how Netty can support NIO with the same API used for asynchronous transports. The answer is that Netty makes use of the `SO_TIMEOUT` `Socket` flag, which specifies the maximum number of milliseconds to wait for an I/O operation to complete. If the operation fails to complete within the specified interval, a `SocketTimeoutException` is thrown. Netty catches this exception and continues the processing loop. On the next `EventLoop` run, it will try again. This is the only way an asynchronous framework like Netty can support OIO.[5] Figure 4.3 illustrates this logic.

4.3.4 Local transport for communication within a JVM

Netty provides a local transport for asynchronous communication between clients and servers running in the same JVM. Again, this transport supports the API common to all Netty transport implementations.

In this transport, the `SocketAddress` associated with a server `Channel` isn't bound to a physical network address; rather, it's stored in a registry for as long as the server is running and is deregistered when the `Channel` is closed. Because the transport doesn't accept real network traffic, it can't interoperate with other transport implementations. Therefore, a client wishing to connect to a server (in the same JVM) that uses this transport must also use it. Apart from this limitation, its use is identical to that of other transports.

---

[5] One problem with this approach is the time required to fill in a stack trace when a `SocketTimeoutException` is thrown, which is costly in terms of performance.

4.3.5 Embedded transport

Netty provides an additional transport that allows you to embed `ChannelHandlers` as helper classes inside other `ChannelHandlers`. In this fashion, you can extend the functionality of a `ChannelHandler` without modifying its internal code.

The key to this embedded transport is a concrete `Channel` implementation called, not surprisingly, `EmbeddedChannel`. In chapter 9 we'll discuss in detail how to use this class to create unit test cases for `ChannelHandler` implementations.

4.4 Transport use cases

Now that we've looked at all the transports in detail, let's consider the factors that go into choosing a protocol for a specific use. As mentioned previously, not all transports support all core protocols, which may limit your choices. Table 4.4 shows the matrix of transports and protocols supported at the time of publication.

Table 4.4 Transports support by network protocols

Transport	TCP	UDP	SCTP*	UDT
NIO	X	X	X	X
Epoll (Linux only)	X	X	—	—
OIO	X	X	X	X

* See the explanation of the Stream Control Transmission Protocol (SCTP) in RFC 2960 at www.ietf.org/rfc/rfc2960.txt.

Enabling SCTP on Linux

SCTP requires kernel support as well as installation of the user libraries.

For example, for Ubuntu you would use the following command:

```
# sudo apt-get install libsctp1
```

For Fedora, you'd use yum:

```
# sudo yum install kernel-modules-extra.x86_64 lksctp-tools.x86_64
```

Please refer to the documentation of your Linux distribution for more information about how to enable SCTP.

Although only SCTP has these specific requirements, other transports may have their own configuration options to consider. Furthermore, a server platform will probably need to be configured differently from a client, if only to support a higher number of concurrent connections.

Here are the use cases that you're likely to encounter.

- *Non-blocking code base*—If you don't have blocking calls in your code base—or you can limit them—it's always a good idea to use NIO or epoll when on Linux.

While NIO/epoll is intended to handle many concurrent connections, it also works quite well with a smaller number, especially given the way it shares threads among connections.

- *Blocking code base*—As we've already remarked, if your code base relies heavily on blocking I/O and your applications have a corresponding design, you're likely to encounter problems with blocking operations if you try to convert directly to Netty's NIO transport. Rather than rewriting your code to accomplish this, consider a phased migration: start with OIO and move to NIO (or epoll if you're on Linux) once you have revised your code.
- *Communications within the same JVM*—Communications within the same JVM with no need to expose a service over the network present the perfect use case for local transport. This will eliminate all the overhead of real network operations while still employing your Netty code base. If the need arises to expose the service over the network, you'll simply replace the transport with NIO or OIO.
- *Testing your* `ChannelHandler` *implementations*—If you want to write unit tests for your `ChannelHandler` implementations, consider using the embedded transport. This will make it easy to test your code without having to create many mock objects. Your classes will still conform to the common API event flow, guaranteeing that the `ChannelHandler` will work correctly with live transports. You'll find more information about testing `ChannelHandlers` in chapter 9.

Table 4.5 summarizes the use cases we've examined.

Table 4.5 Optimal transport for an application

Application needs	Recommended transport
Non-blocking code base or general starting point	NIO (or epoll on Linux)
Blocking code base	OIO
Communication within the same JVM	Local
Testing `ChannelHandler` implementations	Embedded

4.5 Summary

In this chapter we studied transports, their implementation and use, and how Netty presents them to the developer.

We went through the transports that ship with Netty and explained their behavior. We also looked at their minimum requirements, because not all transports work with the same Java version and some may be usable only on specific OSes. Finally, we discussed how you can match transports to the requirements of specific use cases.

In the next chapter, we'll focus on `ByteBuf` and `ByteBufHolder`, Netty's data containers. We'll show how to use them and how to get the best performance from them.

5 ByteBuf

This chapter covers

- ByteBuf—Netty's data container
- API details
- Use cases
- Memory allocation

As we noted earlier, the fundamental unit of network data is always the byte. Java NIO provides ByteBuffer as its byte container, but this class makes usage overly complex and somewhat cumbersome to use.

Netty's alternative to ByteBuffer is ByteBuf, a powerful implementation that addresses the limitations of the JDK API and provides a better API for network application developers.

In this chapter we'll illustrate the superior functionality and flexibility of ByteBuf as compared to the JDK's ByteBuffer. This will also give you a better understanding of Netty's approach to data handling in general and prepare you for our discussion of ChannelPipeline and ChannelHandler in chapter 6.

5.1 The ByteBuf API

Netty's API for data handling is exposed through two components—`abstract class ByteBuf` and `interface ByteBufHolder`.

These are some of the advantages of the `ByteBuf` API:

- It's extensible to user-defined buffer types.
- Transparent zero-copy is achieved by a built-in composite buffer type.
- Capacity is expanded on demand (as with the JDK `StringBuilder`).
- Switching between reader and writer modes doesn't require calling `ByteBuffer`'s `flip()` method.
- Reading and writing employ distinct indices.
- Method chaining is supported.
- Reference counting is supported.
- Pooling is supported.

Other classes are available for managing the allocation of `ByteBuf` instances and for performing a variety of operations on the container and the data it holds. We'll explore these features as we study `ByteBuf` and `ByteBufHolder` in detail.

5.2 Class ByteBuf—Netty's data container

Because all network communications involve the movement of sequences of bytes, an efficient and easy-to-use data structure is an obvious necessity. Netty's `ByteBuf` implementation meets and exceeds these requirements. Let's start by looking at how it uses indices to simplify access to the data it contains.

5.2.1 How it works

`ByteBuf` maintains two distinct indices: one for reading and one for writing. When you read from a `ByteBuf`, its `readerIndex` is incremented by the number of bytes read. Similarly, when you write to a `ByteBuf`, its `writerIndex` is incremented. Figure 5.1 shows the layout and state of an empty `ByteBuf`.

To understand the relationship between these indices, consider what would happen if you were to read bytes until the `readerIndex` reached the same value as the `writerIndex`. At that point, you would have reached the end of readable data. Attempting to read beyond that point would trigger an `IndexOutOfBoundsException`, just as when you attempt to access data beyond the end of an array.

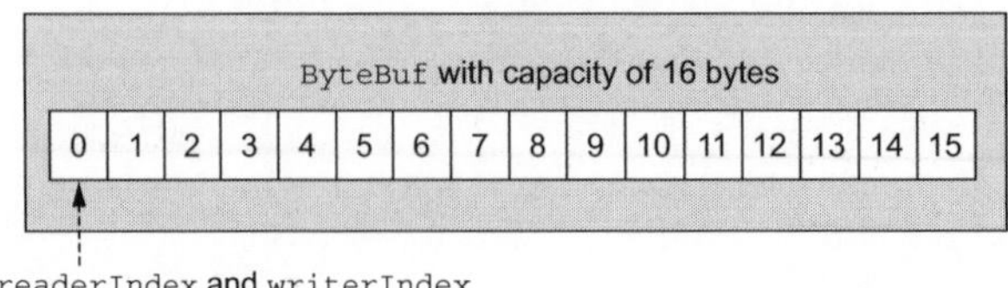

Figure 5.1 A 16-byte `ByteBuf` with its indices set to 0

ByteBuf methods whose names begin with read or write advance the corresponding index, whereas operations that begin with set and get *do not.* The latter methods operate on a relative index that's passed as an argument to the method.

The maximum capacity of a ByteBuf can be specified, and attempting to move the write index past this value will trigger an exception. (The default limit is Integer .MAX_VALUE.)

5.2.2 *ByteBuf usage patterns*

While working with Netty, you'll encounter several common usage patterns built around ByteBuf. As we examine them, it will help to keep figure 5.1 in mind—an array of bytes with distinct indices to control read and write access.

HEAP BUFFERS

The most frequently used ByteBuf pattern stores the data in the heap space of the JVM. Referred to as a *backing array*, this pattern provides fast allocation and deallocation in situations where pooling isn't in use. This approach, shown in listing 5.1, is well suited to cases where you have to handle legacy data.

Listing 5.1 Backing array

```
ByteBuf heapBuf = ...;
if (heapBuf.hasArray()) {
    byte[] array = heapBuf.array();
    int offset = heapBuf.arrayOffset() + heapBuf.readerIndex();
    int length = heapBuf.readableBytes();
    handleArray(array, offset, length);
}
```

Checks whether ByteBuf has a backing array... (at `if (heapBuf.hasArray())`)

...if so, gets a reference to the array (at `byte[] array = heapBuf.array();`)

Calculates the offset of the first byte (at `int offset = ...`)

Gets the number of readable bytes (at `int length = ...`)

Calls your method using array, offset, and length as parameters (at `handleArray(...)`)

NOTE Attempting to access a backing array when hasArray() returns false will trigger an UnsupportedOperationException. This pattern is similar to uses of the JDK's ByteBuffer.

DIRECT BUFFERS

Direct buffer is another ByteBuf pattern. We expect that memory allocated for object creation will always come from the heap, but it doesn't have to—the ByteBuffer class that was introduced in JDK 1.4 with NIO allows a JVM implementation to allocate memory via native calls. This aims to avoid copying the buffer's contents to (or from) an intermediate buffer before (or after) each invocation of a native I/O operation.

The Javadoc for ByteBuffer states explicitly, "The contents of direct buffers will reside outside of the normal garbage-collected heap."[1] This explains why direct buffers

---

[1] Java Platform, Standard Edition 8 API Specification, java.nio, Class ByteBuffer, http://docs.oracle.com/javase/8/docs/api/java/nio/ByteBuffer.html.

are ideal for network data transfer. If your data were contained in a heap-allocated buffer, the JVM would, in fact, copy your buffer to a direct buffer internally before sending it through the socket.

The primary disadvantage of direct buffers is that they're somewhat more expensive to allocate and release than are heap-based buffers. You may also encounter another drawback if you're working with legacy code: because the data isn't on the heap, you may have to make a copy, as shown next.

Listing 5.2 Direct buffer data access

```
ByteBuf directBuf = ...;
if (!directBuf.hasArray()) {
    int length = directBuf.readableBytes();
    byte[] array = new byte[length];
    directBuf.getBytes(directBuf.readerIndex(), array);
    handleArray(array, 0, length);
}
```

Checks if ByteBuf isn't backed by an array. If not, this is a direct buffer.

Gets the number of readable bytes

Allocates a new array to hold length bytes

Copies bytes into the array

Calls some method with array, offset, and length parameters

Clearly, this involves a bit more work than using a backing array, so if you know in advance that the data in the container will be accessed as an array, you may prefer to use heap memory.

COMPOSITE BUFFERS

The third and final pattern uses a *composite buffer*, which presents an aggregated view of multiple `ByteBuf`s. Here you can add and delete `ByteBuf` instances as needed, a feature entirely absent from the JDK's `ByteBuffer` implementation.

Netty implements this pattern with a subclass of `ByteBuf`, `CompositeByteBuf`, which provides a virtual representation of multiple buffers as a single, merged buffer.

> **WARNING** The `ByteBuf` instances in a `CompositeByteBuf` may include both direct and nondirect allocations. If there is only one instance, calling `hasArray()` on a `CompositeByteBuf` will return the `hasArray()` value of that component; otherwise it will return `false`.

To illustrate, let's consider a message composed of two parts, header and body, to be transmitted via HTTP. The two parts are produced by different application modules and assembled when the message is sent out. The application has the option of reusing the same message body for multiple messages. When this happens, a new header is created for each message.

Because we don't want to reallocate both buffers for each message, `CompositeByteBuf` is a perfect fit; it eliminates unnecessary copying while exposing the common `ByteBuf` API. Figure 5.2 shows the resulting message layout.

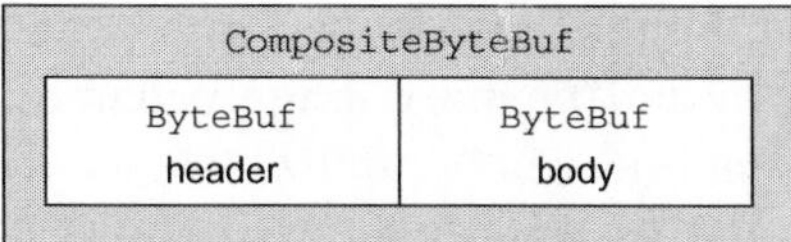

Figure 5.2 `CompositeByteBuf` **holding a header and body**

The following listing shows how this requirement would be implemented using the JDK's `ByteBuffer`. An array of two `ByteBuffers` is created to hold the message components, and a third one is created to hold a copy of all the data.

Listing 5.3 Composite buffer pattern using `ByteBuffer`

```
// Use an array to hold the message parts
ByteBuffer[] message = new ByteBuffer[] { header, body };
// Create a new ByteBuffer and use copy to merge the header and body
ByteBuffer message2 =
    ByteBuffer.allocate(header.remaining() + body.remaining());
message2.put(header);
message2.put(body);
message2.flip();
```

The allocation and copy operations, along with the need to manage the array, make this version inefficient as well as awkward. The next listing shows a version using `CompositeByteBuf`.

Listing 5.4 Composite buffer pattern using `CompositeByteBuf`

```
CompositeByteBuf messageBuf = Unpooled.compositeBuffer();
ByteBuf headerBuf = ...; // can be backing or direct
ByteBuf bodyBuf = ...;   // can be backing or direct
messageBuf.addComponents(headerBuf, bodyBuf);
.....
messageBuf.removeComponent(0); // remove the header
for (ByteBuf buf : messageBuf) {
    System.out.println(buf.toString());
}
```

- Appends ByteBuf instances to the CompositeByteBuf
- Removes ByteBuf at index 0 (first component)
- Loops over all the ByteBuf instances

`CompositeByteBuf` may not allow access to a backing array, so accessing the data in a `CompositeByteBuf` resembles the direct buffer pattern, as shown next.

Listing 5.5 Accessing the data in a `CompositeByteBuf`

```
CompositeByteBuf compBuf = Unpooled.compositeBuffer();
int length = compBuf.readableBytes();
byte[] array = new byte[length];
compBuf.getBytes(compBuf.readerIndex(), array);
handleArray(array, 0, array.length);
```

- Gets the number of readable bytes
- Allocates a new array with length of readable bytes
- Reads bytes into the array
- Uses the array with offset and length parameters

Note that Netty optimizes socket I/O operations that employ `CompositeByteBuf`, eliminating whenever possible the performance and memory usage penalties that are incurred with the JDK's buffer implementation.[2] This optimization takes place in Netty's core code and is therefore not exposed, but you should be aware of its impact.

> **THE COMPOSITEBYTEBUF API** Beyond the methods it inherits from `ByteBuf`, `CompositeByteBuf` offers a great deal of added functionality. Refer to the Netty Javadocs for a full listing of the API.

5.3 Byte-level operations

`ByteBuf` provides numerous methods beyond the basic read and write operations for modifying its data. In the next sections we'll discuss the most important of these.

5.3.1 Random access indexing

Just as in an ordinary Java byte array, `ByteBuf` indexing is zero-based: the index of the first byte is 0 and that of the last byte is always `capacity() - 1`. The next listing shows that the encapsulation of storage mechanisms makes it very simple to iterate over the contents of a `ByteBuf`.

Listing 5.6 Access data

```
ByteBuf buffer = ...;
for (int i = 0; i < buffer.capacity(); i++) {
    byte b = buffer.getByte(i);
    System.out.println((char) b);
}
```

Note that accessing the data using one of the methods that takes an index argument doesn't alter the value of either `readerIndex` or `writerIndex`. Either can be moved manually if necessary by calling `readerIndex(index)` or `writerIndex(index)`.

5.3.2 Sequential access indexing

While `ByteBuf` has both reader and writer indices, the JDK's `ByteBuffer` has only one, which is why you have to call `flip()` to switch between read and write modes. Figure 5.3 shows how a `ByteBuf` is partitioned by its two indices into three areas.

---

[2] This applies particularly to the JDK's use of a technique known as *Scatter/Gather I/O*, defined as "a method of input and output where a single system call writes to a vector of buffers from a single data stream, or, alternatively, reads into a vector of buffers from a single data stream." Robert Love, *Linux System Programming* (O'Reilly, 2007).

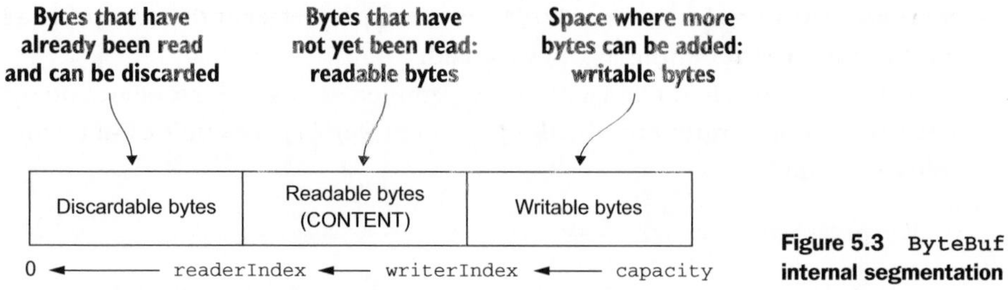

Figure 5.3 `ByteBuf` internal segmentation

5.3.3 *Discardable bytes*

The segment labeled discardable bytes in figure 5.3 contains bytes that have already been read. They can be discarded and the space reclaimed by calling `discardReadBytes()`. The initial size of this segment, stored in `readerIndex`, is 0, increasing as `read` operations are executed (`get*` operations don't move the `readerIndex`).

Figure 5.4 shows the result of calling `discardReadBytes()` on the buffer shown in figure 5.3. You can see that the space in the discardable bytes segment has become available for writing. Note that there's no guarantee about the contents of the writable segment after `discardReadBytes()` has been called.

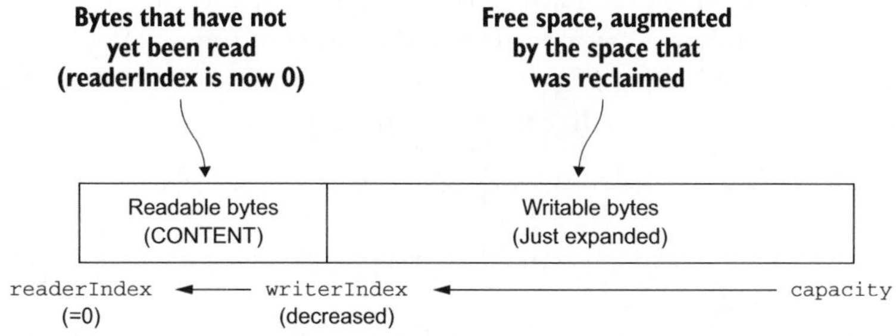

Figure 5.4 `ByteBuf` after discarding read bytes

While you may be tempted to call `discardReadBytes()` frequently to maximize the writable segment, please be aware that this will most likely cause memory copying because the readable bytes (marked CONTENT in the figures) have to be moved to the start of the buffer. We advise doing this only when it's really needed; for example, when memory is at a premium.

5.3.4 *Readable bytes*

The readable bytes segment of a `ByteBuf` stores the actual data. The default value of a newly allocated, wrapped, or copied buffer's `readerIndex` is 0. Any operation whose name starts with read or skip will retrieve or skip the data at the current readerIndex and increase it by the number of bytes read.

If the method called takes a ByteBuf argument as a write target and doesn't have a destination index argument, the destination buffer's writerIndex will be increased as well; for example,

```
readBytes(ByteBuf dest);
```

If an attempt is made to read from the buffer when readable bytes have been exhausted, an IndexOutOfBoundsException is raised.

This listing shows how to read all readable bytes.

Listing 5.7 Read all data

```
ByteBuf buffer = ...;
while (buffer.isReadable()) {
    System.out.println(buffer.readByte());
}
```

5.3.5 *Writable bytes*

The writable bytes segment is an area of memory with undefined contents, ready for writing. The default value of a newly allocated buffer's writerIndex is 0. Any operation whose name starts with write will start writing data at the current writerIndex, increasing it by the number of bytes written. If the target of the write operation is also a ByteBuf and no source index is specified, the source buffer's readerIndex will be increased by the same amount. This call would appear as follows:

```
writeBytes(ByteBuf dest);
```

If an attempt is made to write beyond the target's capacity, an IndexOutOfBound-Exception will be raised.

The following listing is an example that fills the buffer with random integer values until it runs out of space. The method writableBytes() is used here to determine whether there is sufficient space in the buffer.

Listing 5.8 Write data

```
// Fills the writable bytes of a buffer with random integers.
ByteBuf buffer = ...;
while (buffer.writableBytes() >= 4) {
    buffer.writeInt(random.nextInt());
}
```

5.3.6 *Index management*

The JDK's InputStream defines the methods mark(int readlimit) and reset(). These are used to mark the current position in the stream to a specified value and to reset the stream to that position, respectively.

Similarly, you can set and reposition the `ByteBuf` `readerIndex` and `writerIndex` by calling `markReaderIndex()`, `markWriterIndex()`, `resetReaderIndex()`, and `resetWriterIndex()`. These are similar to the `InputStream` calls, except that there's no `readlimit` parameter to specify when the mark becomes invalid.

You can also move the indices to specified positions by calling `readerIndex(int)` or `writerIndex(int)`. Attempting to set either index to an invalid position will cause an `IndexOutOfBoundsException`.

You can set both `readerIndex` and `writerIndex` to 0 by calling `clear()`. Note that this doesn't clear the *contents* of memory. Figure 5.5 (which repeats figure 5.3) shows how it works.

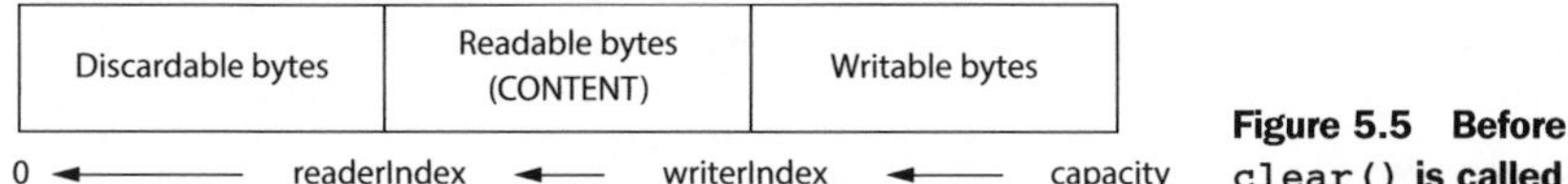

Figure 5.5 Before `clear()` is called

As before, the `ByteBuf` contains three segments. Figure 5.6 shows the `ByteBuf` after `clear()` is called.

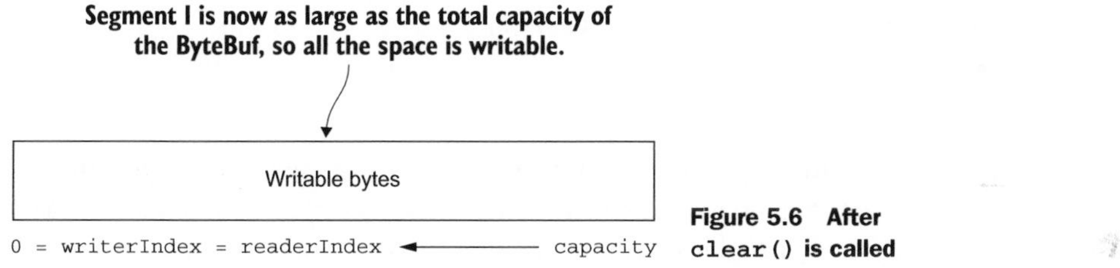

Figure 5.6 After `clear()` is called

Calling `clear()` is much less expensive than `discardReadBytes()` because it resets the indices without copying any memory.

5.3.7 *Search operations*

There are several ways to determine the index of a specified value in a `ByteBuf`. The simplest of these uses the `indexOf()` methods. More complex searches can be executed with methods that take a `ByteBufProcessor` argument. This interface defines a single method,

```
boolean process(byte value)
```

which reports whether the input value is the one being sought.

ByteBufProcessor defines numerous convenience methods targeting common values. Suppose your application needs to integrate with so-called Flash sockets,[3] which have NULL-terminated content. Calling

```
forEachByte(ByteBufProcessor.FIND_NUL)
```

consumes the Flash data simply and efficiently, because fewer bounds checks are executed during processing.

This listing shows an example of searching for a carriage return character (`\r`).

Listing 5.9 Using `ByteBufProcessor` to find `\r`

```
ByteBuf buffer = ...;
int index = buffer.forEachByte(ByteBufProcessor.FIND_CR);
```

5.3.8 Derived buffers

A *derived buffer* provides a view of a `ByteBuf` that represents its contents in a specialized way. Such views are created by the following methods:

- `duplicate()`
- `slice()`
- `slice(int, int)`
- `Unpooled.unmodifiableBuffer(…)`
- `order(ByteOrder)`
- `readSlice(int)`

Each returns a new `ByteBuf` instance with its own reader, writer, and marker indices. The internal storage is shared just as in a JDK `ByteBuffer`. This makes a derived buffer inexpensive to create, but it also means that if you modify its contents you are modifying the source instance as well, so beware.

> **BYTEBUF COPYING** If you need a true copy of an existing buffer, use `copy()` or `copy(int, int)`. Unlike a derived buffer, the `ByteBuf` returned by this call has an independent copy of the data.

The next listing shows how to work with a `ByteBuf` segment using `slice(int, int)`.

[3] Flash sockets are discussed in the Flash ActionScript 3.0 Developer's Guide, Networking and communication, Sockets page at http://help.adobe.com/en_US/as3/dev/WSb2ba3b1aad8a27b0-181c51321220efd9d1c-8000.html.

Listing 5.10 Slice a ByteBuf

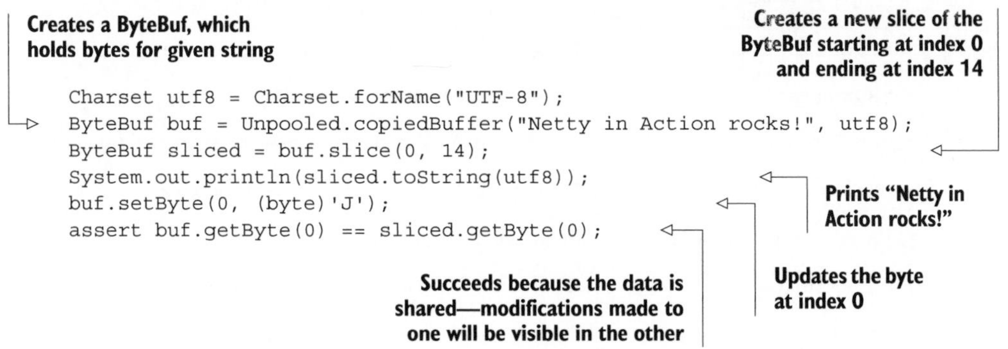

Creates a ByteBuf, which holds bytes for given string
Creates a new slice of the ByteBuf starting at index 0 and ending at index 14
Charset utf8 = Charset.forName("UTF-8");
ByteBuf buf = Unpooled.copiedBuffer("Netty in Action rocks!", utf8);
ByteBuf sliced = buf.slice(0, 14);
System.out.println(sliced.toString(utf8));
buf.setByte(0, (byte)'J');
assert buf.getByte(0) == sliced.getByte(0);
Prints "Netty in Action rocks!"
Updates the byte at index 0
Succeeds because the data is shared—modifications made to one will be visible in the other

Now let's see how a *copy* of a ByteBuf segment differs from a *slice*.

Listing 5.11 Copying a ByteBuf

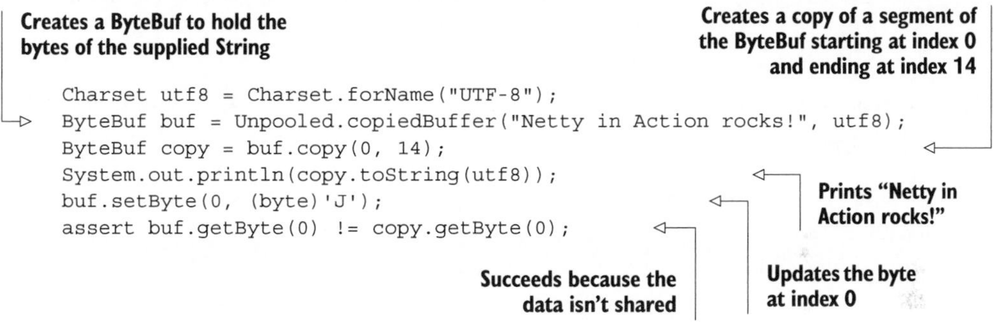

Creates a ByteBuf to hold the bytes of the supplied String
Creates a copy of a segment of the ByteBuf starting at index 0 and ending at index 14
Charset utf8 = Charset.forName("UTF-8");
ByteBuf buf = Unpooled.copiedBuffer("Netty in Action rocks!", utf8);
ByteBuf copy = buf.copy(0, 14);
System.out.println(copy.toString(utf8));
buf.setByte(0, (byte)'J');
assert buf.getByte(0) != copy.getByte(0);
Prints "Netty in Action rocks!"
Updates the byte at index 0
Succeeds because the data isn't shared

The two cases are identical except for the effect of modifying a slice or a copy of the original ByteBuf. Whenever possible, use slice() to avoid the cost of copying memory.

5.3.9 Read/write operations

As we've mentioned, there are two categories of read/write operations:

- get() and set() operations that start at a given index and leave it unchanged
- read() and write() operations that start at a given index and adjust it by the number of bytes accessed

Table 5.1 lists the most frequently used get() methods. For a complete list, refer to the API docs.

Table 5.1 `get()` operations

Name	Description
`getBoolean(int)`	Returns the `Boolean` value at the given index
`getByte(int)`	Returns the byte at the given index
`getUnsignedByte(int)`	Returns the unsigned byte value at the given index as a `short`
`getMedium(int)`	Returns the 24-bit medium `int` value at the given index
`getUnsignedMedium(int)`	Returns the unsigned 24-bit medium `int` value at the given index
`getInt(int)`	Returns the `int` value at the given index
`getUnsignedInt(int)`	Returns the unsigned `int` value at the given index as a long
`getLong(int)`	Returns the `long` value at the given index
`getShort(int)`	Returns the `short` value at the given index
`getUnsignedShort(int)`	Returns the unsigned `short` value at the given index as an int
`getBytes(int, ...)`	Transfers this buffer's data to a specified destination starting at the given index

Most of these operations have a corresponding `set()` method. These are listed in table 5.2.

Table 5.2 `set()` operations

Name	Description
`setBoolean(int, boolean)`	Sets the `Boolean` value at the given index
`setByte(int index, int value)`	Sets byte value at the given index
`setMedium(int index, int value)`	Sets the 24-bit medium value at the given index
`setInt(int index, int value)`	Sets the `int` value at the given index
`setLong(int index, long value)`	Sets the `long` value at the given index
`setShort(int index, int value)`	Sets the `short` value at the given index

The following listing illustrates the use of `get()` and `set()` methods, showing that they don't alter the read and write indices.

Listing 5.12 get() and set() usage

```
Charset utf8 = Charset.forName("UTF-8");
ByteBuf buf = Unpooled.copiedBuffer("Netty in Action rocks!", utf8);
System.out.println((char)buf.getByte(0));
int readerIndex = buf.readerIndex();
int writerIndex = buf.writerIndex();
buf.setByte(0, (byte)'B');
System.out.println((char)buf.getByte(0));
assert readerIndex == buf.readerIndex();
assert writerIndex == buf.writerIndex();
```

Creates a new ByteBuf to hold the bytes for the given String

Prints the first char, 'N'

Stores the current readerIndex and writerIndex

Updates the byte at index 0 with the char 'B'

Prints the first char, now 'B'

Succeeds because these operations don't modify the indices

Now let's examine the `read()` operations, which act on the current `readerIndex` or `writerIndex`. These methods are used to read from the `ByteBuf` as if it were a stream. Table 5.3 shows the most commonly used methods.

Table 5.3 `read()` operations

Name	Description
`readBoolean()`	Returns the `Boolean` value at the current `readerIndex` and increases the `readerIndex` by 1.
`readByte()`	Returns the byte value at the current `readerIndex` and increases the `readerIndex` by 1.
`readUnsignedByte()`	Returns the unsigned byte value at the current `readerIndex` as a short and increases the `readerIndex` by 1.
`readMedium()`	Returns the 24-bit medium value at the current `readerIndex` and increases the `readerIndex` by 3.
`readUnsignedMedium()`	Returns the unsigned 24-bit medium value at the current `readerIndex` and increases the `readerIndex` by 3.
`readInt()`	Returns the `int` value at the current `readerIndex` and increases the `readerIndex` by 4.
`readUnsignedInt()`	Returns the unsigned `int` value at the current `readerIndex` as a long and increases the `readerIndex` by 4.
`readLong()`	Returns the `long` value at the current `readerIndex` and increases the `readerIndex` by 8.
`readShort()`	Returns the `short` value at the current `readerIndex` and increases the `readerIndex` by 2.

Table 5.3 `read()` **operations *(continued)***

Name	Description
`readUnsignedShort()`	Returns the unsigned `short` value at the current `readerIndex` as an int and increases the `readerIndex` by 2.
`readBytes(ByteBuf | byte[] destination, int dstIndex [,int length])`	Transfers data from the current `ByteBuf` starting at the current `readerIndex` (for, if specified, `length` bytes) to a destination `ByteBuf` or `byte[]`, starting at the destination's `dstIndex`. The local `readerIndex` is incremented by the number of bytes transferred.

Almost every `read()` method has a corresponding `write()` method, used to append to a `ByteBuf`. Note that the arguments to these methods, listed in table 5.4, are the values to be written, not index values.

Table 5.4 Write operations

Name	Description
`writeBoolean(boolean)`	Writes the Boolean value at the current `writerIndex` and increases the `writerIndex` by 1.
`writeByte(int)`	Writes the byte value at the current `writerIndex` and increases the `writerIndex` by 1.
`writeMedium(int)`	Writes the medium value at the current `writerIndex` and increases the `writerIndex` by 3.
`writeInt(int)`	Writes the `int` value at the current `writerIndex` and increases the `writerIndex` by 4.
`writeLong(long)`	Writes the `long` value at the current `writerIndex` and increases the `writerIndex` by 8.
`writeShort(int)`	Writes the `short` value at the current `writerIndex` and increases the `writerIndex` by 2.
`writeBytes(source ByteBuf | byte[] [,int srcIndex ,int length])`	Transfers data starting at the current `writerIndex` from the specified source (`ByteBuf` or `byte[]`). If `srcIndex` and `length` are provided, reading starts at `srcIndex` and proceeds for `length` bytes. The current `writerIndex` is incremented by the number of bytes written.

Listing 5.13 shows these methods in use.

Listing 5.13 read() and write() operations on the ByteBuf

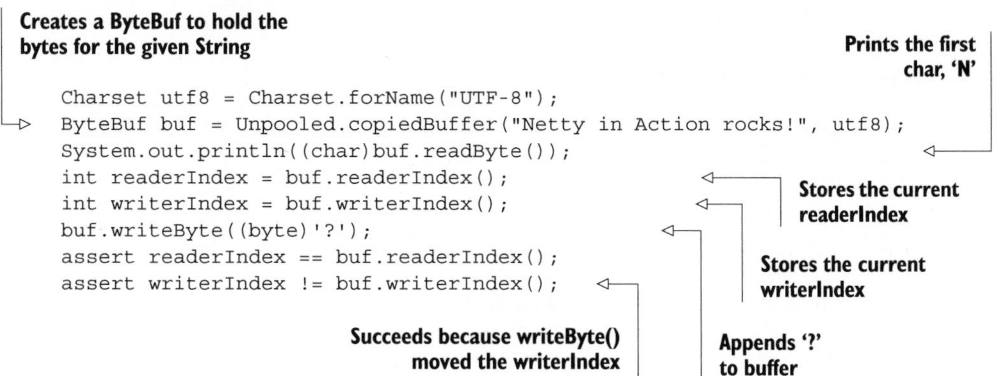
Creates a ByteBuf to hold the bytes for the given String
Prints the first char, 'N'
Stores the current readerIndex
Stores the current writerIndex
Succeeds because writeByte() moved the writerIndex
Appends '?' to buffer

```
Charset utf8 = Charset.forName("UTF-8");
ByteBuf buf = Unpooled.copiedBuffer("Netty in Action rocks!", utf8);
System.out.println((char)buf.readByte());
int readerIndex = buf.readerIndex();
int writerIndex = buf.writerIndex();
buf.writeByte((byte)'?');
assert readerIndex == buf.readerIndex();
assert writerIndex != buf.writerIndex();
```

5.3.10 More operations

Table 5.5 lists additional useful operations provided by `ByteBuf`.

Table 5.5 Other useful operations

Name	Description
`isReadable()`	Returns `true` if at least one byte can be read.
`isWritable()`	Returns `true` if at least one byte can be written.
`readableBytes()`	Returns the number of bytes that can be read.
`writableBytes()`	Returns the number of bytes that can be written.
`capacity()`	Returns the number of bytes that the `ByteBuf` can hold. After this it will try to expand again until `maxCapacity()` is reached.
`maxCapacity()`	Returns the maximum number of bytes the `ByteBuf` can hold.
`hasArray()`	Returns `true` if the `ByteBuf` is backed by a byte array.
`array()`	Returns the byte array if the `ByteBuf` is backed by a byte array; otherwise it throws an `UnsupportedOperationException`.

5.4 Interface ByteBufHolder

We often find that we need to store a variety of property values in addition to the actual data payload. An HTTP response is a good example; along with the content represented as bytes, there are status code, cookies, and so on.

Netty provides `ByteBufHolder` to handle this common use case. `ByteBufHolder` also provides support for advanced features of Netty, such as buffer pooling, where a `ByteBuf` can be borrowed from a pool and also be released automatically if required.

ByteBufHolder has just a handful of methods for access to the underlying data and reference counting. Table 5.6 lists them (leaving aside those it inherits from ReferenceCounted).

Table 5.6 ByteBufHolder operations

Name	Description
content()	Returns the ByteBuf held by this ByteBufHolder
copy()	Returns a deep copy of this ByteBufHolder, including an unshared copy of the contained ByteBuf's data
duplicate()	Returns a shallow copy of this ByteBufHolder, including a shared copy of the contained ByteBuf's data

ByteBufHolder is a good choice if you want to implement a message object that stores its payload in a ByteBuf.

5.5 ByteBuf allocation

In this section we'll describe ways of managing ByteBuf instances.

5.5.1 On-demand: interface ByteBufAllocator

To reduce the overhead of allocating and deallocating memory, Netty implements pooling with the interface ByteBufAllocator, which can be used to allocate instances of any of the ByteBuf varieties we've described. The use of pooling is an application-specific decision that doesn't alter the ByteBuf API in any way.

Table 5.7 lists the operations provided by ByteBufAllocator.

Table 5.7 ByteBufAllocator methods

Name	Description

buffer()
buffer(int initialCapacity);
buffer(int initialCapacity, int maxCapacity);
	Returns a ByteBuf with heap-based or direct data storage

heapBuffer() heapBuffer(int initialCapacity) heapBuffer(int initialCapacity, int maxCapacity)	Returns a ByteBuf with heap-based storage
directBuffer() directBuffer(int initialCapacity) directBuffer(int initialCapacity, int maxCapacity)	Returns a ByteBuf with direct storage

Table 5.7 `ByteBufAllocator` methods

Name	Description

`compositeBuffer()`
`compositeBuffer(int maxNumComponents);`
`compositeDirectBuffer()`
`compositeDirectBuffer(int maxNumComponents);`
`compositeHeapBuffer()`
`compositeHeapBuffer(int maxNumComponents);`
	Returns a `CompositeByteBuf` that can be expanded by adding heap-based or direct buffers up to the specified number of components

`ioBuffer()`	Returns a `ByteBuf` that will be used for I/O operations on a socket

You can obtain a reference to a `ByteBufAllocator` either from a `Channel` (each of which can have a distinct instance) or through the `ChannelHandlerContext` that is bound to a `ChannelHandler`. The following listing illustrates both of these methods.

Listing 5.14 Obtaining a `ByteBufAllocator` reference

```
Channel channel = ...;
ByteBufAllocator allocator = channel.alloc();      <-- Gets a ByteBufAllocator from a Channel
....
ChannelHandlerContext ctx = ...;
ByteBufAllocator allocator2 = ctx.alloc();      <-- Gets a ByteBufAllocator from a ChannelHandlerContext
...
```

Netty provides two implementations of `ByteBufAllocator`: `PooledByteBufAllocator` and `UnpooledByteBufAllocator`. The former pools `ByteBuf` instances to improve performance and minimize memory fragmentation. This implementation uses an efficient approach to memory allocation known as *jemalloc*[4] that has been adopted by a number of modern OSes. The latter implementation doesn't pool `ByteBuf` instances and returns a new instance every time it's called.

Although Netty uses the `PooledByteBufAllocator` by default, this can be changed easily via the `ChannelConfig` API or by specifying a different allocator when bootstrapping your application. More details can be found in chapter 8.

5.5.2 Unpooled buffers

There may be situations where you don't have a reference to a `ByteBufAllocator`. For this case, Netty provides a utility class called `Unpooled`, which provides static helper

[4] Jason Evans, "A Scalable Concurrent malloc(3) Implementation for FreeBSD" (2006), http://people.freebsd.org/~jasone/jemalloc/bsdcan2006/jemalloc.pdf.

methods to create unpooled ByteBuf instances. Table 5.8 lists the most important of these methods.

Table 5.8 Unpooled methods

Name	Description
buffer() buffer(int initialCapacity) buffer(int initialCapacity, int maxCapacity)	Returns an unpooled ByteBuf with heap-based storage
directBuffer() directBuffer(int initialCapacity) directBuffer(int initialCapacity, int maxCapacity)	Returns an unpooled ByteBuf with direct storage
wrappedBuffer()	Returns a ByteBuf, which wraps the given data.
copiedBuffer()	Returns a ByteBuf, which copies the given data

The Unpooled class also makes ByteBuf available to non-networking projects that can benefit from a high-performance extensible buffer API and that don't require other Netty components.

5.5.3 Class ByteBufUtil

ByteBufUtil provides static helper methods for manipulating a ByteBuf. Because this API is generic and unrelated to pooling, these methods have been implemented outside the allocation classes.

The most valuable of these static methods is probably hexdump(), which prints a hexadecimal representation of the contents of a ByteBuf. This is useful in a variety of situations, such as logging the contents of a ByteBuf for debugging purposes. A hex representation will generally provide a more usable log entry than would a direct representation of the byte values. Furthermore, the hex version can easily be converted back to the actual byte representation.

Another useful method is boolean equals(ByteBuf, ByteBuf), which determines the equality of two ByteBuf instances. You may find other methods of ByteBufUtil useful if you implement your own ByteBuf subclasses.

5.6 Reference counting

Reference counting is a technique for optimizing memory use and performance by releasing the resources held by an object when it is no longer referenced by other objects. Netty introduced reference counting in version 4 for ByteBuf and ByteBufHolder, both of which implement interface ReferenceCounted.

The idea behind reference counting isn't particularly complex; mostly it involves tracking the number of active references to a specified object. A `ReferenceCounted` implementation instance will normally start out with an active reference count of 1. As long as the reference count is greater than 0, the object is guaranteed not to be released. When the number of active references decreases to 0, the instance will be released. Note that while the precise meaning of release may be implementation-specific, at the very least an object that has been released should no longer be available for use.

Reference counting is essential to pooling implementations, such as `PooledByteBufAllocator`, which reduces the overhead of memory allocation. Examples are shown in the next two listings.

Listing 5.15 Reference counting

```
Channel channel = ...;
ByteBufAllocator allocator = channel.alloc();
....
ByteBuf buffer = allocator.directBuffer();
assert buffer.refCnt() == 1;
...
```

- Gets ByteBufAllocator from a channel
- Allocates a ByteBuf from the ByteBufAllocator
- Checks for the expected reference count of 1

Listing 5.16 Release reference-counted object

```
ByteBuf buffer = ...;
boolean released = buffer.release();
...
```

- Decrements the active references to the object. At 0, the object is released and the method returns true.

Trying to access a reference-counted object that's been released will result in an `IllegalReferenceCountException`.

Note that a specific class can define its release-counting contract in its own unique way. For example, we can envision a class whose implementation of `release()` always sets the reference count to zero whatever its current value, thus invalidating all active references at once.

> **WHO IS RESPONSIBLE FOR RELEASE?** In general, the last party to access an object is responsible for releasing it. In chapter 6 we'll explain the relevance of this conept to `ChannelHandler` and `ChannelPipeline`.

5.7 Summary

This chapter was devoted to Netty's data containers, based on `ByteBuf`. We started out by explaining the advantages of `ByteBuf` over the implementation provided by the JDK. We also highlighted the APIs of the available variants and indicated which are best suited to specific use cases.

These are the main points we covered:

- The use of distinct read and write indices to control data access
- Different approaches to memory usage—backing arrays and direct buffers
- The aggregate view of multiple `ByteBufs` using `CompositeByteBuf`
- Data-access methods: searching, slicing, and copying
- The read, write, get, and set APIs
- `ByteBufAllocator` pooling and reference counting

In the next chapter, we'll focus on `ChannelHandler`, which provides the vehicle for your data-processing logic. Because `ChannelHandler` makes heavy use of `ByteBuf`, you'll begin to see important pieces of the overall architecture of Netty coming together.

ChannelHandler and ChannelPipeline

6

This chapter covers

- The `ChannelHandler` and `ChannelPipeline` APIs
- Detecting resource leaks
- Exception handling

In the previous chapter you studied `ByteBuf`, Netty's data container. As we explore Netty's dataflow and processing components in this chapter, we'll build on what you've learned and you'll begin to see important elements of the framework coming together.

You already know that `ChannelHandlers` can be chained together in a `ChannelPipeline` to organize processing logic. We'll examine a variety of use cases involving these classes and an important relation, `ChannelHandlerContext`.

Understanding the interactions among all of these components is essential to building modular, reusable implementations with Netty.

6.1 The ChannelHandler family

To prepare for our detailed study of `ChannelHandler`, we'll spend time on some of the underpinnings of this part of Netty's component model.

6.1.1 The Channel lifecycle

Interface Channel defines a simple but powerful state model that's closely related to the ChannelInboundHandler API. The four Channel states are listed in table 6.1.

Table 6.1 Channel lifecycle states

State	Description
ChannelUnregistered	The Channel was created, but isn't registered to an EventLoop.
ChannelRegistered	The Channel is registered to an EventLoop.
ChannelActive	The Channel is active (connected to its remote peer). It's now possible to receive and send data.
ChannelInactive	The Channel isn't connected to the remote peer.

The normal lifecycle of a Channel is shown in figure 6.1. As these state changes occur, corresponding events are generated. These are forwarded to ChannelHandlers in the ChannelPipeline, which can then act on them.

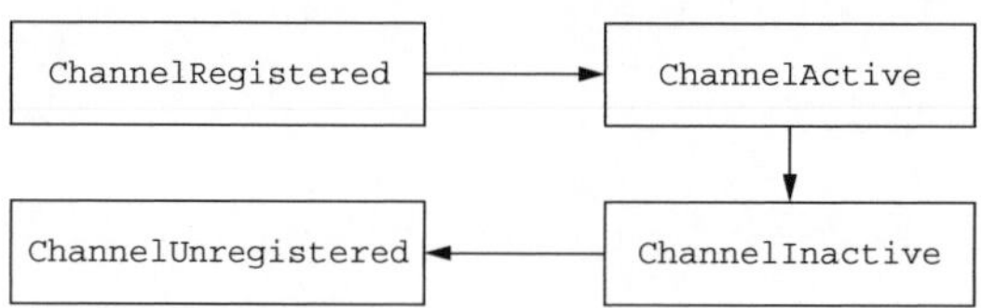

Figure 6.1 Channel state model

6.1.2 The ChannelHandler lifecycle

The lifecycle operations defined by interface ChannelHandler, listed in table 6.2, are called after a ChannelHandler has been added to, or removed from, a ChannelPipeline. Each method accepts a ChannelHandlerContext argument.

Table 6.2 ChannelHandler lifecycle methods

Type	Description
handlerAdded	Called when a ChannelHandler is added to a ChannelPipeline
handlerRemoved	Called when a ChannelHandler is removed from a ChannelPipeline
exceptionCaught	Called if an error occurs in the ChannelPipeline during processing

Netty defines the following two important subinterfaces of ChannelHandler:

- ChannelInboundHandler—Processes inbound data and state changes of all kinds
- ChannelOutboundHandler—Processes outbound data and allows interception of all operations

In the next sections, we'll discuss these interfaces in detail.

6.1.3 Interface ChannelInboundHandler

Table 6.3 lists the lifecycle methods of interface ChannelInboundHandler. These are called when data is received or when the state of the associated Channel changes. As we mentioned earlier, these methods map closely to the Channel lifecycle.

Table 6.3 `ChannelInboundHandler` methods

Type	Description
`channelRegistered`	Invoked when a `Channel` is registered to its `EventLoop` and is able to handle I/O.
`channelUnregistered`	Invoked when a `Channel` is deregistered from its `EventLoop` and can't handle any I/O.
`channelActive`	Invoked when a `Channel` is active; the `Channel` is connected/bound and ready.
`channelInactive`	Invoked when a `Channel` leaves active state and is no longer connected to its remote peer.
`channelReadComplete`	Invoked when a read operation on the `Channel` has completed.
`channelRead`	Invoked if data is read from the `Channel`.
`channelWritabilityChanged`	Invoked when the writability state of the `Channel` changes. The user can ensure writes are not done too quickly (to avoid an `OutOfMemoryError`) or can resume writes when the `Channel` becomes writable again. The `Channel` method `isWritable()` can be called to detect the writability of the channel. The threshold for writability can be set via `Channel.config().setWriteHighWaterMark()` and `Channel.config().setWriteLowWaterMark()`.
`userEventTriggered`	Invoked when `ChannelnboundHandler.fireUser-EventTriggered()` is called because a POJO was passed through the `ChannelPipeline`.

When a `ChannelInboundHandler` implementation overrides `channelRead()`, it is responsible for explicitly releasing the memory associated with pooled `ByteBuf` instances. Netty provides a utility method for this purpose, `ReferenceCountUtil.release()`, as shown next.

Listing 6.1 Releasing message resources

```
@Sharable
public class DiscardHandler extends ChannelInboundHandlerAdapter {     <-- Extends ChannelInbound-HandlerAdapter
    @Override
    public void channelRead(ChannelHandlerContext ctx, Object msg) {
```

```
        ReferenceCountUtil.release(msg);       <-- Discards received message
    }
}
```

Netty logs unreleased resources with a `WARN`-level log message, making it fairly simple to find offending instances in the code. But managing resources in this way can be cumbersome. A simpler alternative is to use `SimpleChannelInboundHandler`. The next listing is a variation of listing 6.1 that illustrates this.

Listing 6.2 Using `SimpleChannelInboundHandler`

```
@Sharable
public class SimpleDiscardHandler
    extends SimpleChannelInboundHandler<Object> {     <-- Extends SimpleChannelInboundHandler
    @Override
    public void channelRead0(ChannelHandlerContext ctx,
        Object msg) {
        // No need to do anything special     <-- No need for any explicit release of resources
    }
}
```

Because `SimpleChannelInboundHandler` releases resources automatically, you shouldn't store references to any messages for later use, as these will become invalid.

Section 6.1.6 provides a more detailed discussion of reference handling.

6.1.4 Interface ChannelOutboundHandler

Outbound operations and data are processed by `ChannelOutboundHandler`. Its methods are invoked by `Channel`, `ChannelPipeline`, and `ChannelHandlerContext`.

A powerful capability of `ChannelOutboundHandler` is to defer an operation or event on demand, which allows for sophisticated approaches to request handling. If writing to the remote peer is suspended, for example, you can defer flush operations and resume them later.

Table 6.4 shows all of the methods defined locally by `ChannelOutboundHandler` (leaving out those inherited from `ChannelHandler`).

Table 6.4 `ChannelOutboundHandler` methods

Type	Description
`bind(ChannelHandlerContext, SocketAddress,ChannelPromise)`	Invoked on request to bind the `Channel` to a local address
`connect(ChannelHandlerContext, SocketAddress,SocketAddress,ChannelPromise)`	Invoked on request to connect the `Channel` to the remote peer
`disconnect(ChannelHandlerContext, ChannelPromise)`	Invoked on request to disconnect the `Channel` from the remote peer
`close(ChannelHandlerContext,ChannelPromise)`	Invoked on request to close the `Channel`

Table 6.4 `ChannelOutboundHandler` methods

Type	Description
`deregister(ChannelHandlerContext, ChannelPromise)`	Invoked on request to deregister the `Channel` from its `EventLoop`
`read(ChannelHandlerContext)`	Invoked on request to read more data from the `Channel`
`flush(ChannelHandlerContext)`	Invoked on request to flush queued data to the remote peer through the `Channel`
`write(ChannelHandlerContext,Object, ChannelPromise)`	Invoked on request to write data through the `Channel` to the remote peer

CHANNELPROMISE VS. CHANNELFUTURE Most of the methods in `ChannelOutboundHandler` take a `ChannelPromise` argument to be notified when the operation completes. `ChannelPromise` is a subinterface of `ChannelFuture` that defines the writable methods, such as `setSuccess()` or `setFailure()`, thus making `ChannelFuture` immutable.

Next we'll look at classes that simplify the task of writing `ChannelHandlers`.

6.1.5 *ChannelHandler adapters*

You can use the classes `ChannelInboundHandlerAdapter` and `ChannelOutboundHandlerAdapter` as starting points for your own `ChannelHandlers`. These adapters provide basic implementations of `ChannelInboundHandler` and `ChannelOutboundHandler` respectively. They acquire the methods of their common superinterface, `ChannelHandler`, by extending the abstract class `ChannelHandlerAdapter`. The resulting class hierarchy is shown in figure 6.2.

`ChannelHandlerAdapter` also provides the utility method `isSharable()`. This method returns `true` if the implementation is annotated as `Sharable`, indicating that it can be added to multiple `ChannelPipelines` (as discussed in section 2.3.1).

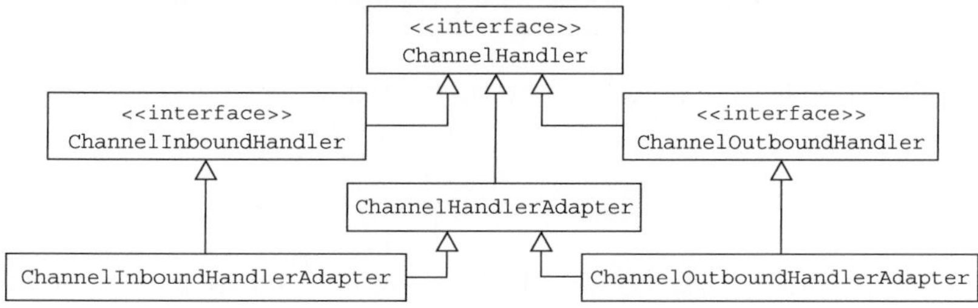

Figure 6.2 `ChannelHandlerAdapter` class hierarchy

The method bodies provided in `ChannelInboundHandlerAdapter` and `ChannelOutboundHandlerAdapter` call the equivalent methods on the associated `ChannelHandlerContext`, thereby forwarding events to the next `ChannelHandler` in the pipeline.

To use these adapter classes in your own handlers, simply extend them and override the methods you want to customize.

6.1.6 *Resource management*

Whenever you act on data by calling `ChannelInboundHandler.channelRead()` or `ChannelOutboundHandler.write()`, you need to ensure that there are no resource leaks. As you may remember from the previous chapter, Netty uses reference counting to handle pooled `ByteBuf`s. So it's important to adjust the reference count after you have finished using a `ByteBuf`.

To assist you in diagnosing potential problems, Netty provides `class ResourceLeakDetector`, which will sample about 1% of your application's buffer allocations to check for memory leaks. The overhead involved is very small.

If a leak is detected, a log message similar to the following will be produced:

```
LEAK: ByteBuf.release() was not called before it's garbage-collected. Enable
advanced leak reporting to find out where the leak occurred. To enable
advanced leak reporting, specify the JVM option
'-Dio.netty.leakDetectionLevel=ADVANCED' or call
ResourceLeakDetector.setLevel().
```

Netty currently defines the four leak detection levels, as listed in table 6.5.

Table 6.5 Leak-detection levels

Level	Description
`DISABLED`	Disables leak detection. Use this only after extensive testing.
`SIMPLE`	Reports any leaks found using the default sampling rate of 1%. This is the default level and is a good fit for most cases.
`ADVANCED`	Reports leaks found and where the message was accessed. Uses the default sampling rate.
`PARANOID`	Like `ADVANCED` except that *every* access is sampled. This has a heavy impact on performance and should be used only in the debugging phase.

The leak-detection level is defined by setting the following Java system property to one of the values in the table:

```
java -Dio.netty.leakDetectionLevel=ADVANCED
```

If you relaunch your application with the JVM option you'll see the recent locations of your application where the leaked buffer was accessed. The following is a typical leak report generated by a unit test:

```
Running io.netty.handler.codec.xml.XmlFrameDecoderTest
15:03:36.886 [main] ERROR io.netty.util.ResourceLeakDetector - LEAK:
     ByteBuf.release() was not called before it's garbage-collected.
Recent access records: 1
#1: io.netty.buffer.AdvancedLeakAwareByteBuf.toString(
    AdvancedLeakAwareByteBuf.java:697)
io.netty.handler.codec.xml.XmlFrameDecoderTest.testDecodeWithXml(
    XmlFrameDecoderTest.java:157)
io.netty.handler.codec.xml.XmlFrameDecoderTest.testDecodeWithTwoMessages(
    XmlFrameDecoderTest.java:133)
...
```

How do you use this diagnostic tool to prevent leaks when you implement `ChannelInboundHandler.channelRead()` and `ChannelOutboundHandler.write()`? Let's examine the case where your `channelRead()` operation consumes an inbound message; that is, without passing it on to the next `ChannelInboundHandler` by calling `ChannelHandlerContext.fireChannelRead()`. This listing shows how to release the message.

Listing 6.3 Consuming and releasing an inbound message

```
@Sharable
public class DiscardInboundHandler extends ChannelInboundHandlerAdapter {
    @Override
    public void channelRead(ChannelHandlerContext ctx, Object msg) {
        ReferenceCountUtil.release(msg);
    }
}
```

Extends ChannelInboundHandlerAdapter

Releases resource by using ReferenceCountUtil.release()

CONSUMING INBOUND MESSAGES THE EASY WAY Because consuming inbound data and releasing it is such a common task, Netty provides a special `ChannelInboundHandler` implementation called `SimpleChannelInboundHandler`. This implementation will automatically release a message once it's consumed by `channelRead0()`.

On the outbound side, if you handle a `write()` operation and discard a message, you're responsible for releasing it. The next listing shows an implementation that discards all written data.

Listing 6.4 Discarding and releasing outbound data

```
@Sharable
public class DiscardOutboundHandler
    extends ChannelOutboundHandlerAdapter {
    @Override
    public void write(ChannelHandlerContext ctx,
        Object msg, ChannelPromise promise) {
        ReferenceCountUtil.release(msg);
        promise.setSuccess();
    }
}
```

Extends ChannelOutboundHandlerAdapter

Releases resource by using ReferenceCountUtil.release(...)

Notifies ChannelPromise that data was handled

It's important not only to release resources but also to notify the `ChannelPromise`. Otherwise a situation might arise where a `ChannelFutureListener` has not been notified about a message that has been handled.

In sum, it is the responsibility of the user to call `ReferenceCountUtil.release()` if a message is consumed or discarded and not passed to the next `ChannelOutboundHandler` in the `ChannelPipeline`. If the message reaches the actual transport layer, it will be released automatically when it's written or the `Channel` is closed.

6.2 *Interface ChannelPipeline*

If you think of a `ChannelPipeline` as a chain of `ChannelHandler` instances that intercept the inbound and outbound events that flow through a `Channel`, it's easy to see how the interaction of these `ChannelHandlers` can make up the core of an application's data and event-processing logic.

Every new `Channel` that's created is assigned a new `ChannelPipeline`. This association is permanent; the `Channel` can neither attach another `ChannelPipeline` nor detach the current one. This is a fixed operation in Netty's component lifecycle and requires no action on the part of the developer.

Depending on its origin, an event will be handled by either a `ChannelInboundHandler` or a `ChannelOutboundHandler`. Subsequently it will be forwarded to the next handler of the same supertype by a call to a `ChannelHandlerContext` implementation.

> **ChannelHandlerContext**
>
> A `ChannelHandlerContext` enables a `ChannelHandler` to interact with its `ChannelPipeline` and with other handlers. A handler can notify the next `ChannelHandler` in the `ChannelPipeline` and even dynamically modify the `ChannelPipeline` it belongs to.
>
> `ChannelHandlerContext` has a rich API for handling events and performing I/O operations. Section 6.3 will provide more information on `ChannelHandlerContext`.

Figure 6.3 illustrates a typical `ChannelPipeline` layout with both inbound and outbound `ChannelHandlers` and illustrates our earlier statement that a `ChannelPipeline`

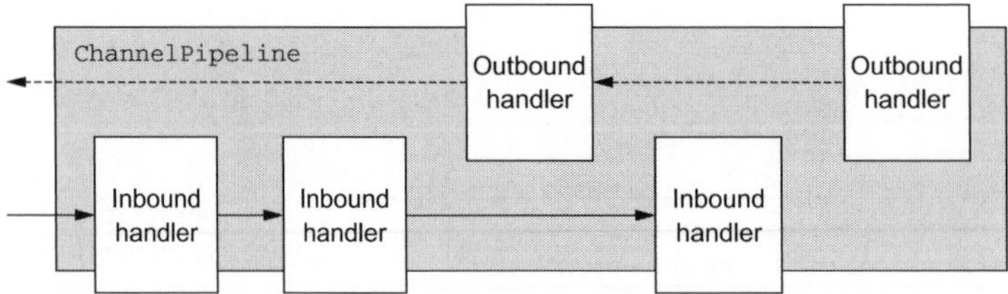

Figure 6.3 **`ChannelPipeline` and `ChannelHandlers`**

is primarily a series of ChannelHandlers. ChannelPipeline also provides methods for propagating events through the ChannelPipeline itself. If an inbound event is triggered, it's passed from the beginning to the end of the ChannelPipeline. In figure 6.3, an outbound I/O event will start at the right end of the ChannelPipeline and proceed to the left.

> **ChannelPipeline relativity**
>
> You might say that from the point of view of an event traveling through the ChannelPipeline, the starting end depends on whether the event is inbound or outbound. But Netty always identifies the inbound entry to the ChannelPipeline (the left side in figure 6.3) as the beginning and the outbound entry (the right side) as the end.
>
> When you've finished adding your mix of inbound and outbound handlers to a ChannelPipeline using the ChannelPipeline.add*() methods, the ordinal of each ChannelHandler is its position from beginning to end as we just defined them. Thus, if you number the handlers in figure 6.3 from left to right, the first ChannelHandler seen by an inbound event will be 1; the first handler seen by an outbound event will be 5.

As the pipeline propagates an event, it determines whether the type of the next ChannelHandler in the pipeline matches the direction of movement. If not, the ChannelPipeline skips that ChannelHandler and proceeds to the next one, until it finds one that matches the desired direction. (Of course, a handler might implement both ChannelInboundHandler and ChannelOutboundHandler interfaces.)

6.2.1 *Modifying a ChannelPipeline*

A ChannelHandler can modify the layout of a ChannelPipeline in real time by adding, removing, or replacing other ChannelHandlers. (It can remove itself from the ChannelPipeline as well.) This is one of the most important capabilities of the ChannelHandler, so we'll take a close look at how it's done. The relevant methods are listed in table 6.6.

Table 6.6 ChannelHandler methods for modifying a ChannelPipeline

Name	Description
addFirst addBefore addAfter addLast	Adds a ChannelHandler to the ChannelPipeline
remove	Removes a ChannelHandler from the ChannelPipeline
replace	Replaces a ChannelHandler in the ChannelPipeline with another ChannelHandler

This listing shows these methods in use.

Listing 6.5 Modify the ChannelPipeline

```
ChannelPipeline pipeline = ..;
FirstHandler firstHandler = new FirstHandler();
pipeline.addLast("handler1", firstHandler);
pipeline.addFirst("handler2", new SecondHandler());
pipeline.addLast("handler3", new ThirdHandler());
...
pipeline.remove("handler3");
pipeline.remove(firstHandler);
pipeline.replace("handler2", "handler4", new FourthHandler());
```

Creates a FirstHandler instance

Adds this instance to the ChannelPipeline as "handler1"

Adds an instance of a SecondHandler to the ChannelPipeline in the first slot, as "handler2". It will be placed before the existing "handler1".

Adds a ThirdHandler instance to the ChannelPipeline in the last slot as "handler3".

Removes "handler3" by name.

Removes the FirstHandler by reference (it's unique, so its name is not needed).

Replaces the SecondHandler ("handler2") with a FourthHandler: "handler4".

You'll see later on that this ability to reorganize `ChannelHandlers` with ease lends itself to the implementation of extremely flexible logic.

ChannelHandler execution and blocking

Normally each `ChannelHandler` in the `ChannelPipeline` processes events that are passed to it by its `EventLoop` (the I/O thread). It's critically important not to block this thread as it would have a negative effect on the overall handling of I/O.

Sometimes it may be necessary to interface with legacy code that uses blocking APIs. For this case, the `ChannelPipeline` has `add()` methods that accept an `EventExecutorGroup`. If an event is passed to a custom `EventExecutorGroup`, it will be handled by one of the `EventExecutors` contained in this `EventExecutorGroup` and thus be removed from the `EventLoop` of the `Channel` itself. For this use case Netty provides an implementation called `DefaultEventExecutorGroup`.

In addition to these operations, there are others for accessing `ChannelHandlers` either by type or by name. These are listed in table 6.7.

Table 6.7 `ChannelPipeline` operations for accessing `ChannelHandlers`

Name	Description
`get`	Returns a `ChannelHandler` by type or name
`context`	Returns the `ChannelHandlerContext` bound to a `ChannelHandler`
`names`	Returns the names of all the `ChannelHandlers` in the `ChannelPipeline`

6.2.2 *Firing events*

The `ChannelPipeline` API exposes additional methods for invoking inbound and outbound operations. Table 6.8 lists the inbound operations, which notify `ChannelInboundHandlers` of events occurring in the `ChannelPipeline`.

Table 6.8 `ChannelPipeline` inbound operations

Method name	Description
`fireChannelRegistered`	Calls `channelRegistered(ChannelHandlerContext)` on the next `ChannelInboundHandler` in the `ChannelPipeline`
`fireChannelUnregistered`	Calls `channelUnregistered(ChannelHandlerContext)` on the next `ChannelInboundHandler` in the `ChannelPipeline`
`fireChannelActive`	Calls `channelActive(ChannelHandlerContext)` on the next `ChannelInboundHandler` in the `ChannelPipeline`
`fireChannelInactive`	Calls `channelInactive(ChannelHandlerContext)` on the next `ChannelInboundHandler` in the `ChannelPipeline`
`fireExceptionCaught`	Calls `exceptionCaught(ChannelHandlerContext, Throwable)` on the next `ChannelHandler` in the `ChannelPipeline`
`fireUserEventTriggered`	Calls `userEventTriggered(ChannelHandlerContext, Object)` on the next `ChannelInboundHandler` in the `ChannelPipeline`
`fireChannelRead`	Calls `channelRead(ChannelHandlerContext, Object msg)` on the next `ChannelInboundHandler` in the `ChannelPipeline`
`fireChannelReadComplete`	Calls `channelReadComplete(ChannelHandlerContext)` on the next `ChannelStateHandler` in the `ChannelPipeline`

On the outbound side, handling an event will cause some action to be taken on the underlying socket. Table 6.9 lists the outbound operations of the `ChannelPipeline` API.

Table 6.9 `ChannelPipeline` outbound operations

Method name	Description
`bind`	Binds the `Channel` to a local address. This will call `bind(ChannelHandlerContext, SocketAddress, ChannelPromise)` on the next `ChannelOutboundHandler` in the `ChannelPipeline`.
`connect`	Connects the `Channel` to a remote address. This will call `connect(ChannelHandlerContext, SocketAddress, ChannelPromise)` on the next `ChannelOutboundHandler` in the `ChannelPipeline`.
`disconnect`	Disconnects the `Channel`. This will call `disconnect(ChannelHandlerContext, ChannelPromise)` on the next `ChannelOutboundHandler` in the `ChannelPipeline`.
`close`	Closes the `Channel`. This will call `close(ChannelHandlerContext, ChannelPromise)` on the next `ChannelOutboundHandler` in the `ChannelPipeline`.
`deregister`	Deregisters the `Channel` from the previously assigned `EventExecutor` (the `EventLoop`). This will call `deregister(ChannelHandlerContext, ChannelPromise)` on the next `ChannelOutboundHandler` in the `ChannelPipeline`.
`flush`	Flushes all pending writes of the `Channel`. This will call `flush(ChannelHandlerContext)` on the next `ChannelOutboundHandler` in the `ChannelPipeline`.
`write`	Writes a message to the `Channel`. This will call `write(ChannelHandlerContext, Object msg, ChannelPromise)` on the next `ChannelOutboundHandler` in the `ChannelPipeline`. Note: this does not write the message to the underlying `Socket`, but only queues it. To write it to the `Socket`, call `flush()` or `writeAndFlush()`.
`writeAndFlush`	This is a convenience method for calling `write()` then `flush()`.
`read`	Requests to read more data from the `Channel`. This will call `read(ChannelHandlerContext)` on the next `ChannelOutboundHandler` in the `ChannelPipeline`.

In summary,

- A `ChannelPipeline` holds the `ChannelHandlers` associated with a `Channel`.
- A `ChannelPipeline` can be modified dynamically by adding and removing `ChannelHandlers` as needed.
- `ChannelPipeline` has a rich API for invoking actions in response to inbound and outbound events.

6.3 Interface ChannelHandlerContext

A ChannelHandlerContext represents an association between a ChannelHandler and a ChannelPipeline and is created whenever a ChannelHandler is added to a ChannelPipeline. The primary function of a ChannelHandlerContext is to manage the interaction of its associated ChannelHandler with others in the same ChannelPipeline.

ChannelHandlerContext has numerous methods, some of which are also present on Channel and on ChannelPipeline itself, but there is an important difference. If you invoke these methods on a Channel or ChannelPipeline instance, they propagate through the entire pipeline. The same methods called on a ChannelHandlerContext will start at the current associated ChannelHandler and propagate only to the next ChannelHandler in the pipeline that is capable of handling the event.

Table 6.10 summarizes the ChannelHandlerContext API.

Table 6.10 The ChannelHandlerContext API

Method name	Description
bind	Binds to the given SocketAddress and returns a ChannelFuture
channel	Returns the Channel that is bound to this instance
close	Closes the Channel and returns a ChannelFuture
connect	Connects to the given SocketAddress and returns a ChannelFuture
deregister	Deregisters from the previously assigned EventExecutor and returns a ChannelFuture
disconnect	Disconnects from the remote peer and returns a ChannelFuture
executor	Returns the EventExecutor that dispatches events
fireChannelActive	Triggers a call to channelActive() (connected) on the next ChannelInboundHandler
fireChannelInactive	Triggers a call to channelInactive() (closed) on the next ChannelInboundHandler
fireChannelRead	Triggers a call to channelRead() (message received) on the next ChannelInboundHandler
fireChannelReadComplete	Triggers a channelWritabilityChanged event to the next ChannelInboundHandler
handler	Returns the ChannelHandler bound to this instance
isRemoved	Returns true if the associated ChannelHandler was removed from the ChannelPipeline
name	Returns the unique name of this instance

Table 6.10 The `ChannelHandlerContext` API *(continued)*

Method name	Description
`pipeline`	Returns the associated `ChannelPipeline`
`read`	Reads data from the `Channel` into the first inbound buffer; triggers a `channelRead` event if successful and notifies the handler of `channelReadComplete`
`write`	Writes a message via this instance through the pipeline

When using the `ChannelHandlerContext` API, please keep the following points in mind:

- The `ChannelHandlerContext` associated with a `ChannelHandler` never changes, so it's safe to cache a reference to it.
- `ChannelHandlerContext` methods, as we explained at the start of this section, involve a shorter event flow than do the identically named methods available on other classes. This should be exploited where possible to provide maximum performance.

6.3.1 *Using ChannelHandlerContext*

In this section we'll discuss the use of `ChannelHandlerContext` and the behaviors of methods available on `ChannelHandlerContext`, `Channel`, and `ChannelPipeline`. Figure 6.4 shows the relationships among them.

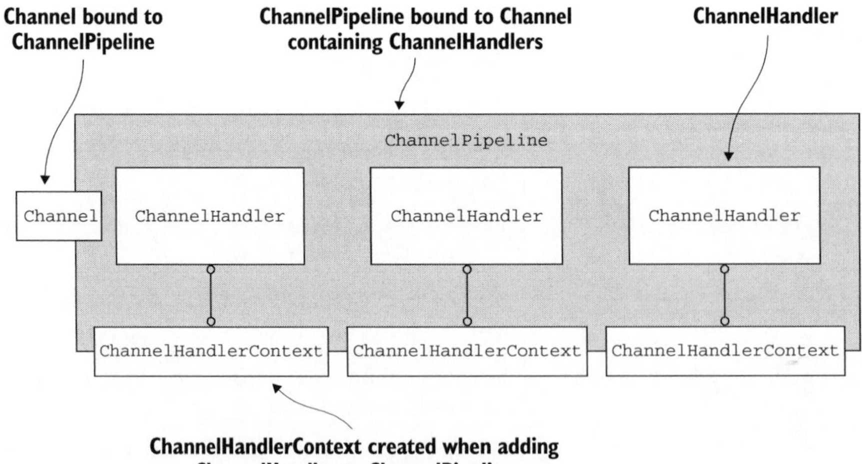

Figure 6.4 The relationships among `Channel`, `ChannelPipeline`, `ChannelHandler`, and `ChannelHandlerContext`

In the following listing you acquire a reference to the Channel from a ChannelHandlerContext. Calling write() on the Channel causes a write event to flow all the way through the pipeline.

Listing 6.6 Accessing the Channel from a ChannelHandlerContext

```
ChannelHandlerContext ctx = ..;
Channel channel = ctx.channel();
channel.write(Unpooled.copiedBuffer("Netty in Action",
   CharsetUtil.UTF_8));
```

Gets a reference to the Channel associated with the ChannelHandlerContext

Writes buffer via the Channel

The next listing shows a similar example, but writing this time to a ChannelPipeline. Again, the reference is retrieved from the ChannelHandlerContext.

Listing 6.7 Accessing the ChannelPipeline from a ChannelHandlerContext

```
ChannelHandlerContext ctx = ..;
ChannelPipeline pipeline = ctx.pipeline();
pipeline.write(Unpooled.copiedBuffer("Netty in Action",
   CharsetUtil.UTF_8));
```

Gets a reference to the ChannelPipeline associated with the ChannelHandlerContext

Writes the buffer via the ChannelPipeline

As you can see in figure 6.5, the flows in listings 6.6 and 6.7 are identical. It's important to note that although the write() invoked on either the Channel or the ChannelPipeline operation propagates the event all the way through the pipeline, the movement from one handler to the next at the ChannelHandler level is invoked on the ChannelHandlerContext.

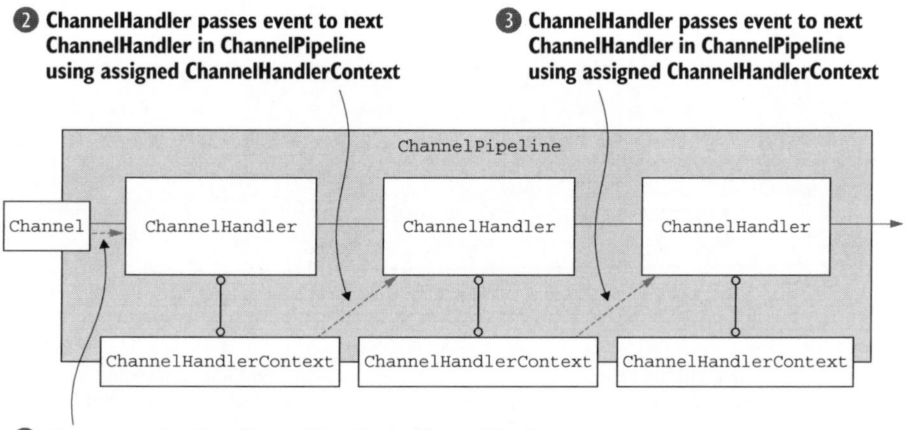

2 ChannelHandler passes event to next ChannelHandler in ChannelPipeline using assigned ChannelHandlerContext
3 ChannelHandler passes event to next ChannelHandler in ChannelPipeline using assigned ChannelHandlerContext
ChannelPipeline
Channel
ChannelHandler
ChannelHandler
ChannelHandler
ChannelHandlerContext
ChannelHandlerContext
ChannelHandlerContext
1 Event passed to first ChannelHandler in ChannelPipeline

Figure 6.5 Event propagation via the Channel or the ChannelPipeline

Why would you want to propagate an event starting at a specific point in the `ChannelPipeline`?

- To reduce the overhead of passing the event through `ChannelHandlers` that are not interested in it
- To prevent processing of the event by handlers that *would* be interested in the event

To invoke processing starting with a specific `ChannelHandler`, you must refer to the `ChannelHandlerContext` that's associated with the `ChannelHandler` *before* that one. This `ChannelHandlerContext` will invoke the `ChannelHandler` that *follows* the one with which it's associated.

The following listing and figure 6.6 illustrate this use.

Listing 6.8 Calling `ChannelHandlerContext write()`

```
ChannelHandlerContext ctx = ..;
ctx.write(Unpooled.copiedBuffer("Netty in Action", CharsetUtil.UTF_8));
```

Gets a reference to a ChannelHandlerContext

write() sends the buffer to the next ChannelHandler

As shown in figure 6.6, the message flows through the `ChannelPipeline` starting at the *next* `ChannelHandler`, bypassing all the preceding ones.

The use case we just described is a common one, and it's especially useful for calling operations on a specific `ChannelHandler` instance.

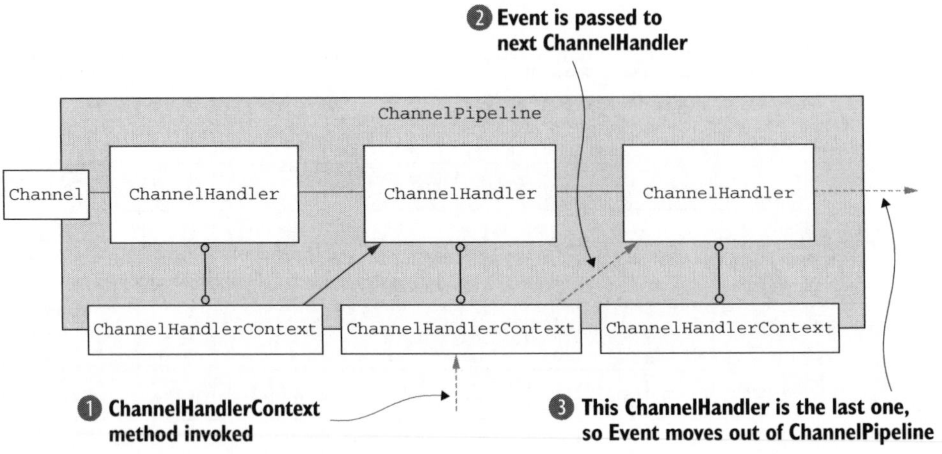
2 Event is passed to next ChannelHandler
ChannelPipeline
Channel
ChannelHandler
ChannelHandler
ChannelHandler
ChannelHandlerContext
ChannelHandlerContext
ChannelHandlerContext
1 ChannelHandlerContext method invoked
3 This ChannelHandler is the last one, so Event moves out of ChannelPipeline

Figure 6.6 Event flow for operations triggered via the `ChannelHandlerContext`

6.3.2 Advanced uses of ChannelHandler and ChannelHandlerContext

As you saw in listing 6.6, you can acquire a reference to the enclosing `ChannelPipeline` by calling the `pipeline()` method of a `ChannelHandlerContext`. This enables runtime manipulation of the pipeline's `ChannelHandlers`, which can be exploited to implement sophisticated designs. For example, you could add a `ChannelHandler` to a pipeline to support a dynamic protocol change.

Other advanced uses can be supported by caching a reference to a `ChannelHandlerContext` for later use, which might take place outside any `ChannelHandler` methods and could even originate from a different thread. This listing shows this pattern being used to trigger an event.

Listing 6.9 Caching a `ChannelHandlerContext`

```
public class WriteHandler extends ChannelHandlerAdapter {
    private ChannelHandlerContext ctx;
    @Override
    public void handlerAdded(ChannelHandlerContext ctx) {
        this.ctx = ctx;
    }
    public void send(String msg) {
        ctx.writeAndFlush(msg);
    }
}
```

Stores reference to ChannelHandlerContext for later use

Sends message using previously stored ChannelHandlerContext

Because a `ChannelHandler` can belong to more than one `ChannelPipeline`, it can be bound to multiple `ChannelHandlerContext` instances. A `ChannelHandler` intended for this use must be annotated with `@Sharable`; otherwise, attempting to add it to more than one `ChannelPipeline` will trigger an exception. Clearly, to be safe for use with multiple concurrent channels (that is, connections), such a `ChannelHandler` must be thread-safe.

This listing shows a correct implementation of this pattern.

Listing 6.10 A sharable `ChannelHandler`

```
@Sharable
public class SharableHandler extends ChannelInboundHandlerAdapter {
    @Override
    public void channelRead(ChannelHandlerContext ctx, Object msg) {
        System.out.println("Channel read message: " + msg);
        ctx.fireChannelRead(msg);
    }
}
```

Annotates with @Sharable

Log method calls and forwards to next ChannelHandler

The preceding `ChannelHandler` implementation meets all the requirements for inclusion in multiple pipelines; namely, it's annotated with `@Sharable` and doesn't hold any state. Conversely, the code in listing 6.11 will cause problems.

Listing 6.11 Invalid usage of @Sharable

```
@Sharable                                                          <-- Annotates with @Sharable
public class UnsharableHandler extends ChannelInboundHandlerAdapter {
    private int count;
    @Override
    public void channelRead(ChannelHandlerContext ctx, Object msg) {
        count++;                                                   <-- Increments the count field
        System.out.println("channelRead(...) called the "
            + count + " time");          <-- Logs method call and forwards to next ChannelHandler
        ctx.fireChannelRead(msg();
    }
}
```

The problem with this code is that it has state; namely the instance variable `count`, which tracks the number of method invocations. Adding an instance of this class to the `ChannelPipeline` will very likely produce errors when it's accessed by concurrent channels. (Of course, this simple case could be corrected by making `channelRead()` synchronized.)

In summary, use `@Sharable` only if you're certain that your `ChannelHandler` is thread-safe.

> **WHY SHARE A CHANNELHANDLER?** A common reason for installing a single `ChannelHandler` in multiple `ChannelPipelines` is to gather statistics across multiple `Channels`.

This concludes our discussion of `ChannelHandlerContext` and its relationship to other framework components. Next we'll look at exception handling.

6.4 Exception handling

Exception handling is an important part of any substantial application, and it can be approached in a variety of ways. Accordingly, Netty provides several options for handling exceptions thrown during inbound or outbound processing. This section will help you understand how to design the approach that best suits your needs.

6.4.1 Handling inbound exceptions

If an exception is thrown during processing of an inbound event, it will start to flow through the `ChannelPipeline` starting at the point in the `ChannelInboundHandler` where it was triggered. To handle such an inbound exception, you need to override the following method in your `ChannelInboundHandler` implementation.

```
public void exceptionCaught(
    ChannelHandlerContext ctx, Throwable cause) throws Exception
```

The following listing shows a simple example that closes the `Channel` and prints the exception's stack trace.

Listing 6.12 Basic inbound exception handling

```
public class InboundExceptionHandler extends ChannelInboundHandlerAdapter {
    @Override
    public void exceptionCaught(ChannelHandlerContext ctx,
        Throwable cause) {
        cause.printStackTrace();
        ctx.close();
    }
}
```

Because the exception will continue to flow in the inbound direction (just as with all inbound events), the `ChannelInboundHandler` that implements the preceding logic is usually placed last in the `ChannelPipeline`. This ensures that all inbound exceptions are always handled, wherever in the `ChannelPipeline` they may occur.

How you should react to an exception is likely to be quite specific to your application. You may want to close the `Channel` (and connections) or you may attempt to recover. If you don't implement any handling for inbound exceptions (or don't consume the exception), Netty will log the fact that the exception wasn't handled.

To summarize,

- The default implementation of `ChannelHandler.exceptionCaught()` forwards the current exception to the next handler in the pipeline.
- If an exception reaches the end of the pipeline, it's logged as unhandled.
- To define custom handling, you override `exceptionCaught()`. It's then your decision whether to propagate the exception beyond that point.

6.4.2 Handling outbound exceptions

The options for handling normal completion and exceptions in outbound operations are based on the following notification mechanisms:

- Every outbound operation returns a `ChannelFuture`. The `ChannelFutureListeners` registered with a `ChannelFuture` are notified of success or error when the operation completes.
- Almost all methods of `ChannelOutboundHandler` are passed an instance of `ChannelPromise`. As a subclass of `ChannelFuture`, `ChannelPromise` can also be assigned listeners for asynchronous notification. But `ChannelPromise` also has writable methods that provide for immediate notification:

```
ChannelPromise setSuccess();
ChannelPromise setFailure(Throwable cause);
```

Adding a `ChannelFutureListener` is a matter of calling `addListener(ChannelFutureListener)` on a `ChannelFuture` instance, and there are two ways to do this. The one most commonly used is to invoke `addListener()` on the `ChannelFuture` that is returned by an outbound operation (for example `write()`).

The following listing uses this approach to add a ChannelFutureListener that will print the stack trace and then close the Channel.

Listing 6.13 Adding a ChannelFutureListener to a ChannelFuture

```
ChannelFuture future = channel.write(someMessage);
future.addListener(new ChannelFutureListener() {
    @Override
    public void operationComplete(ChannelFuture f) {
        if (!f.isSuccess()) {
            f.cause().printStackTrace();
            f.channel().close();
        }
    }
});
```

The second option is to add a ChannelFutureListener to the ChannelPromise that is passed as an argument to the ChannelOutboundHandler methods. The code shown next will have the same effect as the previous listing.

Listing 6.14 Adding a ChannelFutureListener to a ChannelPromise

```
public class OutboundExceptionHandler extends ChannelOutboundHandlerAdapter {
    @Override
    public void write(ChannelHandlerContext ctx, Object msg,
        ChannelPromise promise) {
        promise.addListener(new ChannelFutureListener() {
            @Override
            public void operationComplete(ChannelFuture f) {
                if (!f.isSuccess()) {
                    f.cause().printStackTrace();
                    f.channel().close();
                }
            }
        });
    }
}
```

ChannelPromise writable methods

By calling setSuccess() and setFailure() on ChannelPromise, you can make the status of an operation known as soon as the ChannelHandler method returns to the caller.

Why choose one approach over the other? For detailed handling of an exception, you'll probably find it more appropriate to add the ChannelFutureListener when calling the outbound operation, as shown in listing 6.13. For a less specialized approach to handling exceptions, you might find the custom ChannelOutboundHandler implementation shown in listing 6.14 to be simpler.

What happens if your `ChannelOutboundHandler` itself throws an exception? In this case, Netty itself will notify any listeners that have been registered with the corresponding `ChannelPromise`.

6.5 Summary

In this chapter we took a close look at Netty's data processing component, `ChannelHandler`. We discussed how `ChannelHandlers` are chained together and how they interact with the `ChannelPipeline` as `ChannelInboundHandlers` and `ChannelOutboundHandlers`.

The next chapter will focus on Netty's codec abstraction, which makes writing protocol encoders and decoders much easier than using the underlying `ChannelHandler` implementations directly.

EventLoop and threading model

7

This chapter covers

- Threading model overview
- Event loop concept and implementation
- Task scheduling
- Implementation details

Simply stated, a *threading model* specifies key aspects of thread management in the context of an OS, programming language, framework, or application. How and when threads are created obviously has a significant impact on the execution of application code, so developers need to understand the trade-offs associated with different models. This is true whether they choose the model themselves or acquire it implicitly via the adoption of a language or framework.

In this chapter we'll examine Netty's threading model in detail. It's powerful but easy to use and, as usual with Netty, aims to simplify your application code and maximize performance and maintainability. We'll also discuss the experiences that led to the choice of the current model.

If you have a good general understanding of Java's concurrency API (`java.util.concurrent`), you should find the discussion in this chapter straightforward. If you're new to these concepts or need to refresh your memory, *Java*

Concurrency in Practice by Brian Goetz, et al. (Addison-Wesley Professional, 2006) is an excellent resource.

7.1 Threading model overview

In this section we'll introduce threading models in general and then discuss Netty's past and present threading models, reviewing the benefits and limitations of each.

As we pointed out at the start of the chapter, a threading model specifies how code is going to be executed. Because we must always guard against the possible side effects of concurrent execution, it's important to understand the implications of the model being applied (there are single-thread models as well). Ignoring these matters and merely hoping for the best is tantamount to gambling—with the odds definitely against you.

Because computers with multiple cores or CPUs are commonplace, most modern applications employ sophisticated multithreading techniques to make efficient use of system resources. By contrast, our approach to multithreading in the early days of Java wasn't much more than creating and starting new `Threads` on demand to execute concurrent units of work, a primitive approach that works poorly under heavy load. Java 5 then introduced the `Executor` API, whose thread pools greatly improved performance through `Thread` caching and reuse.

The basic thread pooling pattern can be described as:

- A `Thread` is selected from the pool's free list and assigned to run a submitted task (an implementation of `Runnable`).
- When the task is complete, the `Thread` is returned to the list and becomes available for reuse.

This pattern is illustrated in figure 7.1.

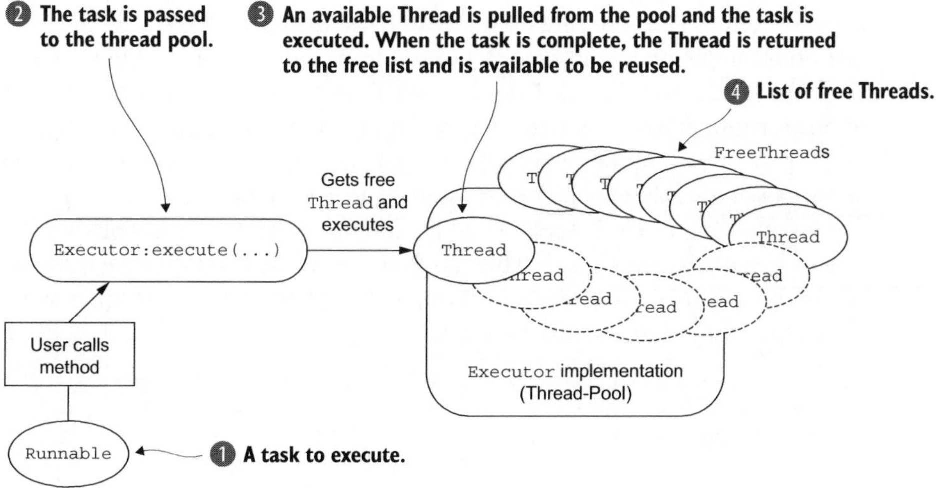

Figure 7.1 Executor execution logic

Pooling and reusing threads is an improvement over creating and destroying a thread with each task, but it doesn't eliminate the cost of context switching, which quickly becomes apparent as the number of threads increases and can be severe under heavy load. In addition, other thread-related problems can arise during the lifetime of a project simply because of the overall complexity or concurrency requirements of an application.

In short, multithreading can be complex. In the next sections we'll see how Netty helps to simplify it.

7.2 Interface EventLoop

Running tasks to handle events that occur during the lifetime of a connection, a basic function of any networking framework. The corresponding programming construct is often referred to as an *event loop*, a term Netty adopts with `interface io.netty.channel.EventLoop`.

The basic idea of an event loop is illustrated in the following listing, where each task is an instance of `Runnable` (as in figure 7.1).

Listing 7.1 Executing tasks in an event loop

```
while (!terminated) {
    List<Runnable> readyEvents = blockUntilEventsReady();    <-- Blocks until there are events that are ready to run
    for (Runnable ev: readyEvents) {
        ev.run();                                            <-- Loops over and runs all the events
    }
}
```

Netty's `EventLoop` is part of a collaborative design that employs two fundamental APIs: concurrency and networking. First, the package `io.netty.util.concurrent` builds on the JDK package `java.util.concurrent` to provide thread executors. Second, the classes in the package `io.netty.channel` extend these in order to interface with `Channel` events. The resulting class hierarchy is seen in figure 7.2.

In this model, an `EventLoop` is powered by exactly one `Thread` that never changes, and tasks (`Runnable` or `Callable`) can be submitted directly to `EventLoop` implementations for immediate or scheduled execution. Depending on the configuration and the available cores, multiple `EventLoop`s may be created in order to optimize resource use, and a single `EventLoop` may be assigned to service multiple `Channel`s.

Note that Netty's `EventLoop`, while it extends `ScheduledExecutorService`, defines only one method, `parent()`.[1] This method, shown in the following code snippet, is intended to return a reference to the `EventLoopGroup` to which the current `EventLoop` implementation instance belongs.

```
public interface EventLoop extends EventExecutor, EventLoopGroup {
    @Override
    EventLoopGroup parent();
}
```

[1] This method overrides the `EventExecutor` method `EventExecutorGroup parent()`.

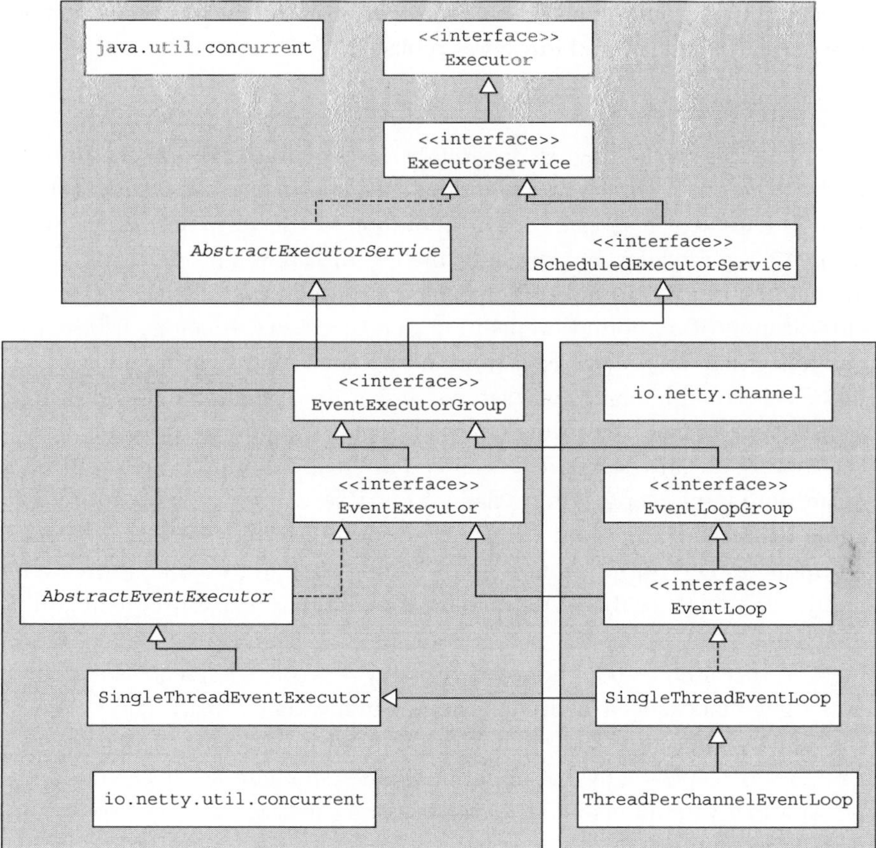

Figure 7.2 `EventLoop` **class hierarchy**

> **EVENT/TASK EXECUTION ORDER** Events and tasks are executed in FIFO (first-in-first-out) order. This eliminates the possibility of data corruption by guaranteeing that byte contents are processed in the correct order.

7.2.1 *I/O and event handling in Netty 4*

As we described in detail in chapter 6, events triggered by I/O operations flow through a `ChannelPipeline` that has one or more installed `ChannelHandlers`. The method calls that propagate these events can then be intercepted by the `ChannelHandlers` and the events processed as required.

The nature of an event usually determines how it is to be handled; it may transfer data from the network stack into your application, do the reverse, or do something entirely different. But event-handling logic must be generic and flexible enough to handle all possible use cases. Therefore, in Netty 4 *all I/O operations and events are handled by the* `Thread` *that has been assigned to the* `EventLoop`.

This differs from the model that was used in Netty 3. In the next section we'll discuss the earlier model and why it was replaced.

7.2.2 I/O operations in Netty 3

The threading model used in previous releases guaranteed only that inbound (previously called upstream) events would be executed in the so-called I/O thread (corresponding to Netty 4's `EventLoop`). All outbound (downstream) events were handled by the calling thread, which might be the I/O thread or any other. This seemed a good idea at first but was found to be problematical because of the need for careful synchronization of outbound events in `ChannelHandlers`. In short, it wasn't possible to guarantee that multiple threads wouldn't try to access an outbound event at the same time. This could happen, for example, if you fired simultaneous downstream events for the same `Channel` by calling `Channel.write()` in different threads.

Another negative side effect occurred when an inbound event was fired as a result of an outbound event. When `Channel.write()` causes an exception, you need to generate and fire an `exceptionCaught` event. But in the Netty 3 model, because this is an inbound event, you wound up executing code in the calling thread, then handing the event over to the I/O thread for execution, with a consequent additional context switch.

The threading model adopted in Netty 4 resolves these problems by handling everything that occurs in a given `EventLoop` in the same thread. This provides a simpler execution architecture and eliminates the need for synchronization in the `ChannelHandlers` (except for any that might be shared among multiple `Channels`).

Now that you understand the role of the `EventLoop`, let's see how tasks are scheduled for execution.

7.3 Task scheduling

Occasionally you'll need to schedule a task for later (deferred) or periodic execution. For example, you might want to register a task to be fired after a client has been connected for five minutes. A common use case is to send a heartbeat message to a remote peer to check whether the connection is still alive. If there is no response, you know you can close the channel.

In the next sections, we'll show you how to schedule tasks with both the core Java API and Netty's `EventLoop`. Then, we'll examine the internals of Netty's implementation and discuss its advantages and limitations.

7.3.1 JDK scheduling API

Before Java 5, task scheduling was built on `java.util.Timer`, which uses a background `Thread` and has the same limitations as standard threads. Subsequently, the JDK provided the package `java.util.concurrent`, which defines the interface `ScheduledExecutorService`. Table 7.1 shows the relevant factory methods of `java.util.concurrent.Executors`.

Table 7.1 The `java.util.concurrent.Executors` factory methods

Methods	Description

`newScheduledThreadPool( int corePoolSize)`
 	
`newScheduledThreadPool( int corePoolSize, ThreadFactorythreadFactory)`
	Creates a `ScheduledThreadExecutorService` that can schedule commands to run after a delay or to execute periodically. It uses the argument `corePoolSize` to calculate the number of threads.

`newSingleThreadScheduledExecutor()`
 	
`newSingleThreadScheduledExecutor( ThreadFactorythreadFactory)`
	Creates a `ScheduledThreadExecutorService` that can schedule commands to run after a delay or to execute periodically. It uses one thread to execute the scheduled tasks.

Although there are not many choices,[2] those provided are sufficient for most use cases. The next listing shows how to use `ScheduledExecutorService` to run a task after a 60-second delay.

Listing 7.2 Scheduling a task with a `ScheduledExecutorService`

```
ScheduledExecutorService executor =
    Executors.newScheduledThreadPool(10);

ScheduledFuture<?> future = executor.schedule(
    new Runnable() {
    @Override
    public void run() {
        System.out.println("60 seconds later");
    }
}, 60, TimeUnit.SECONDS);
...
executor.shutdown();
```

- Creates a ScheduledExecutorService with a pool of 10 threads
- Creates a Runnable to schedule for later execution
- The message to be printed by the task
- Schedules task to run 60 seconds from now
- Shuts down ScheduledExecutorService to release resources once the task is complete

Although the `ScheduledExecutorService` API is straightforward, under heavy load it can introduce performance costs. In the next section we'll see how Netty provides the same functionality with greater efficiency.

7.3.2 Scheduling tasks using EventLoop

The `ScheduledExecutorService` implementation has limitations, such as the fact that extra threads are created as part of pool management. This can become a bottleneck if many tasks are aggressively scheduled. Netty addresses this by implementing scheduling using the channel's `EventLoop`, as shown in the following listing.

[2] The only concrete implementation of this interface provided by the JDK is `java.util.concurrent.ScheduledThreadPoolExecutor`.

Listing 7.3 Scheduling a task with EventLoop

```
Channel ch = ...
ScheduledFuture<?> future = ch.eventLoop().schedule(
    new Runnable() {
    @Override
    public void run() {
        System.out.println("60 seconds later");
    }
}, 60, TimeUnit.SECONDS);
```

Creates a Runnable to schedule for later execution

The code to run

Schedule to run 60 seconds from now

After 60 seconds have elapsed, the `Runnable` instance will be executed by the `EventLoop` assigned to the channel. To schedule a task to be executed every 60 seconds, use `scheduleAtFixedRate()`, as shown next.

Listing 7.4 Scheduling a recurring task with EventLoop

```
Channel ch = ...
ScheduledFuture<?> future = ch.eventLoop().scheduleAtFixedRate(
    new Runnable() {
    @Override
    public void run() {
        System.out.println("Run every 60 seconds");
    }
}, 60, 60, TimeUnit.Seconds);
```

Creates a Runnable to schedule for later execution

This will run until the ScheduledFuture is canceled.

Schedule to run in 60 seconds and every 60 seconds thereafter

As we noted earlier, Netty's `EventLoop` extends `ScheduledExecutorService` (see figure 7.2), so it provides all of the methods available with the JDK implementation, including `schedule()` and `scheduleAtFixedRate()`, used in the preceding examples. The complete list of all the operations can be found in the Javadocs for `ScheduledExecutorService`.[3]

To cancel or check the state of an execution, use the `ScheduledFuture` that's returned for every asynchronous operation. This listing shows a simple cancellation operation.

Listing 7.5 Canceling a task using ScheduledFuture

```
ScheduledFuture<?> future = ch.eventLoop().scheduleAtFixedRate(...);
// Some other code that runs...
boolean mayInterruptIfRunning = false;
future.cancel(mayInterruptIfRunning);
```

Schedules task and obtains the returned ScheduledFuture.

Cancels the task, which prevents it from running again.

[3] Java Platform, Standard Edition 8 API Specification, java.util.concurrent, Interface ScheduledExecutorService, http://docs.oracle.com/javase/8/docs/api/java/util/concurrent/ScheduledExecutorService.html.

These examples illustrate the performance gain that can be achieved by taking advantage of Netty's scheduling capabilities. These depend, in turn, on the underlying threading model, which we'll examine next.

7.4 Implementation details

This section examines in greater detail the principal elements of Netty's threading model and scheduling implementation. We'll also mention limitations to be aware of, as well as areas of ongoing development.

7.4.1 Thread management

The superior performance of Netty's threading model hinges on determining the identity of the currently executing `Thread`; that is, whether or not it is the one assigned to the current `Channel` and its `EventLoop`. (Recall that the `EventLoop` is responsible for handling all events for a `Channel` during its lifetime.)

If the calling `Thread` is that of the `EventLoop`, the code block in question is executed. Otherwise, the `EventLoop` schedules a task for later execution and puts it in an internal queue. When the `EventLoop` next processes its events, it will execute those in the queue. This explains how any `Thread` can interact directly with the `Channel` without requiring synchronization in the `ChannelHandlers`.

Note that each `EventLoop` has its own task queue, independent of that of any other `EventLoop`. Figure 7.3 shows the execution logic used by `EventLoop` to schedule tasks. This is a critical component of Netty's threading model.

We stated earlier the importance of not blocking the current I/O thread. We'll say it again in another way: "Never put a long-running task in the execution queue, because it will block any other task from executing on the same thread." If you must make blocking calls or execute long-running tasks, we advise the use of a dedicated

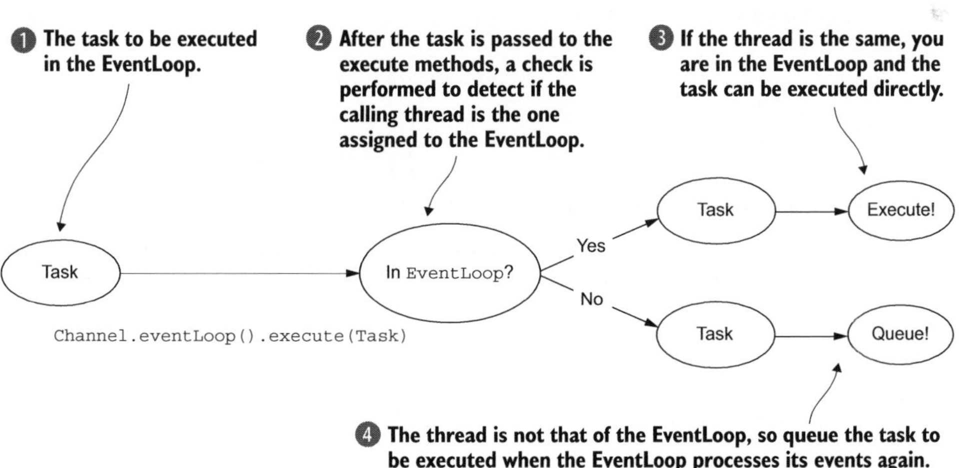

1 The task to be executed in the EventLoop.
2 After the task is passed to the execute methods, a check is performed to detect if the calling thread is the one assigned to the EventLoop.
3 If the thread is the same, you are in the EventLoop and the task can be executed directly.
Task
In EventLoop?
Yes
No
Task
Execute!
Task
Queue!
Channel.eventLoop().execute(Task)
4 The thread is not that of the EventLoop, so queue the task to be executed when the EventLoop processes its events again.

Figure 7.3 `EventLoop` execution logic

EventExecutor. (See the sidebar "ChannelHandler execution and blocking" in section 6.2.1.)

Leaving aside such a limit case, the threading model in use can strongly affect the impact of queued tasks on overall system performance, as can the event-processing implementation of the transport employed. (And as we saw in chapter 4, Netty makes it easy to switch transports without modifying your code base.)

7.4.2 EventLoop/thread allocation

The EventLoops that service I/O and events for Channels are contained in an EventLoopGroup. The manner in which EventLoops are created and assigned varies according to the transport implementation.

Asynchronous transports

Asynchronous implementations use only a few EventLoops (and their associated Threads), and in the current model these may be shared among Channels. This allows many Channels to be served by the smallest possible number of Threads, rather than assigning a Thread per Channel.

Figure 7.4 displays an EventLoopGroup with a fixed size of three EventLoops (each powered by one Thread). The EventLoops (and their Threads) are allocated directly when the EventLoopGroup is created to ensure that they will be available when needed.

The EventLoopGroup is responsible for allocating an EventLoop to each newly created Channel. In the current implementation, using a round-robin approach achieves a balanced distribution, and the same EventLoop may be assigned to multiple Channels. (This may change in future versions.)

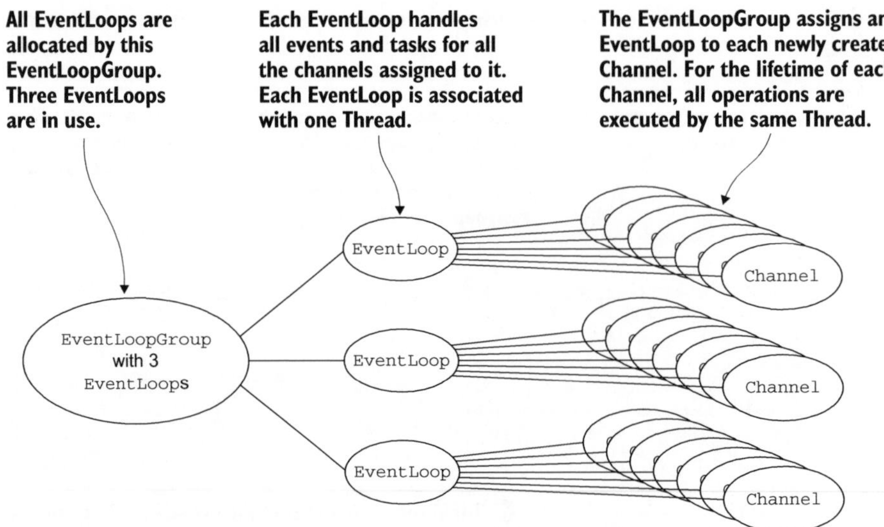

Figure 7.4 EventLoop allocation for non-blocking transports (such as NIO and AIO)

Once a Channel has been assigned an EventLoop, it will use this EventLoop (and the associated Thread) throughout its lifetime. Keep this in mind, because it frees you from worries about thread safety and synchronization in your ChannelHandler implementations.

Also, be aware of the implications of EventLoop allocation for ThreadLocal use. Because an EventLoop usually powers more than one Channel, ThreadLocal will be the same for all associated Channels. This makes it a poor choice for implementing a function such as state tracking. However, in a stateless context it can still be useful for sharing heavy or expensive objects, or even events, among Channels.

BLOCKING TRANSPORTS

The design for other transports such as OIO (old blocking I/O) is a bit different, as illustrated in figure 7.5.

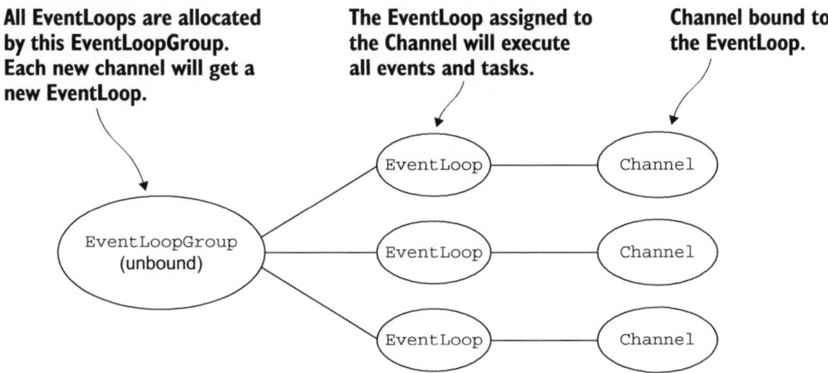

Figure 7.5 `EventLoop` **allocation of blocking transports (such as OIO)**

Here one EventLoop (and its Thread) is assigned to each Channel. You may have encountered this pattern if you've developed applications that use the blocking I/O implementation in the java.io package.

But just as before, it is guaranteed that the I/O events of each Channel will be handled by only one Thread—the one that powers the Channel's EventLoop. This is another example of Netty's consistency of design, and it is one that contributes strongly to Netty's reliability and ease of use.

7.5 Summary

In this chapter you learned about threading models in general and Netty's threading model in particular, whose performance and consistency advantages we discussed in detail.

You saw how to execute your own tasks in the EventLoop (I/O Thread) just as the framework itself does. You learned how to schedule tasks for deferred execution, and we examined the question of scalability under heavy load. You also saw how to verify whether a task has executed and how to cancel it.

This information, augmented by our study of the framework's implementation details, will help you to maximize your application's performance while simplifying its code base. For more information about thread pools and concurrent programming in general, we recommend *Java Concurrency in Practice* by Brian Goetz. His book will give you a deeper understanding of even the most complex multithreading use cases.

We've reached an exciting point—in the next chapter we'll discuss bootstrapping, the process of configuring and connecting all of Netty's components to bring your application to life.

8 Bootstrapping

This chapter covers

- Bootstrapping clients and servers
- Bootstrapping clients from within a Channel
- Adding ChannelHandlers
- Using ChannelOptions and attributes

Having studied ChannelPipelines, ChannelHandlers, and codec classes in depth, your next question is probably, "How do all these pieces add up to a working application?"

The answer? "Bootstrapping." Up to now, we've used the term somewhat vaguely, and the time has come to define it more precisely. Simply stated, *bootstrapping* an application is the process of configuring it to run—though the details of the process may not be as simple as its definition, especially in network applications.

Consistent with its approach to application architecture, Netty handles bootstrapping in a way that insulates your application, whether client or server, from the network layer. As you'll see, all of the framework components are connected and enabled in the background. Bootstrapping is the missing piece of the puzzle we've been assembling; when you put it in place, your Netty application will be complete.

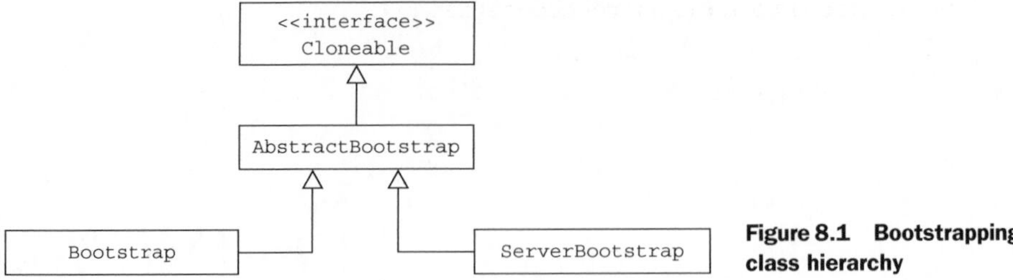

Figure 8.1 Bootstrapping class hierarchy

8.1 Bootstrap classes

The bootstrapping class hierarchy consists of an abstract parent class and two concrete bootstrap subclasses, as shown in figure 8.1.

Rather than thinking of the concrete classes as *server* and *client* bootstraps, it's helpful to keep in mind the distinct application functions they're intended to support. Namely, a *server* devotes a *parent* channel to accepting connections from clients and creating *child* channels for conversing with them, whereas a *client* will most likely require only a single, *non-parent* channel for all network interactions. (As we'll see, this applies also to connectionless transports such as UDP, because they don't require a channel for each connection.)

Several of the Netty components we've studied in previous chapters participate in the bootstrapping process, and some of these are used in both clients and servers. The bootstrapping steps common to both application types are handled by `AbstractBootstrap`, whereas those that are specific to clients or servers are handled by `Bootstrap` or `ServerBootstrap`, respectively.

In the rest of this chapter we'll explore these two classes in detail, beginning with the less complex, `Bootstrap`.

> **Why are the bootstrap classes Cloneable?**
>
> You'll sometimes need to create multiple channels that have similar or identical settings. To support this pattern without requiring a new bootstrap instance to be created and configured for each channel, `AbstractBootstrap` has been marked `Cloneable`.[1] Calling `clone()` on an already configured bootstrap will return another bootstrap instance that's immediately usable.
>
> Note that this creates only a shallow copy of the bootstrap's `EventLoopGroup`, so the latter will be shared among all of the cloned channels. This is acceptable, as the cloned channels are often short-lived, a typical case being a channel created to make an HTTP request.

1 Java Platform, Standard Edition 8 API Specification, java.lang, Interface Cloneable, http://docs.oracle.com/javase/8/docs/api/java/lang/Cloneable.html.

The full declaration of `AbstractBootstrap` is

```
public abstract class AbstractBootstrap
    <B extends AbstractBootstrap<B,C>,C extends Channel>
```

In this signature, the subclass `B` is a type parameter to the superclass, so that a reference to the runtime instance can be returned to support method chaining (so-called *fluent syntax*).

The subclasses are declared as follows:

```
public class Bootstrap
    extends AbstractBootstrap<Bootstrap,Channel>
```

and

```
public class ServerBootstrap
    extends AbstractBootstrap<ServerBootstrap,ServerChannel>
```

8.2 Bootstrapping clients and connectionless protocols

`Bootstrap` is used in clients or in applications that use a connectionless protocol. Table 8.1 gives an overview of the class, many of whose methods are inherited from `AbstractBootstrap`.

Table 8.1 The `Bootstrap` API

Name	Description
`Bootstrap group(EventLoopGroup)`	Sets the `EventLoopGroup` that will handle all events for the `Channel`.
`Bootstrap channel(Class<? extends C>)` `Bootstrap channelFactory(ChannelFactory<? extends C>)`	`channel()` specifies the `Channel` implementation class. If the class doesn't provide a default constructor, you can call `channelFactory()` to specify a factory class to be called by `bind()`.
`Bootstrap localAddress(SocketAddress)`	Specifies the local address to which the `Channel` should be bound. If not provided, a random one will be created by the OS. Alternatively, you can specify the `localAddress` with `bind()` or `connect()`.
`<T> Bootstrap option(ChannelOption<T> option, T value)`	Sets a `ChannelOption` to apply to the `ChannelConfig` of a newly created `Channel`. These options will be set on the `Channel` by `bind()` or `connect()`, whichever is called first. This method has no effect after `Channel` creation. The `ChannelOptions` supported depend on the `Channel` type used. Refer to section 8.6 and to the API docs of the `ChannelConfig` for the `Channel` type used.

Table 8.1 The `Bootstrap` API *(continued)*

Name	Description
`<T> Bootstrap attr( Attribute<T> key, T value)`	Specifies an attribute of a newly created `Channel`. These are set on the `Channel` by `bind()` or `connect()`, depending on which is called first. This method has no effect after `Channel` creation. Please refer to section 8.6.
`Bootstrap handler(ChannelHandler)`	Sets the `ChannelHandler` that's added to the `ChannelPipeline` to receive event notification.
`Bootstrap clone()`	Creates a clone of the current `Bootstrap` with the same settings as the original.
`Bootstrap remoteAddress( SocketAddress)`	Sets the remote address. Alternatively, you can specify it with `connect()`.
`ChannelFuture connect()`	Connects to the remote peer and returns a `ChannelFuture`, which is notified once the connection operation is complete.
`ChannelFuture bind()`	Binds the `Channel` and returns a `ChannelFuture`, which is notified once the bind operation is complete, after which `Channel.connect()` must be called to establish the connection.

The next section presents a step-by-step explanation of client bootstrapping. We'll also discuss the matter of maintaining compatibility when choosing among the available component implementations.

8.2.1 *Bootstrapping a client*

The `Bootstrap` class is responsible for creating channels for clients and for applications that utilize connectionless protocols, as illustrated in figure 8.2.

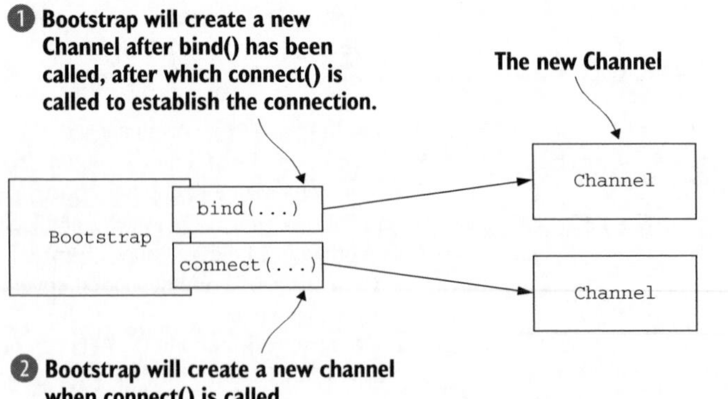
1 Bootstrap will create a new Channel after bind() has been called, after which connect() is called to establish the connection.
The new Channel
Channel
bind(...)
Bootstrap
connect(...)
Channel
2 Bootstrap will create a new channel when connect() is called.

Figure 8.2 Bootstrapping process

The code in the following listing bootstraps a client that uses the NIO TCP transport.

Listing 8.1 Bootstrapping a client

```
EventLoopGroup group = new NioEventLoopGroup();
Bootstrap bootstrap = new Bootstrap();
bootstrap.group(group)
    .channel(NioSocketChannel.class)
    .handler(new SimpleChannelInboundHandler<ByteBuf>() {
        @Override
        protected void channeRead0(
            ChannelHandlerContext channelHandlerContext,
            ByteBuf byteBuf) throws Exception {
            System.out.println("Received data");
        }
    } );
ChannelFuture future = bootstrap.connect(
    new InetSocketAddress("www.manning.com", 80));
future.addListener(new ChannelFutureListener() {
    @Override
    public void operationComplete(ChannelFuture channelFuture)
        throws Exception {
        if (channelFuture.isSuccess()) {
            System.out.println("Connection established");
        } else {
            System.err.println("Connection attempt failed");
            channelFuture.cause().printStackTrace();
        }
    }
} );
```

Creates a Bootstrap to create and connect new client channels

Sets the EventLoopGroup that provides EventLoops for processing Channel events

Specifies the Channel implementation to be used

Sets the handler for Channel events and data

Connects to the remote host

This example uses the fluent syntax mentioned earlier; the methods (except `connect()`) are chained by the reference to the `Bootstrap` instance that each one returns.

8.2.2 *Channel and EventLoopGroup compatibility*

The following directory listing is from the package `io.netty.channel`. You can see from the package names and the matching class-name prefixes that there are related `EventLoopGroup` and `Channel` implementations for both the NIO and OIO transports.

Listing 8.2 Compatible `EventLoopGroups` and `Channels`

```
channel
├───nio
│       NioEventLoopGroup
├───oio
│       OioEventLoopGroup
└───socket
    ├───nio
    │       NioDatagramChannel
```

```
    |       NioServerSocketChannel
    |       NioSocketChannel
    └──oio
            OioDatagramChannel
            OioServerSocketChannel
            OioSocketChannel
```

This compatibility must be maintained; you can't mix components having different prefixes, such as `NioEventLoopGroup` and `OioSocketChannel`. The following listing shows an attempt to do just that.

Listing 8.3 Incompatible `Channel` and `EventLoopGroup`

```
EventLoopGroup group = new NioEventLoopGroup();
Bootstrap bootstrap = new Bootstrap();
bootstrap.group(group)
    .channel(OioSocketChannel.class)
    .handler(new SimpleChannelInboundHandler<ByteBuf>() {
        @Override
        protected void channelRead0(
            ChannelHandlerContext channelHandlerContext,
            ByteBuf byteBuf) throws Exception {
            System.out.println("Received data");
        }
    } );
ChannelFuture future = bootstrap.connect(
    new InetSocketAddress("www.manning.com", 80));
future.syncUninterruptibly();
```

Creates a new Bootstrap to create new client channels

Specifies an NIO EventLoopGroup implementation

Specifies an OIO Channel implementation class

Sets a handler for channel I/O events and data

Tries to connect to the remote peer

This code will cause an `IllegalStateException` because it mixes incompatible transports:

```
Exception in thread "main" java.lang.IllegalStateException:
incompatible event loop type: io.netty.channel.nio.NioEventLoop at
io.netty.channel.AbstractChannel$AbstractUnsafe.register(
AbstractChannel.java:571)
```

More on IllegalStateException

When bootstrapping, before you call `bind()` or `connect()` you must call the following methods to set up the required components.

- `group()`
- `channel()` or `channnelFactory()`
- `handler()`

Failure to do so will cause an `IllegalStateException`. The `handler()` call is particularly important because it's needed to configure the `ChannelPipeline`.

8.3 Bootstrapping servers

We'll begin our overview of server bootstrapping with an outline of the `ServerBootstrap` API. We'll then examine the steps involved in bootstrapping servers, and several related topics, including the special case of bootstrapping a client from a server channel.

8.3.1 The ServerBootstrap class

Table 8.2 lists the methods of `ServerBootstrap`.

Table 8.2 Methods of the `ServerBootstrap` class

Name	Description
`group`	Sets the `EventLoopGroup` to be used by the `ServerBootstrap`. This `EventLoopGroup` serves the I/O of the `ServerChannel` and accepted `Channels`.
`channel`	Sets the class of the `ServerChannel` to be instantiated.
`channelFactory`	If the `Channel` can't be created via a default constructor, you can provide a `ChannelFactory`.
`localAddress`	Specifies the local address the `ServerChannel` should be bound to. If not specified, a random one will be used by the OS. Alternatively, you can specify the `localAddress` with `bind()` or `connect()`.
`option`	Specifies a `ChannelOption` to apply to the `ChannelConfig` of a newly created `ServerChannel`. Those options will be set on the `Channel` by `bind()` or `connect()`, depending on which is called first. Setting or changing a `ChannelOption` after those methods have been called has no effect. Which `ChannelOptions` are supported depends on the channel type used. Refer to the API docs for the `ChannelConfig` you're using.
`childOption`	Specifies a `ChannelOption` to apply to a `Channel`'s `ChannelConfig` when the channel has been accepted. Which `ChannelOptions` are supported depends on the channel type used. Please refer to the API docs for the `ChannelConfig` you're using.
`attr`	Specifies an attribute on the `ServerChannel`. Attributes will be set on the channel by `bind()`. Changing them after calling `bind()` has no effect.
`childAttr`	Applies an attribute to accepted `Channels`. Subsequent calls have no effect.
`handler`	Sets the `ChannelHandler` that's added to the `ChannelPipeline` of the `ServerChannel`. See `childHandler()` for a more frequently used approach.
`childHandler`	Sets the `ChannelHandler` that's added to the `ChannelPipeline` of accepted `Channels`. The difference between `handler()` and `childHandler()` is that the former adds a handler that's processed by the *accepting* `ServerChannel`, whereas `childHandler()` adds a handler that's processed by an *accepted* `Channel`, which represents a socket bound to a remote peer.
`clone`	Clones the `ServerBootstrap` for connecting to a different remote peer with settings identical to those of the original `ServerBootstrap`.
`bind`	Binds the `ServerChannel` and returns a `ChannelFuture`, which is notified once the connection operation is complete (with the success or error result).

The next section explains the details of server bootstrapping.

8.3.2 Bootstrapping a server

You may have noticed that table 8.2 lists several methods not present in table 8.1: `childHandler()`, `childAttr()`, and `childOption()`. These calls support operations that are typical of server applications. Specifically, `ServerChannel` implementations are responsible for creating child `Channel`s, which represent accepted connections. Thus `ServerBootstrap`, which bootstraps `ServerChannel`s, provides these methods to simplify the task of applying settings to the `ChannelConfig` member of an accepted `Channel`.

Figure 8.3 shows a `ServerBootstrap` creating a `ServerChannel` on `bind()`, and the `ServerChannel` managing a number of child `Channel`s.

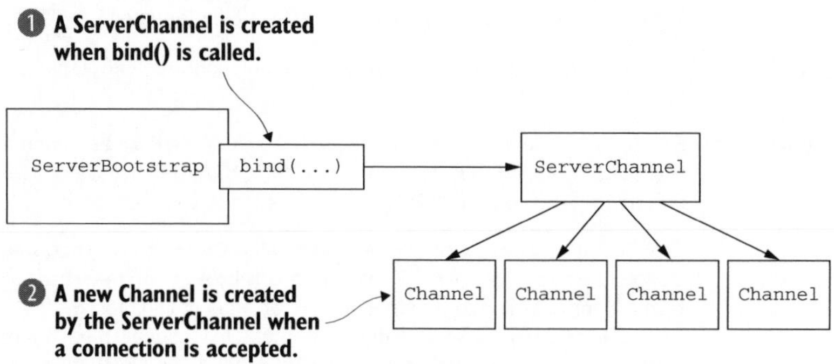

Figure 8.3 `ServerBootstrap` **and** `ServerChannel`

The code in this listing implements the server bootstrapping shown in figure 8.3.

Listing 8.4 Bootstrapping a server

```
NioEventLoopGroup group = new NioEventLoopGroup();
ServerBootstrap bootstrap = new ServerBootstrap();
bootstrap.group(group)
    .channel(NioServerSocketChannel.class)
    .childHandler(new SimpleChannelInboundHandler<ByteBuf>() {
        @Override
        protected void channelRead0(ChannelHandlerContext ctx,
            ByteBuf byteBuf) throws Exception {
            System.out.println("Received data");
        }
    } );
```

Creates a ServerBootstrap

Sets the EventLoopGroup that provides EventLoops for processing Channel events

Specifies the Channel implementation to be used

Sets a ChannelInboundHandler for I/O and data for the accepted channels

```
ChannelFuture future = bootstrap.bind(new InetSocketAddress(8080)); <-- Binds the channel with the configured bootstrap
future.addListener(new ChannelFutureListener() {
    @Override
    public void operationComplete(ChannelFuture channelFuture)
        throws Exception {
        if (channelFuture.isSuccess()) {
            System.out.println("Server bound");
        } else {
            System.err.println("Bound attempt failed");
            channelFuture.cause().printStackTrace();
        }
    }
} );
```

8.4 Bootstrapping clients from a Channel

Suppose your server is processing a client request that requires it to act as a client to a third system. This can happen when an application, such as a proxy server, has to integrate with an organization's existing systems, such as web services or databases. In such cases you'll need to bootstrap a client `Channel` from a `ServerChannel`.

You could create a new `Bootstrap` as described in section 8.2.1, but this is not the most efficient solution, as it would require you to define another `EventLoop` for the new client `Channel`. This would produce additional threads, necessitating context switching when exchanging data between the accepted `Channel` and the client `Channel`.

A better solution is to share the `EventLoop` of the accepted `Channel` by passing it to the `group()` method of the `Bootstrap`. Because all `Channel`s assigned to an `EventLoop` use the same thread, this avoids the extra thread creation and related context-switching mentioned previously. This sharing solution is illustrated in figure 8.4.

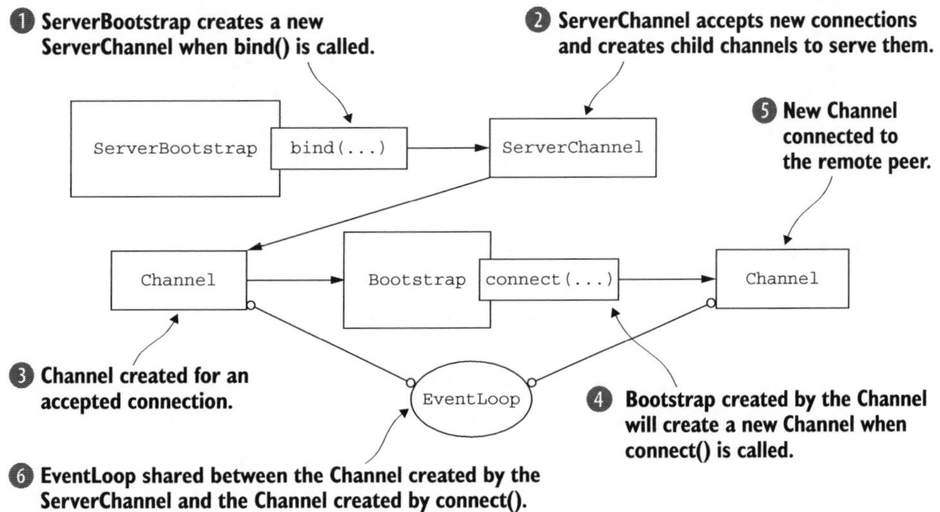

Figure 8.4 `EventLoop` **shared between channels**

Implementing EventLoop sharing involves setting the EventLoop by calling the group() method, as shown in the following listing.

Listing 8.5 Bootstrapping a server

```
ServerBootstrap bootstrap = new ServerBootstrap();
bootstrap.group(new NioEventLoopGroup(), new NioEventLoopGroup())
    .channel(NioServerSocketChannel.class)
    .childHandler(
        new SimpleChannelInboundHandler<ByteBuf>() {
            ChannelFuture connectFuture;
            @Override
            public void channelActive(ChannelHandlerContext ctx)
                throws Exception {
                Bootstrap bootstrap = new Bootstrap();
                bootstrap.channel(NioSocketChannel.class).handler(
                    new SimpleChannelInboundHandler<ByteBuf>() {
                        @Override
                        protected void channelRead0(
                            ChannelHandlerContext ctx, ByteBuf in)
                            throws Exception {
                            System.out.println("Received data");
                        }
                    } );
                bootstrap.group(ctx.channel().eventLoop());
                connectFuture = bootstrap.connect(
                    new InetSocketAddress("www.manning.com", 80));
            }
            @Override
            protected void channelRead0(
                ChannelHandlerContext channelHandlerContext,
                    ByteBuf byteBuf) throws Exception {
                if (connectFuture.isDone()) {
                    // do something with the data
                }
            }
        } );
ChannelFuture future = bootstrap.bind(new InetSocketAddress(8080));
future.addListener(new ChannelFutureListener() {
    @Override
    public void operationComplete(ChannelFuture channelFuture)
        throws Exception {
        if (channelFuture.isSuccess()) {
            System.out.println("Server bound");
        } else {
            System.err.println("Bind attempt failed");
            channelFuture.cause().printStackTrace();
        }
    }
} );
```

Annotations:

- Creates a ServerBootstrap to create SocketChannels and bind them
- Sets the EventLoopGroups that provide EventLoops for processing Channel events
- Specifies the Channel implementation to be used
- Sets a ChannelInbound-Handler for I/O and data for accepted channels
- Creates a Bootstrap to connect to remote host
- Specifies the channel implementation
- Sets a handler for inbound I/O
- Uses the same EventLoop as the one assigned to the accepted channel
- Connects to remote peer
- When the connection is complete performs some data operation (such as proxying)
- Binds the channel via configured Bootstrap

The topic we've discussed in this section and the solution presented reflect a general guideline in coding Netty applications: reuse EventLoops wherever possible to reduce the cost of thread creation.

8.5 Adding multiple ChannelHandlers during a bootstrap

In all of the code examples we've shown, we've called `handler()` or `childHandler()` during the bootstrap process to add a single `ChannelHandler`. This may be sufficient for simple applications, but it won't meet the needs of more complex ones. For example, an application that has to support multiple protocols will have many `ChannelHandlers`, the alternative being a large and unwieldy class.

As you've seen repeatedly, you can deploy as many `ChannelHandlers` as you require by chaining them together in a `ChannelPipeline`. But how can you do this if you can set only one `ChannelHandler` during the bootstrapping process?

For exactly this use case, Netty supplies a special subclass of `ChannelInboundHandlerAdapter`,

```
public abstract class ChannelInitializer<C extends Channel>
    extends ChannelInboundHandlerAdapter
```

which defines the following method:

```
protected abstract void initChannel(C ch) throws Exception;
```

This method provides an easy way to add multiple `ChannelHandlers` to a `ChannelPipeline`. You simply provide your implementation of `ChannelInitializer` to the bootstrap, and once the `Channel` is registered with its `EventLoop` your version of `initChannel()` is called. After the method returns, the `ChannelInitializer` instance removes itself from the `ChannelPipeline`.

The following listing defines the class `ChannelInitializerImpl` and registers it using the bootstrap's `childHandler()`. You can see that this apparently complex operation is quite straightforward.

Listing 8.6 Bootstrapping and using `ChannelInitializer`

```
ServerBootstrap bootstrap = new ServerBootstrap();
bootstrap.group(new NioEventLoopGroup(), new NioEventLoopGroup())
    .channel(NioServerSocketChannel.class)
    .childHandler(new ChannelInitializerImpl());
ChannelFuture future = bootstrap.bind(new InetSocketAddress(8080));
future.sync();
```

- Creates a ServerBootstrap to create and bind new Channels (line 1)
- Sets the EventLoopGroup that provides EventLoops for processing Channel events (line 2)
- Specifies the Channel implementation (line 3)
- Registers an instance of ChannelInitializerImpl to set up the ChannelPipeline (line 4)
- Binds to an address (line 5)

```
final class ChannelInitializerImpl extends ChannelInitializer<Channel> {
    @Override
    protected void initChannel(Channel ch) throws Exception {
        ChannelPipeline pipeline = ch.pipeline();
        pipeline.addLast(new HttpClientCodec());
        pipeline.addLast(new HttpObjectAggregator(Integer.MAX_VALUE));
    }
}
```

Adds the required handlers to the ChannelPipeline

Custom implementation of ChannelInitializerImpl to set up the ChannelPipeline

If your application makes use of numerous `ChannelHandlers`, define your own `ChannelInitializer` to install them in the pipeline.

8.6 Using Netty ChannelOptions and attributes

Manually configuring every channel when it's created could become quite tedious. Fortunately, you don't have to. Instead, you can use `option()` to apply `ChannelOptions` to a bootstrap. The values you provide will be applied automatically to all `Channels` created in the bootstrap. The `ChannelOptions` available include low-level connection details such as keep-alive or timeout properties and buffer settings.

Netty applications are often integrated with an organization's proprietary software, and components such as `Channel` may even be utilized outside the normal Netty lifecycle. In the event that some of the usual properties and data aren't available, Netty offers the `AttributeMap` abstraction, a collection provided by the channel and bootstrap classes, and `AttributeKey<T>`, a generic class for inserting and retrieving attribute values. With these tools, you can safely associate any kind of data item with both client and server `Channels`.

Consider, for example, a server application that tracks the relationship between users and `Channels`. This can be accomplished by storing the user's ID as an attribute of a `Channel`. A similar technique could be used to route messages to users based on their ID or to shut down a channel if there is low activity.

The next listing shows how you can use `ChannelOptions` to configure a `Channel` and an attribute to store an integer value.

Listing 8.7 Using attributes

Creates a Bootstrap to create client channels and connect them

Creates an AttributeKey to identify the attribute

```
final AttributeKey<Integer> id = new AttributeKey<Integer>("ID");
Bootstrap bootstrap = new Bootstrap();
bootstrap.group(new NioEventLoopGroup())
.channel(NioSocketChannel.class)
.handler(
    new SimpleChannelInboundHandler<ByteBuf>() {
```

Sets the EventLoopGroup that provides EventLoops for processing Channel events

Specifies the Channel implementation

Sets a ChannelInboundHandler to handle I/O and data for the channel

```
            @Override
            public void channelRegistered(ChannelHandlerContext ctx)
                throws Exception {
                Integer idValue = ctx.channel().attr(id).get();
                // do something  with the idValue
            }

            @Override
            protected void channelRead0(
                ChannelHandlerContext channelHandlerContext,
                ByteBuf byteBuf) throws Exception {
                System.out.println("Received data");
            }
        }
    );
    bootstrap.option(ChannelOption.SO_KEEPALIVE,true)
        .option(ChannelOption.CONNECT_TIMEOUT_MILLIS, 5000);
    bootstrap.attr(id, 123456);
    ChannelFuture future = bootstrap.connect(
        new InetSocketAddress("www.manning.com", 80));
    future.syncUninterruptibly();
```

Retrieves the attribute with the AttributeKey and its value

Sets the ChannelOptions that will be set on the created channels on connect() or bind()

Stores the id attribute

Connects to the remote host with the configured Bootstrap

8.7 Bootstrapping DatagramChannels

The previous bootstrap code examples used a `SocketChannel`, which is TCP-based, but a `Bootstrap` can be used for connectionless protocols as well. Netty provides various `DatagramChannel` implementations for this purpose. The only difference is that you don't call `connect()` but only `bind()`, as shown next.

Listing 8.8 Using `Bootstrap` with `DatagramChannel`

Sets the EventLoopGroup that provides EventLoops for processing Channel events

Creates a Bootstrap to create and bind new datagram channels

```
Bootstrap bootstrap = new Bootstrap();
bootstrap.group(new OioEventLoopGroup()).channel(
    OioDatagramChannel.class).handler(
    new SimpleChannelInboundHandler<DatagramPacket>(){
        @Override
        public void channelRead0(ChannelHandlerContext ctx,
            DatagramPacket msg) throws Exception {
            // Do something with the packet
        }
    }
);
ChannelFuture future = bootstrap.bind(new InetSocketAddress(0));
future.addListener(new ChannelFutureListener() {
      @Override
      public void operationComplete(ChannelFuture channelFuture)
         throws Exception {
         if (channelFuture.isSuccess()) {
             System.out.println("Channel bound");
         } else {
             System.err.println("Bind attempt failed");
```

Specifies the Channel implementation

Sets a Channel-InboundHandler to handle I/O and data for the channel

Calls bind() because the protocol is connectionless

```
                channelFuture.cause().printStackTrace();
            }
        }
    });
```

8.8 Shutdown

Bootstrapping gets your application up and running, but sooner or later you'll need to shut it down gracefully. You could, of course, just let the JVM handle everything on exiting, but this wouldn't meet the definition of graceful, which refers to releasing resources cleanly. There isn't much magic needed to shut down a Netty application, but there are a few things to keep in mind.

Above all, you need to shut down the `EventLoopGroup`, which will handle any pending events and tasks and subsequently release all active threads. This is a matter of calling `EventLoopGroup.shutdownGracefully()`. This call will return a `Future`, which is notified when the shutdown completes. Note that `shutdownGracefully()` is also an asynchronous operation, so you'll need to either block until it completes or register a listener with the returned `Future` to be notified of completion.

The following listing meets the definition of a graceful shutdown.

Listing 8.9 Graceful shutdown

```
EventLoopGroup group = new NioEventLoopGroup();        <-- Creates the EventLoop-Group that handles I/O
Bootstrap bootstrap = new Bootstrap();                 <-- Creates a Bootstrap and configures it
bootstrap.group(group)
     .channel(NioSocketChannel.class);
...
Future<?> future = group.shutdownGracefully();         <-- shutdownGracefully() releases resources and closes all Channels currently in use
// block until the group has shutdown
future.syncUninterruptibly();
```

Alternatively, you can call `Channel.close()` explicitly on all active channels before calling `EventLoopGroup.shutdownGracefully()`. But in all cases, remember to shut down the `EventLoopGroup` itself.

8.9 Summary

In this chapter you learned how to bootstrap Netty server and client applications, including those that use connectionless protocols. We covered a number of special cases, including bootstrapping client channels in server applications and using a `ChannelInitializer` to handle the installation of multiple `ChannelHandlers` during bootstrapping. You saw how to specify configuration options on channels and how to attach information to a channel using attributes. Finally, you learned how to shut down an application gracefully to release all resources in an orderly fashion.

In the next chapter we'll examine the tools Netty provides to help you test your `ChannelHandler` implementations.

9 Unit testing

This chapter covers

- Unit testing
- Overview of EmbeddedChannel
- Testing ChannelHandlers with EmbeddedChannel

ChannelHandlers are the critical elements of a Netty application, so testing them thoroughly should be a standard part of your development process. Best practices dictate that you test not only to prove that your implementation is correct, but also to make it easy to isolate problems that crop up as code is modified. This type of testing is called *unit testing*.

Although there's no universal definition of unit testing, most practitioners agree on the fundamentals. The basic idea is to test your code in the smallest possible chunks, isolated as much as possible from other code modules and from runtime dependencies such as databases and networks. If you can verify through testing that each unit works correctly by itself, it will be much easier to find the culprit when something goes awry.

In this chapter we'll study a special Channel implementation, EmbeddedChannel, that Netty provides specifically to facilitate unit testing of ChannelHandlers.

Because the code module or unit being tested is going to be executed outside its normal runtime environment, you need a framework or harness within which to run it. In our examples we'll use JUnit 4 as our testing framework, so you'll need a basic understanding of its use. If it's new to you, have no fear; though powerful it's simple, and you'll find all the information you need on the JUnit website (www.junit.org).

You may find it useful to review the previous chapters on `ChannelHandler` and codecs, as these will provide the material for our examples.

9.1 Overview of EmbeddedChannel

You already know that `ChannelHandler` implementations can be chained together in a `ChannelPipeline` to build up your application's business logic. We explained previously that this design supports the decomposition of potentially complex processing into small and reusable components, each of which handles a well-defined task or step. In this chapter we'll show you how it simplifies testing as well.

Netty provides what it calls an *embedded transport* for testing `ChannelHandlers`. This transport is a feature of a special `Channel` implementation, `EmbeddedChannel`, which provides a simple way to pass events through the pipeline.

The idea is straightforward: you write inbound or outbound data into an `EmbeddedChannel` and then check whether anything reached the end of the `ChannelPipeline`. In this way you can determine whether messages were encoded or decoded and whether any `ChannelHandler` actions were triggered.

The relevant methods of `EmbeddedChannel` are listed in table 9.1.

Table 9.1 Special `EmbeddedChannel` methods

Name	Responsibility
`writeInbound(Object... msgs)`	Writes an inbound message to the `EmbeddedChannel`. Returns `true` if data can be read from the `EmbeddedChannel` via `readInbound()`.
`readInbound()`	Reads an inbound message from the `EmbeddedChannel`. Anything returned traversed the entire `ChannelPipeline`. Returns `null` if nothing is ready to read.
`writeOutbound(Object... msgs)`	Writes an outbound message to the `EmbeddedChannel`. Returns `true` if something can now be read from the `EmbeddedChannel` via `readOutbound()`.
`readOutbound()`	Reads an outbound message from the `EmbeddedChannel`. Anything returned traversed the entire `ChannelPipeline`. Returns `null` if nothing is ready to read.
`finish()`	Marks the `EmbeddedChannel` as complete and returns `true` if either inbound or outbound data can be read. This will also call `close()` on the `EmbeddedChannel`.

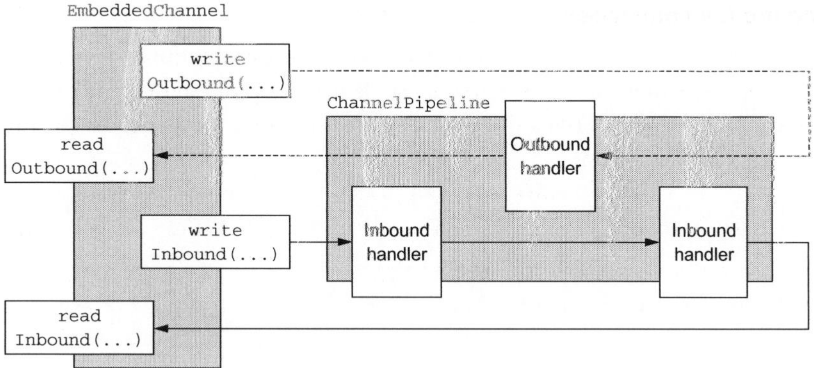

Figure 9.1 `EmbeddedChannel` data flow

Inbound data is processed by `ChannelInboundHandlers` and represents data read from the remote peer. Outbound data is processed by `ChannelOutboundHandlers` and represents data to be written to the remote peer. Depending on the `ChannelHandler` you're testing, you'll use the `*Inbound()` or `*Outbound()` pairs of methods, or perhaps both.

Figure 9.1 shows how data flows through the `ChannelPipeline` using the methods of `EmbeddedChannel`. You can use `writeOutbound()` to write a message to the `Channel` and pass it through the `ChannelPipeline` in the outbound direction. Subsequently you can read the processed message with `readOutbound()` to determine whether the result is as expected. Similarly, for inbound data you use `writeInbound()` and `readInbound()`.

In each case, messages are passed through the `ChannelPipeline` and processed by the relevant `ChannelInboundHandlers` or `ChannelOutboundHandlers`. If the message isn't consumed, you can use `readInbound()` or `readOutbound()` as appropriate to read the messages out of the `Channel` after processing them.

Let's take a closer look at both scenarios and see how they apply to testing your application logic.

9.2 Testing ChannelHandlers with EmbeddedChannel

In this section we'll explain how to test a `ChannelHandler` with `EmbeddedChannel`.

JUnit assertions

The class `org.junit.Assert` provides many static methods for use in tests. A failed assertion will cause an exception to be thrown and will terminate the currently executing test. The most efficient way to import these assertions is by way of an `import static` statement:

```
import static org.junit.Assert.*;
```

Once you have done this you can call the `Assert` methods directly:

```
assertEquals(buf.readSlice(3), read);
```

9.2.1 Testing inbound messages

Figure 9.2 represents a simple `ByteToMessageDecoder` implementation. Given sufficient data, this will produce frames of a fixed size. If not enough data is ready to read, it will wait for the next chunk of data and check again whether a frame can be produced.

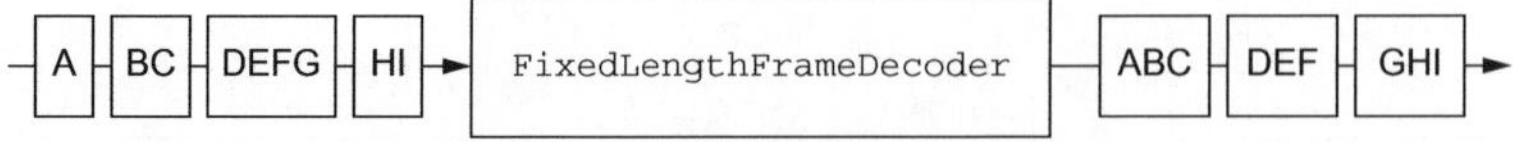

Figure 9.2 Decoding via `FixedLengthFrameDecoder`

As you can see from the frames on the right side of the figure, this particular decoder produces frames with a fixed size of 3 bytes. Thus it may require more than one event to provide enough bytes to produce a frame.

Finally, each frame will be passed to the next `ChannelHandler` in the `ChannelPipeline`.

The implementation of the decoder is shown in the following listing.

Listing 9.1 `FixedLengthFrameDecoder`

```
public class FixedLengthFrameDecoder extends ByteToMessageDecoder {
    private final int frameLength;

    public FixedLengthFrameDecoder(int frameLength) {
        if (frameLength <= 0) {
            throw new IllegalArgumentException(
                "frameLength must be a positive integer: " + frameLength);
        }
        this.frameLength = frameLength;
    }

    @Override
    protected void decode(ChannelHandlerContext ctx, ByteBuf in,
        List<Object> out) throws Exception {
        while (in.readableBytes() >= frameLength) {
            ByteBuf buf = in.readBytes(frameLength);
            out.add(buf);
        }
    }
}
```

Annotations: **Extends ByteToMessageDecoder to handle inbound bytes and decode them to messages** (class declaration); **Specifies the length of the frames to be produced** (constructor); **Checks if enough bytes can be read to produce the next frame** (while loop); **Reads a new frame out of the ByteBuf** (readBytes); **Adds the frame to the List of decoded messages** (out.add).

Now let's create a unit test to make sure this code works as expected. As we pointed out earlier, even in simple code, unit tests help to prevent problems that might occur if the code is refactored in the future and to diagnose them if they do.

This listing shows a test of the preceding code using `EmbeddedChannel`.

Listing 9.2 Testing the FixedLengthFrameDecoder

```
public class FixedLengthFrameDecoderTest {
    @Test
    public void testFramesDecoded() {
        ByteBuf buf = Unpooled.buffer();
        for (int i = 0; i < 9; i++) {
            buf.writeByte(i);
        }
        ByteBuf input = buf.duplicate();
        EmbeddedChannel channel = new EmbeddedChannel(
            new FixedLengthFrameDecoder(3));
        // write bytes
        assertTrue(channel.writeInbound(input.retain()));
        assertTrue(channel.finish());

        // read messages
        ByteBuf read = (ByteBuf) channel.readInbound();
        assertEquals(buf.readSlice(3), read);
        read.release();

        read = (ByteBuf) channel.readInbound();
        assertEquals(buf.readSlice(3), read);
        read.release();

        read = (ByteBuf) channel.readInbound();
        assertEquals(buf.readSlice(3), read);
        read.release();

        assertNull(channel.readInbound());
        buf.release();
    }

    @Test
    public void testFramesDecoded2() {
        ByteBuf buf = Unpooled.buffer();
        for (int i = 0; i < 9; i++) {
            buf.writeByte(i);
        }
        ByteBuf input = buf.duplicate();

        EmbeddedChannel channel = new EmbeddedChannel(
            new FixedLengthFrameDecoder(3));
        assertFalse(channel.writeInbound(input.readBytes(2)));
        assertTrue(channel.writeInbound(input.readBytes(7)));

        assertTrue(channel.finish());
        ByteBuf read = (ByteBuf) channel.readInbound();
        assertEquals(buf.readSlice(3), read);
        read.release();

        read = (ByteBuf) channel.readInbound();
        assertEquals(buf.readSlice(3), read);
        read.release();
```

Annotations:

- **Annotated with @Test so JUnit will execute the method**
- **The first test method: testFramesDecoded()**
- **Creates a ByteBuf and stores 9 bytes**
- **Creates an EmbeddedChannel and adds a FixedLengthFrameDecoder to be tested with a frame length of 3 bytes**
- **Writes data to the EmbeddedChannel**
- **Marks the Channel finished**
- **Reads the produced messages and verifies that there are 3 frames (slices) with 3 bytes each**
- **The second test method: testFramesDecoded2()**
- **Returns false because a complete frame is not ready to be read.**

```
            read = (ByteBuf) channel.readInbound();
            assertEquals(buf.readSlice(3), read);
            read.release();

            assertNull(channel.readInbound());
            buf.release();
        }
    }
```

The method `testFramesDecoded()` verifies that a `ByteBuf` containing 9 readable bytes is decoded into 3 `ByteBufs`, each containing 3 bytes. Notice how the `ByteBuf` is populated with 9 readable bytes in one call of `writeInbound()`. After this, `finish()` is executed to mark the `EmbeddedChannel` complete. Finally, `readInbound()` is called to read exactly three frames and a `null` from the `EmbeddedChannel`.

The method `testFramesDecoded2()` is similar, with one difference: the inbound `ByteBufs` are written in two steps. When `writeInbound(input.readBytes(2))` is called, `false` is returned. Why? As stated in table 9.1, `writeInbound()` returns `true` if a subsequent call to `readInbound()` would return data. But the `FixedLengthFrameDecoder` will produce output only when three or more bytes are readable. The rest of the test is identical to `testFramesDecoded()`.

9.2.2 Testing outbound messages

Testing the processing of outbound messages is similar to what you've just seen. In the next example we'll show how you can use `EmbeddedChannel` to test a `ChannelOutboundHandler` in the form of an encoder, a component that transforms one message format to another. You'll study encoders and decoders in great detail in the next chapter, so for now we'll just mention that the handler we're testing, `AbsIntegerEncoder`, is a specialization of Netty's `MessageToMessageEncoder` that converts negative-valued integers to absolute values.

The example will work as follows:

- An `EmbeddedChannel` that holds an `AbsIntegerEncoder` will write outbound data in the form of 4-byte negative integers.
- The decoder will read each negative integer from the incoming `ByteBuf` and will call `Math.abs()` to get the absolute value.
- The decoder will write the absolute value of each integer to the `ChannelHandlerPipeline`.

Figure 9.3 shows the logic.

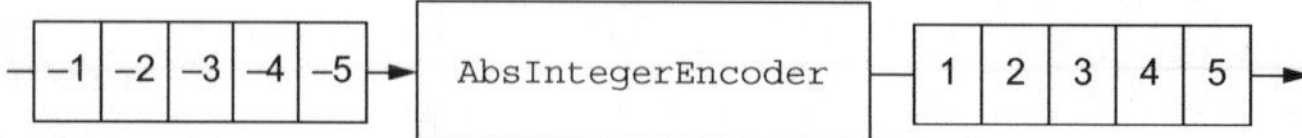

Figure 9.3 Encoding via `AbsIntegerEncoder`

The next listing implements this logic, illustrated in figure 9.3. The `encode()` method writes the produced values to a `List`.

Listing 9.3 `AbsIntegerEncoder`

```
public class AbsIntegerEncoder extends
    MessageToMessageEncoder<ByteBuf> {
    @Override
    protected void encode(ChannelHandlerContext channelHandlerContext,
        ByteBuf in, List<Object> out) throws Exception {
        while (in.readableBytes() >= 4) {
            int value = Math.abs(in.readInt());
            out.add(value);
        }
    }
}
```

Extends MessageToMessageEncoder to encode a message to another format

Checks if there are enough bytes to encode

Reads the next int out of the input ByteBuf and calculates the absolute value

Writes the int to the List of encoded messages

The next listing tests the code using `EmbeddedChannel`.

Listing 9.4 Testing the `AbsIntegerEncoder`

```
public class AbsIntegerEncoderTest {
    @Test
    public void testEncoded() {
        ByteBuf buf = Unpooled.buffer();
        for (int i = 1; i < 10; i++) {
            buf.writeInt(i * -1);
        }

        EmbeddedChannel channel = new EmbeddedChannel(
            new AbsIntegerEncoder());
        assertTrue(channel.writeOutbound(buf));
        assertTrue(channel.finish());

        // read bytes
        for (int i = 1; i < 10; i++) {
            assertEquals(i, channel.readOutbound());
        }
        assertNull(channel.readOutbound());
    }
}
```

❶ Creates a ByteBuf and writes 9 negative ints

❷ Creates an EmbeddedChannel and installs an AbsIntegerEncoder to be tested

❸ Writes the ByteBuf and asserts that readOutbound() will produce data

❹ Marks the channel finished

❺ Reads the produced messages and asserts that they contain absolute values

Here are the steps executed in the code:

❶ Writes negative 4-byte integers to a new `ByteBuf`.

❷ Creates an `EmbeddedChannel` and assigns an `AbsIntegerEncoder` to it.

❸ Calls `writeOutbound()` on the `EmbeddedChannel` to write the `ByteBuf`.

❹ Marks the channel finished.

❺ Reads all the integers from the outbound side of the `EmbeddedChannel` and verifies that only absolute values were produced.

9.3 *Testing exception handling*

Applications usually have additional tasks to execute beyond transforming data. For example, you may need to handle malformed input or an excessive volume of data. In the next example we'll throw a `TooLongFrameException` if the number of bytes read exceeds a specified limit. This is an approach often used to guard against resource exhaustion.

In figure 9.4 the maximum frame size has been set to 3 bytes. If the size of a frame exceeds that limit, its bytes are discarded and a `TooLongFrameException` is thrown. The other `ChannelHandlers` in the pipeline can either handle the exception in `exceptionCaught()` or ignore it.

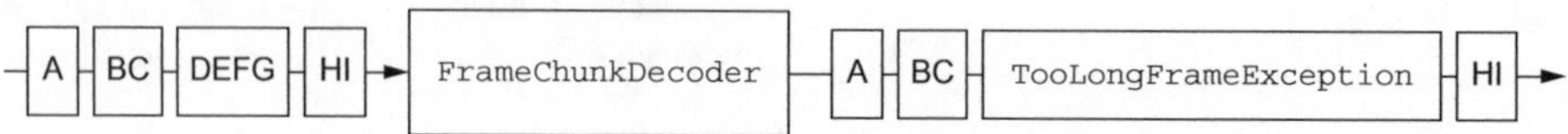

Figure 9.4 Decoding via `FrameChunkDecoder`

The implementation is shown in the following listing.

Listing 9.5 `FrameChunkDecoder`

```
public class FrameChunkDecoder extends ByteToMessageDecoder {
    private final int maxFrameSize;

    public FrameChunkDecoder(int maxFrameSize) {
        this.maxFrameSize = maxFrameSize;
    }

    @Override
    protected void decode(ChannelHandlerContext ctx, ByteBuf in,
        List<Object> out) throws Exception {
        int readableBytes = in.readableBytes();
        if (readableBytes > maxFrameSize)  {
            // discard the bytes
            in.clear();
            throw new TooLongFrameException();
        }
        ByteBuf buf = in.readBytes(readableBytes);
        out.add(buf);
    }
}
```

Extends ByteToMessageDecoder to decode inbound bytes to messages

Specifies the maximum allowable size of the frames to be produced

Discards the frame if it's too large and throws a TooLongFrameException...

...otherwise, reads the new frame from the ByteBuf

Adds the frame to the List of decoded messages

Again, we'll test the code using `EmbeddedChannel`.

Listing 9.6 Testing FrameChunkDecoder

```
public class FrameChunkDecoderTest {
    @Test
    public void testFramesDecoded() {
        ByteBuf buf = Unpooled.buffer();
        for (int i = 0; i < 9; i++) {
            buf.writeByte(i);
        }
        ByteBuf input = buf.duplicate();

        EmbeddedChannel channel = new EmbeddedChannel(
            new FrameChunkDecoder(3));

        assertTrue(channel.writeInbound(input.readBytes(2)));
        try {
            channel.writeInbound(input.readBytes(4));
            Assert.fail();
        } catch (TooLongFrameException e) {
            // expected exception
        }
        assertTrue(channel.writeInbound(input.readBytes(3)));
        assertTrue(channel.finish());

        // Read frames
        ByteBuf read = (ByteBuf) channel.readInbound();
        assertEquals(buf.readSlice(2), read);
        read.release();

        read = (ByteBuf) channel.readInbound();
        assertEquals(buf.skipBytes(4).readSlice(3), read);
        read.release();
        buf.release();
    }
}
```

Creates a ByteBuf and writes 9 bytes to it

Creates an EmbeddedChannel and installs a FixedLengthFrameDecoder with a frame size of 3

Writes 2 bytes to it and asserts that they produced a new frame

Writes a 4-byte frame and catches the expected TooLongFrameException

If the exception isn't thrown this assertion is reached and the test fails.

Writes the remaining 2 bytes and asserts a valid frame

Marks the channel finished

Reads the produced messages and verifies the values

At first glance this looks quite similar to the test in listing 9.2, but it has an interesting twist; namely, the handling of the `TooLongFrameException`. The `try/catch` block used here is a special feature of `EmbeddedChannel`. If one of the `write*` methods produces a checked `Exception`, it will be thrown wrapped in a `RuntimeException`.[1] This makes it easy to test whether an `Exception` was handled during processing of the data.

The testing approach illustrated here can be used with any `ChannelHandler` implementation that throws an `Exception`.

[1] Note that if the class implements `exceptionCaught()` and handles the exception, then it will not be caught by the catch block.

9.4 Summary

Unit testing with a test harness such as JUnit is an extremely effective way to guarantee the correctness of your code and enhance its maintainability. In this chapter you learned how to use the testing tools provided by Netty to test your custom `ChannelHandlers`.

In the next chapters we'll focus on writing real-world applications with Netty. We won't be presenting any further examples of test code, so we hope you'll keep in mind the importance of the testing approach we've demonstrated here.

Part 2

Codecs

A network sees data as just a sequence of raw bytes. Our applications, however, structure these bytes in a way that has meaning as *information.* Converting data to and from the network byte stream is one of the most common programming tasks. You may, for example, need to work with a standard format or protocol such as FTP or Telnet, implement a proprietary binary protocol defined by a third party, or extend a legacy message format created by your own organization.

Components that handle the conversion of application data to and from a network format are called encoders and decoders, respectively, and a single component with both capabilities is referred to as a codec. Netty provides a range of tools for creating all of these, from prebuilt classes specialized for well-known protocols such as HTTP and base64 to generic message transformation codecs that you can customize for your specific needs.

Chapter 10 provides an introduction to encoders and decoders. You'll learn about Netty's basic codec classes by studying some typical use cases. As you learn how these classes fit into the overall framework, you'll find that they are built on the same APIs you've already studied, so you'll be able to use them right away.

In chapter 11 you'll explore some of the encoders and decoders Netty provides to handle more specialized scenarios. The section on WebSocket is of particular interest, and it will prepare you for the detailed discussion of advanced network protocols in part 3.

10 The codec framework

This chapter covers

- An overview of decoders, encoders and codecs
- Netty's codec classes

Just as many standard architectural patterns are supported by dedicated frameworks, common data-processing patterns are often good candidates for targeted implementations, which can save developers considerable time and effort.

This certainly applies to the subject of this chapter: encoding and decoding, or the conversion of data from one protocol-specific format to another. These tasks are handled by components commonly called codecs. Netty provides components that simplify the creation of custom codecs for a broad range of protocols. For example, if you're building a Netty-based mail server, you'll find Netty's codec support invaluable for implementing the POP3, IMAP, and SMTP protocols.

10.1 What is a codec?

Every network application has to define how raw bytes transferred between peers are to be parsed and converted to—and from—the target program's data format. This conversion logic is handled by a *codec*, which consists of an encoder and a decoder, each of which transforms a stream of bytes from one format to another. What distinguishes them?

Think of a message as a structured sequence of bytes having meaning for a specific application—its data. An *encoder* converts that message to a format suitable for transmission (most likely a byte stream); the corresponding *decoder* converts the network stream back to the program's message format. An encoder, then, operates on *outbound* data and a decoder handles *inbound* data.

With this background information in mind, let's examine the classes Netty provides for implementing both kinds of components.

10.2 Decoders

In this section we'll survey Netty's decoder classes and present concrete examples of when and how you might use them. These classes cover two distinct use cases:

- Decoding bytes to messages—`ByteToMessageDecoder` and `ReplayingDecoder`
- Decoding one message type to another—`MessageToMessageDecoder`

Because decoders are responsible for transforming inbound data from one format to another, it won't surprise you to learn that Netty's decoders implement `ChannelInboundHandler`.

When would you use a decoder? Simple: whenever you need to transform inbound data for the next `ChannelInboundHandler` in the `ChannelPipeline`. Furthermore, thanks to the design of `ChannelPipeline`, you can chain together multiple decoders to implement arbitrarily complex transformation logic, a prime example of how Netty supports code modularity and reuse.

10.2.1 Abstract class ByteToMessageDecoder

Decoding from bytes to messages (or to another sequence of bytes) is such a common task that Netty provides an abstract base class for it: `ByteToMessageDecoder`. Since you can't know whether the remote peer will send a complete message all at once, this class buffers inbound data until it's ready for processing. Table 10.1 explains its two most important methods.

Table 10.1 `ByteToMessageDecoder` API

Method	Description
`decode(ChannelHandlerContext ctx, ByteBuf in, List<Object> out)`	This is the only abstract method you have to implement. `decode()` is called with a `ByteBuf` containing incoming data and a `List` to which decoded messages are added. This call is repeated until it is determined that no new items have been added to the `List` or no more bytes are readable in the ByteBuf. Then, if the `List` is not empty, its contents are passed to the next handler in the pipeline.
`decodeLast(ChannelHandlerContext ctx, ByteBuf in, List<Object> out)`	The default implementation provided by Netty simply calls `decode()`. This method is called once, when the `Channel` goes inactive. Override the method to provide special handling.

For an example of how to use this class, suppose you receive a byte stream containing simple `int`s, each to be handled separately. In this case, you'll read each `int` from the inbound `ByteBuf` and pass it to the next `ChannelInboundHandler` in the pipeline. To decode the byte stream, you'll extend `ByteToMessageDecoder`. (Note that the primitive `int` will be autoboxed to an `Integer` when it is added to the `List`.)

The design is illustrated in figure 10.1.

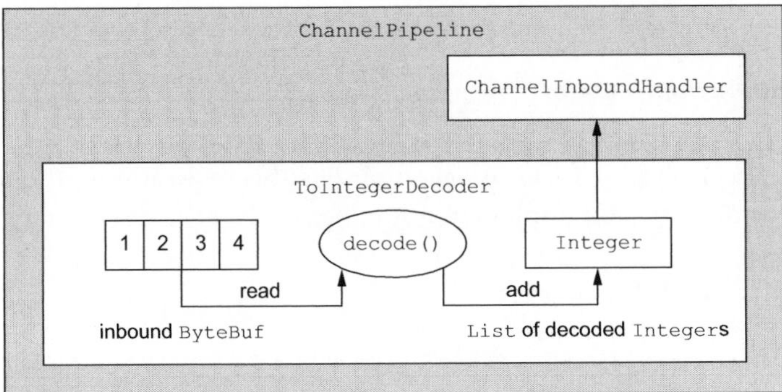

Figure 10.1 `ToIntegerDecoder`

Four bytes at a time are read from the inbound `ByteBuf`, decoded to an `int`, and added to a `List`. When no more items are available to add to the `List`, its contents will be sent to the next `ChannelInboundHandler`.

This listing shows the code for `ToIntegerDecoder`.

Listing 10.1 Class `ToIntegerDecoder` extends `ByteToMessageDecoder`

```
public class ToIntegerDecoder extends ByteToMessageDecoder {
    @Override
    public void decode(ChannelHandlerContext ctx, ByteBuf in,
        List<Object> out) throws Exception {
        if (in.readableBytes() >= 4) {
            out.add(in.readInt());
        }
    }
}
```

- **Extends ByteToMessageDecoder to decode bytes to a specific format**
- **Checks if there are at least 4 bytes readable (length of an int)**
- **Reads an int from the inbound ByteBuf and adds it to the List of decoded messages**

Although `ByteToMessageDecoder` makes this pattern simple to implement, you might find it a bit annoying to have to verify that the input `ByteBuf` has enough data for you to call `readInt()`. In the next section we'll discuss `ReplayingDecoder`, a special decoder that eliminates this step, at the cost of a small amount of overhead.

> **Reference counting in codecs**
>
> As we mentioned in chapters 5 and 6, reference counting requires special attention. In the case of encoders and decoders, the procedure is quite simple: once a message has been encoded or decoded, it will automatically be released by a call to `ReferenceCountUtil.release(message)`. If you need to keep a reference for later use you can call `ReferenceCountUtil.retain(message)`. This increments the reference count, preventing the message from being released.

10.2.2 *Abstract class ReplayingDecoder*

`ReplayingDecoder` extends `ByteToMessageDecoder` and frees us from having to call `readableBytes()` (as in listing 10.1). It accomplishes this by wrapping the incoming `ByteBuf` with a custom `ByteBuf` implementation, `ReplayingDecoderBuffer`, that executes the call internally.

The full declaration of this class is

```
public abstract class ReplayingDecoder<S> extends ByteToMessageDecoder
```

The parameter `S` specifies the type to be used for state management, where `Void` indicates that none is to be performed. The following listing shows a reimplementation of `ToIntegerDecoder` based on `ReplayingDecoder`.

Listing 10.2 Class `ToIntegerDecoder2` extends `ReplayingDecoder`

```
public class ToIntegerDecoder2 extends ReplayingDecoder<Void> {
    @Override
    public void decode(ChannelHandlerContext ctx, ByteBuf in,
        List<Object> out) throws Exception {
        out.add(in.readInt());
    }
}
```

- Extends ReplayingDecoder<Void> to decode bytes to messages
- The incoming ByteBuf is a ReplayingDecoderBuffer.
- Reads an int from the inbound ByteBuf and adds it to the List of decoded messages

As before, `int`s extracted from the `ByteBuf` are added to the `List`. If insufficient bytes are available, this implementation of `readInt()` throws an `Error` that will be caught and handled in the base class. The `decode()` method will be called again when more data is ready for reading. (See the description of `decode()` in table 10.1.)

Please take note of these aspects of `ReplayingDecoderBuffer`:

- Not all `ByteBuf` operations are supported. If an unsupported method is called, an `UnsupportedOperationException` will be thrown.
- `ReplayingDecoder` is slightly slower than `ByteToMessageDecoder`.

If you compare listings 10.1 and 10.2, it's apparent that the latter is simpler. The example itself is very basic, so keep in mind that in a real-life, more complex situation the difference between using one or the other base classes might be significant. Here's a simple guideline: use `ByteToMessageDecoder` if it doesn't introduce excessive complexity; otherwise, use `ReplayingDecoder`.

More decoders

The following classes handle more complex use cases:

- `io.netty.handler.codec.LineBasedFrameDecoder`—This class, used internally by Netty, uses end-of-line control characters (`\n` or `\r\n`) to parse the message data.
- `io.netty.handler.codec.http.HttpObjectDecoder`—A decoder for HTTP data.

You'll find additional encoder and decoder implementations for special use cases in the subpackages of `io.netty.handler.codec`. Please consult the Netty Javadoc for more information.

10.2.3 Abstract class MessageToMessageDecoder

In this section we'll explain how to convert between message formats (for example, from one type of POJO to another) using the abstract base class

```
public abstract class MessageToMessageDecoder<I>
    extends ChannelInboundHandlerAdapter
```

The parameter `I` specifies the type of the input `msg` argument to `decode()`, which is the only method you have to implement. Table 10.2 shows the details of this method.

Table 10.2 `MessageToMessageDecoder` API

Method	Description
`decode( ChannelHandlerContext ctx, I msg, List<Object> out)`	Called for each inbound message to be decoded to another format. The decoded messages are then passed to the next `ChannelInboundHandler` in the pipeline.

In this example, we'll write an `IntegerToStringDecoder` decoder that extends `MessageToMessageDecoder<Integer>`. Its `decode()` method will convert the `Integer` argument to its `String` representation and will have the following signature:

```
public void decode( ChannelHandlerContext ctx,
    Integer msg, List<Object> out ) throws Exception
```

As before, the decoded `String` will be added to the outgoing `List` and forwarded to the next `ChannelInboundHandler`.

The design is illustrated in figure 10.2.

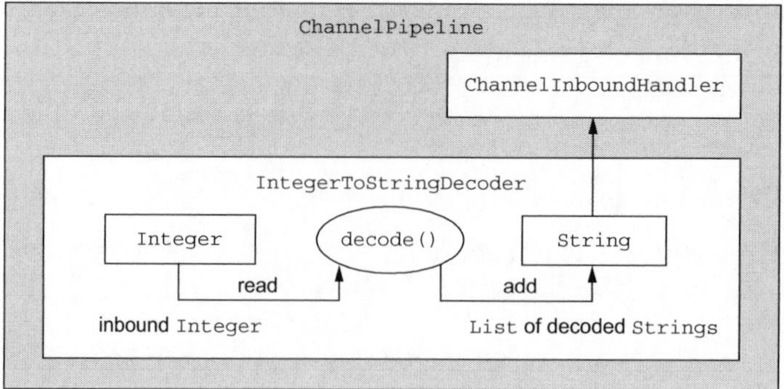

Figure 10.2 `IntegerToStringDecoder`

The following listing is the implementation of `IntegerToStringDecoder`.

Listing 10.3 Class `IntegerToStringDecoder`

```
public class IntegerToStringDecoder extends
    MessageToMessageDecoder<Integer> {
    @Override
    public void decode(ChannelHandlerContext ctx, Integer msg
        List<Object> out) throws Exception {
        out.add(String.valueOf(msg));
    }
}
```

Extends MessageToMessageDecoder<Integer>

Converts the Integer message to its String representation and adds it to the output List

> **HttpObjectAggregator**
>
> For a more complex example, please examine the class `io.netty.handler.codec.http.HttpObjectAggregator`, which extends `MessageToMessageDecoder<HttpObject>`.

10.2.4 *Class TooLongFrameException*

As Netty is an asynchronous framework, you'll need to buffer bytes in memory until you're able to decode them. Consequently, you mustn't allow your decoder to buffer enough data to exhaust available memory. To address this common concern, Netty provides a `TooLongFrameException`, which is intended to be thrown by decoders if a frame exceeds a specified size limit.

To avoid this you can set a threshold of a maximum number of bytes which, if exceeded, will cause a `TooLongFrameException` to be thrown (and caught by `ChannelHandler.exceptionCaught()`). It will then be up to the user of the decoder to decide how to handle the exception. Some protocols, such as HTTP, may allow you to return a special response. In other cases, the only option may be to close the connection.

Listing 10.4 shows how a `ByteToMessageDecoder` can make use of `TooLongFrameException` to notify other `ChannelHandlers` in the `ChannelPipeline` about the occurrence of a frame-size overrun. Note that this kind of protection is especially important if you are working with a protocol that has a variable frame size.

Listing 10.4 TooLongFrameException

```
public class SafeByteToMessageDecoder extends ByteToMessageDecoder {
    private static final int MAX_FRAME_SIZE = 1024;
    @Override
    public void decode(ChannelHandlerContext ctx, ByteBuf in,
        List<Object> out) throws Exception {
            int readable = in.readableBytes();
            if (readable > MAX_FRAME_SIZE) {
                in.skipBytes(readable);
                throw new TooLongFrameException("Frame too big!");
        }
        // do something
        ...
    }
}
```

Extends ByteToMessageDecoder to decode bytes to messages

Checks if the buffer has more than MAX_FRAME_SIZE bytes

Skips all readable bytes, throws TooLongFrameException and notifies ChannelHandlers

So far we've examined common use cases for decoders and the abstract base classes Netty provides for building them. But decoders are only one side of the coin. On the other side are encoders, which transform messages to a format suitable for outgoing transmission. These encoders complete the codec API and they'll be our next topic.

10.3 Encoders

Reviewing our earlier definition, an encoder implements `ChannelOutboundHandler` and transforms outbound data from one format to another, the reverse of the decoder functions we've just studied. Netty provides a set of classes to help you to write encoders with the following capabilities:

- Encoding from messages to bytes
- Encoding from messages to messages

We'll start our examination of these classes with the abstract base class `MessageToByteEncoder`.

10.3.1 Abstract class MessageToByteEncoder

Earlier we looked at how to convert bytes to messages using `ByteToMessageDecoder`. We'll do the reverse now with `MessageToByteEncoder`. Table 10.3 shows the API.

Table 10.3 `MessageToByteEncoder` API

Method	Description
`encode(ChannelHandlerContext ctx, I msg, ByteBuf out)`	The `encode` method is the only abstract method you need to implement. It's called with the outbound message (of type `I`) that this class will encode to a `ByteBuf`. The `ByteBuf` is then forwarded to the next `ChannelOutboundHandler` in the pipeline.

You may have noticed that this class has only one method, while decoders have two. The reason is that decoders often need to produce a last message after the `Channel` has closed (hence the `decodeLast()` method). This is clearly not the case for an encoder—there is no sense in producing a message after the connection has been closed.

Figure 10.3 shows a `ShortToByteEncoder` that receives a `Short` instance as a message, encodes it to a `Short` primitive, and writes it to a `ByteBuf`, which is then forwarded to the next `ChannelOutboundHandler` in the pipeline. Every outgoing `Short` will take up two bytes in the `ByteBuf`.

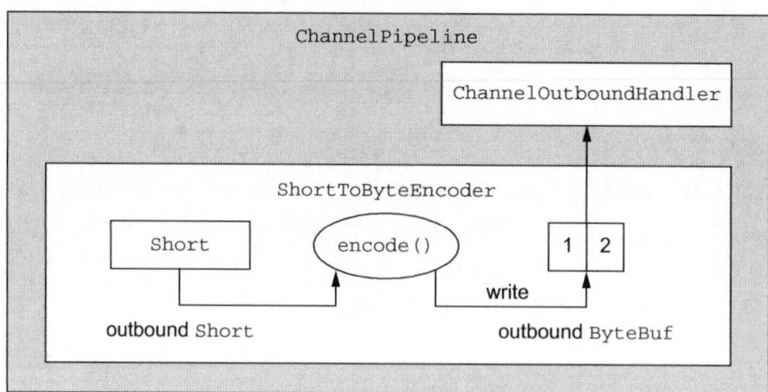

Figure 10.3 `ShortToByteEncoder`

The implementation of `ShortToByteEncoder` is shown in the following listing.

Listing 10.5 Class `ShortToByteEncoder`

```
public class ShortToByteEncoder extends MessageToByteEncoder<Short> {
    @Override
    public void encode(ChannelHandlerContext ctx, Short msg, ByteBuf out)
        throws Exception {
        out.writeShort(msg);
    }
}
```

Annotations: **Extends MessageToByteEncoder** (class declaration); **Writes Short into ByteBuf** (`out.writeShort(msg);`)

Netty provides several specializations of `MessageToByteEncoder` upon which you can base your own implementations. The class `WebSocket08FrameEncoder` provides a good practical example. You'll find it in the package `io.netty.handler.codec.http.websocketx`.

10.3.2 Abstract class MessageToMessageEncoder

You've already seen how to decode inbound data from one message format to another. To complete the picture, we'll show how to encode from one message to another for outbound data. The `encode()` method of `MessageToMessageEncoder` provides this capability, as described in table 10.4.

Table 10.4 `MessageToMessageEncoder` **API**

Name	Description
`encode( ChannelHandlerContext ctx, I msg, List<Object> out)`	This is the only method you need to implement. Each message written with `write()` is passed to `encode()` to be encoded to one or more outbound messages. These are then forwarded to the next `ChannelOutboundHandler` in the pipeline.

To demonstrate, listing 10.6 extends `MessageToMessageEncoder` with an `IntegerToStringEncoder`. The design is shown in figure 10.4.

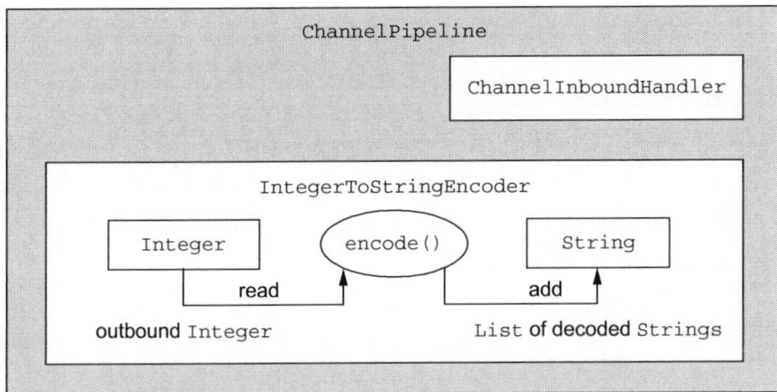

Figure 10.4 `IntegerToStringEncoder`

As shown in the next listing, the encoder adds a `String` representation of each outbound `Integer` to the `List`.

Listing 10.6 Class IntegerToStringEncoder

```
public class IntegerToStringEncoder
    extends MessageToMessageEncoder<Integer> {      <-- Extends MessageToMessageEncoder
    @Override
    public void encode(ChannelHandlerContext ctx, Integer msg
        List<Object> out) throws Exception {
        out.add(String.valueOf(msg));               <-- Converts the Integer to a String and adds it to the List
    }
}
```

For an interesting specialized use of `MessageToMessageEncoder`, look at the class `io.netty.handler.codec.protobuf.ProtobufEncoder`, which handles data formats defined by Google's Protocol Buffers specification.

10.4 Abstract codec classes

Although we've been discussing decoders and encoders as distinct entities, you'll sometimes find it useful to manage transformations of both inbound and outbound data and messages in one class. Netty's abstract codec classes are useful for this purpose, as each bundles together a decoder/encoder pair to handle both types of the operations we've been studying. As you might suspect, these classes implement both `ChannelInboundHandler` and `ChannelOutboundHandler`.

Why would we not use these composite classes all the time in preference to separate decoders and encoders? Because keeping the two functions separate wherever possible maximizes code reusability and extensibility, a basic principle of Netty's design.

As we look at the abstract codec classes we'll compare and contrast them with the corresponding single decoders and encoders.

10.4.1 Abstract class ByteToMessageCodec

Let's examine a case where we need to decode bytes to some kind of message, perhaps a POJO, and then encode it again. `ByteToMessageCodec` will handle this for us, as it combines a `ByteToMessageDecoder` and the reverse, a `MessageToByteEncoder`. The important methods are listed in table 10.5.

Table 10.5 `ByteToMessageCodec` API

Method name	Description
`decode( ChannelHandlerContext ctx, ByteBuf in, List<Object>)`	This method is called as long as bytes are available to be consumed. It converts the inbound `ByteBuf` to the specified message format and forwards to the next `ChannelInboundHandler` in the pipeline.
`decodeLast( ChannelHandlerContext ctx, ByteBuf in, List<Object> out)`	The default implementation of this method delegates to `decode()`. It is called only once, when the `Channel` goes inactive. For special handling it can be overridden.

Table 10.5 `ByteToMessageCodec` API

Method name	Description
`encode( ChannelHandlerContext ctx, I msg, ByteBuf out)`	This method is called for each message (of type `I`) to be encoded and written to an outbound `ByteBuf`.

Any request/response protocol could be a good candidate for using the `ByteToMessageCodec`. For example, in an SMTP implementation, the codec would read incoming bytes and decode them to a custom message type, say `SmtpRequest`. On the receiving side, when a response is created, an `SmtpResponse` will be produced, which will be encoded back to bytes for transmission.

10.4.2 *Abstract class MessageToMessageCodec*

In section 9.2.2 you saw an example of `MessageToMessageEncoder` extended to convert one message format to another. With `MessageToMessageCodec` we can make the round trip with a single class. `MessageToMessageCodec` is a parameterized class, defined as follows:

```
public abstract class MessageToMessageCodec<INBOUND_IN,OUTBOUND_IN>
```

The important methods are listed in table 10.6.

Table 10.6 Methods of `MessageToMessageCodec`

Method name	Description
`protected abstract decode( ChannelHandlerContext ctx, INBOUND_IN msg, List<Object> out)`	This method is called with messages of type `INBOUND_IN`. It decodes them to messages of type `OUTBOUND_IN`, which are forwarded to the next `ChannelInboundHandler` in the `ChannelPipeline`.
`protected abstract encode( ChannelHandlerContext ctx, OUTBOUND_IN msg, List<Object> out)`	This method is called for each message of type `OUTBOUND_IN`. These are encoded to messages of type `INBOUND_IN` and forwarded to the next `ChannelOutboundHandler` in the pipeline.

The `decode()` method transforms an `INBOUND_IN` message to an `OUTBOUND_IN` type and `encode()` does the reverse. It may help to think of `INBOUND_IN` messages as the type sent over the wire, and `OUTBOUND_IN` messages as the type processed by the application.

Although this codec may seem somewhat esoteric, the use case it handles is fairly common: converting data back and forth between two distinct messaging APIs. We often encounter this pattern when we have to interoperate with an API that uses a legacy or proprietary message format.

WebSocket protocol

The following example of MessageToMessageCodec references WebSocket, a recent protocol that enables full bidirectional communications between web browsers and servers. We'll discuss Netty's support for WebSockets at length in chapter 11.

Listing 10.7 shows how such a conversation might take place. Our WebSocketConvertHandler parameterizes MessageToMessageCodec with an INBOUND_IN type of WebSocketFrame and an OUTBOUND_IN type of MyWebSocketFrame, the latter being a static nested class of WebSocketConvertHandler itself.

Listing 10.7 Using MessageToMessageCodec

```
public class WebSocketConvertHandler extends
    MessageToMessageCodec<WebSocketFrame,
    WebSocketConvertHandler.MyWebSocketFrame> {
    @Override
    protected void encode(ChannelHandlerContext ctx,
        WebSocketConvertHandler.MyWebSocketFrame msg,
        List<Object> out) throws Exception {
        ByteBuf payload = msg.getData().duplicate().retain();
        switch (msg.getType()) {
            case BINARY:
                out.add(new BinaryWebSocketFrame(payload));
                break;
            case TEXT:
                out.add(new TextWebSocketFrame(payload));
                break;
            case CLOSE:
                out.add(new CloseWebSocketFrame(true, 0, payload));
                break;
            case CONTINUATION:
                out.add(new ContinuationWebSocketFrame(payload));
                break;
            case PONG:
                out.add(new PongWebSocketFrame(payload));
                break;
            case PING:
                out.add(new PingWebSocketFrame(payload));
                break;
            default:
                throw new IllegalStateException(
                    "Unsupported websocket msg " + msg);
        }
    }

    @Override
    protected void decode(ChannelHandlerContext ctx, WebSocketFrame msg,
        List<Object> out) throws Exception {
            ByteBuf payload = msg.getData().duplicate().retain();
```

Encodes a MyWebSocketFrame to a specified WebSocketFrame subtype

Instantiates a WebSocketFrame of the specified subtype

Decodes a WebSocketFrame to a MyWebSocketFrame and sets the FrameType

```
            if (msg instanceof BinaryWebSocketFrame) {
                out.add(new MyWebSocketFrame(
                    MyWebSocketFrame.FrameType.BINARY, payload));
            } else
            if (msg instanceof CloseWebSocketFrame) {
                out.add(new MyWebSocketFrame (
                    MyWebSocketFrame.FrameType.CLOSE, payload));
            } else
            if (msg instanceof PingWebSocketFrame) {
                out.add(new MyWebSocketFrame (
                    MyWebSocketFrame.FrameType.PING, payload));
            } else
            if (msg instanceof PongWebSocketFrame) {
                out.add(new MyWebSocketFrame (
                    MyWebSocketFrame.FrameType.PONG, payload));
            } else
            if (msg instanceof TextWebSocketFrame) {
                out.add(new MyWebSocketFrame (
                    MyWebSocketFrame.FrameType.TEXT, payload));
            } else
            if (msg instanceof ContinuationWebSocketFrame) {
                out.add(new MyWebSocketFrame (
                    MyWebSocketFrame.FrameType.CONTINUATION, payload));
            } else
            {
                throw new IllegalStateException(
                    "Unsupported websocket msg " + msg);
        }
    }

    public static final class MyWebSocketFrame {
        public enum FrameType {
            BINARY,
            CLOSE,
            PING,
            PONG,
            TEXT,
            CONTINUATION
        }
        private final FrameType type;
        private final ByteBuf data;

        public WebSocketFrame(FrameType type, ByteBuf data) {
            this.type = type;
            this.data = data;
        }

        public FrameType getType() {
            return type;
        }

        public ByteBuf getData() {
            return data;
        }
    }
}
```

Declares the OUTBOUND_IN type used by WebSocket-ConvertHandler

Defines the type of the WebSocketFrame that owns the wrapped payload

10.4.3 Class CombinedChannelDuplexHandler

As we mentioned earlier, combining a decoder and an encoder may have an impact on reusability. However, there is a way to avoid this penalty without sacrificing the convenience of deploying a decoder and an encoder as a single unit. The solution is provided by `CombinedChannelDuplexHandler`, declared as

```
public class CombinedChannelDuplexHandler
    <I extends ChannelInboundHandler,
    O extends ChannelOutboundHandler>
```

This class acts as a container for a `ChannelInboundHandler` and a `ChannelOutboundHandler` (the class parameters `I` and `O`). By providing types that extend a decoder class and an encoder class, respectively, we can implement a codec without having to extend the abstract codec classes directly. We'll illustrate this in the following example.

First, examine `ByteToCharDecoder` in this listing. Notice that the implementation extends `ByteToMessageDecoder` because it reads chars from a `ByteBuf`.

Listing 10.8 Class `ByteToCharDecoder`

```
public class ByteToCharDecoder extends ByteToMessageDecoder {     <-- Extends ByteToMessageDecoder
    @Override
    public void decode(ChannelHandlerContext ctx, ByteBuf in,
        List<Object> out) throws Exception {
            while (in.readableBytes() >= 2) {
                out.add(in.readChar());     <-- Adds one or more Character objects to the outgoing List
        }
    }
}
```

Here `decode()` extracts 2 bytes at a time from the `ByteBuf` and writes them to the `List` as chars, which will be autoboxed as `Character` objects.

This listing has `CharToByteEncoder`, which converts `Characters` back to bytes. This class extends `MessageToByteEncoder` because it needs to encode `char` messages into a `ByteBuf`. This is done by writing directly into the `ByteBuf`.

Listing 10.9 Class `CharToByteEncoder`

```
public class CharToByteEncoder extends
    MessageToByteEncoder<Character> {     <-- Extends MessageToByteEncoder
    @Override
    public void encode(ChannelHandlerContext ctx, Character msg,
        ByteBuf out) throws Exception {
        out.writeChar(msg);     <-- Decodes a Character to a char and writes it into the outbound ByteBuf
    }
}
```

Now that we have a decoder and encoder, we'll combine them to build up a codec. This listing shows how this is done.

Listing 10.10 `CombinedChannelDuplexHandler<I,O>`

```
public class CombinedByteCharCodec extends
    CombinedChannelDuplexHandler<ByteToCharDecoder, CharToByteEncoder> {
    public CombinedByteCharCodec() {
        super(new ByteToCharDecoder(), new CharToByteEncoder());
    }
}
```

Parameterizes CombinedByteCharCodec by the decoder and encoder implementations

Passes the delegate instances to the parent

As you can see, it may be simpler and more flexible in some cases to combine implementations in this way than to use one of the codec classes. It may also come down to a matter of personal preference.

10.5 Summary

In this chapter we studied the use of the Netty codec API to write decoders and encoders. You learned why using this API is preferable to using the `ChannelHandler` API directly.

You saw how the abstract codec classes provide support for handling decoding and encoding in one implementation. If you need greater flexibility or wish to reuse existing implementations, you also have the option of combining them without needing to extend any of the abstract codec classes.

In the next chapter, we'll discuss the `ChannelHandler` implementations and codecs that are part of the Netty framework itself and that you can utilize to handle specific protocols and tasks.

11 Provided ChannelHandlers and codecs

This chapter covers

- Securing Netty applications with SSL/TLS
- Building Netty HTTP/HTTPS applications
- Handling idle connections and timeouts
- Decoding delimited and length-based protocols
- Writing big data

Netty provides codecs and handlers for numerous common protocols that you can use literally out of the box, reducing time and effort you would otherwise spend on fairly tedious matters. In this chapter we'll explore these tools and their benefits, which include support for SSL/TLS and WebSocket, as well as for simply squeezing better performance out of HTTP with data compression.

11.1 Securing Netty applications with SSL/TLS

Data privacy is a matter of great concern today, and as developers we need to be prepared to address it. At a minimum we should be familiar with encryption protocols such as SSL and TLS,[1] which are layered on top of other protocols to implement

[1] The Transport Layer Security (TLS) Protocol, version 1.2, http://tools.ietf.org/html/rfc5246.

data security. We have all encountered these protocols when accessing secure websites, but they are also used in applications that are not HTTP-based, such as Secure SMTP (SMTPS) mail services and even relational database systems.

To support SSL/TLS, Java provides the package `javax.net.ssl`, whose classes `SSLContext` and `SSLEngine` make it quite straightforward to implement decryption and encryption. Netty leverages this API by way of a `ChannelHandler` implementation named `SslHandler`, which employs an `SSLEngine` internally to do the actual work.

Netty's OpenSSL/SSLEngine implementation

Netty also provides an `SSLEngine` implementation that uses the OpenSSL toolkit (www.openssl.org). This class, `OpenSslEngine`, offers better performance than the `SSLEngine` implementation supplied by the JDK.

Netty applications (clients and servers) can be configured to use `OpenSslEngine` by default if the OpenSSL libraries are available. If not, Netty will fall back to the JDK implementation. For detailed instructions on configuring OpenSSL support, please see the Netty documentation at http://netty.io/wiki/forked-tomcat-native.html#wiki-h2-1.

Note that the SSL API and data flow are identical whether you use the JDK's `SSLEngine` or Netty's `OpenSslEngine`.

Figure 11.1 shows data flow using `SslHandler`.

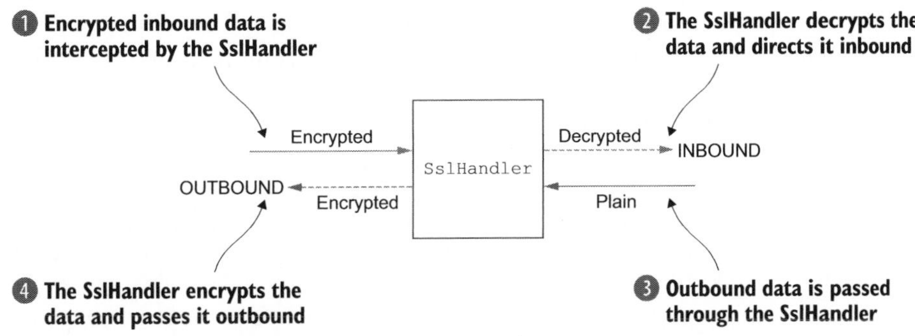

Figure 11.1 Data flow through `SslHandler` for decryption and encryption

Listing 11.1 shows how an `SslHandler` is added to a `ChannelPipeline` using a `ChannelInitializer`. Recall that `ChannelInitializer` is used to set up the `ChannelPipeline` once a `Channel` is registered.

Listing 11.1 Adding SSL/TLS support

```
public class SslChannelInitializer extends ChannelInitializer<Channel>{
    private final SslContext context;
    private final boolean startTls;

    public SslChannelInitializer(SslContext context,
        boolean startTls) {
        this.context = context;
        this.startTls = startTls;
    }

    @Override
    protected void initChannel(Channel ch) throws Exception {
        SSLEngine engine = context.newEngine(ch.alloc());
        ch.pipeline().addFirst("ssl",
            new SslHandler(engine, startTls));
    }
}
```

Passes in the SslContext to use

If true, the first message written is not encrypted (clients should set to true)

For each SslHandler instance, obtains a new SSLEngine from the SslContext using the ByteBufAllocator of the Channel

Adds the SslHandler to the pipeline as the first handler

In most cases the `SslHandler` will be the first `ChannelHandler` in the `ChannelPipeline`. This ensures that encryption will take place only after all other `ChannelHandlers` have applied their logic to the data.

The `SslHandler` has some useful methods, as shown in table 11.1. For example, during the handshake phase, the two peers validate each other and agree upon an encryption method. You can configure `SslHandler` to modify its behavior or provide notification once the SSL/TLS handshake is complete, after which all data will be encrypted. The SSL/TLS handshake will be executed automatically.

Table 11.1 `SslHandler` methods

Name	Description

`setHandshakeTimeout (long,TimeUnit)`
`setHandshakeTimeoutMillis (long)`
`getHandshakeTimeoutMillis()`
	Sets and gets the timeout after which the handshake `ChannelFuture` will be notified of failure.

`setCloseNotifyTimeout (long,TimeUnit)`
`setCloseNotifyTimeoutMillis (long)`
`getCloseNotifyTimeoutMillis()`
	Sets and gets the timeout after which the close notification will be triggered and the connection will close. This also results in notifying the `ChannelFuture` of failure.

`handshakeFuture()`	Returns a `ChannelFuture` that will be notified when the handshake is complete. If the handshake was previously executed, returns a `ChannelFuture` that contains the result of the previous handshake.

Table 11.1 `SslHandler` methods

Name	Description

`close()`
`close(ChannelPromise)`
`close(ChannelHandlerContext,ChannelPromise)`
	Sends the `close_notify` to request close and destroy the underlying `SslEngine`.

11.2 Building Netty HTTP/HTTPS applications

HTTP/HTTPS is one of the most common protocol suites, and with the success of smartphones it's more widely used with each passing day because it has become practically obligatory for any company to have a mobile-accessible website. These protocols are used in other ways too. WebService APIs exported by many organizations for communications with their business partners are generally based on HTTP(S).

Next we'll look at the `ChannelHandlers` that Netty provides so you can use HTTP and HTTPS without having to write custom codecs.

11.2.1 HTTP decoder, encoder, and codec

HTTP is based on a request/response pattern: the client sends an HTTP request to the server, and the server sends back an HTTP response. Netty provides a variety of encoders and decoders to simplify working with this protocol. Figures 11.2 and 11.3 show the methods for producing and consuming HTTP requests and responses, respectively.

As shown in figures 11.2 and 11.3, an HTTP request/response may consist of more than one data part, and it always terminates with a `LastHttpContent` part. The `FullHttpRequest` and `FullHttpResponse` messages are special subtypes that represent a complete request and response, respectively. All types of HTTP messages (`FullHttpRequest`, `LastHttpContent`, and those shown in listing 11.2) implement the `HttpObject` interface.

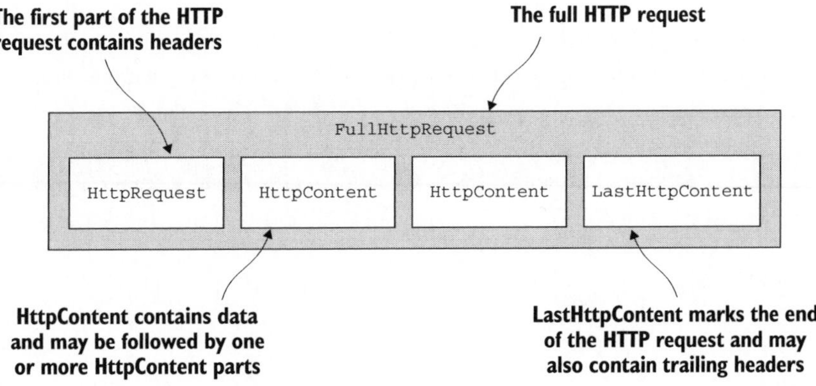

Figure 11.2 HTTP request component parts

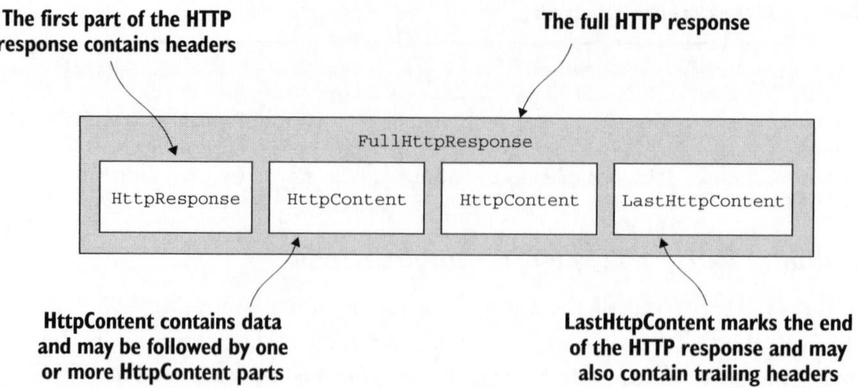

Figure 11.3 HTTP response component parts

Table 11.2 gives an overview of the HTTP decoders and encoders that handle and produce these messages.

Table 11.2 HTTP decoders and encoders

Name	Description
`HttpRequestEncoder`	Encodes `HttpRequest`, `HttpContent`, and `LastHttpContent` messages to bytes.
`HttpResponseEncoder`	Encodes `HttpResponse`, `HttpContent`, and `LastHttpContent` messages to bytes.
`HttpRequestDecoder`	Decodes bytes into `HttpRequest`, `HttpContent`, and `LastHttpContent` messages.
`HttpResponseDecoder`	Decodes bytes into `HttpResponse`, `HttpContent`, and `LastHttpContent` messages.

The class `HttpPipelineInitializer` in the next listing shows how simple it is to add HTTP support to your application—merely add the correct `ChannelHandlers` to the `ChannelPipeline`.

Listing 11.2 Adding support for HTTP

```
public class HttpPipelineInitializer extends ChannelInitializer<Channel> {
    private final boolean client;

    public HttpPipelineInitializer(boolean client) {
        this.client = client;
    }

    @Override
    protected void initChannel(Channel ch) throws Exception {
        ChannelPipeline pipeline = ch.pipeline();
```

```
        if (client) {
            pipeline.addLast("decoder", new HttpResponseDecoder());
            pipeline.addLast("encoder", new HttpRequestEncoder());
        } else {
            pipeline.addLast("decoder", new HttpRequestDecoder());
            pipeline.addLast("encoder", new HttpResponseEncoder());
        }
    }
}
```

If server, adds HttpResponseEncoder to send responses to the client

If client, adds HttpResponseDecoder to handle responses from the server

If server, adds HttpRequestDecoder to receive requests from the client

If client, adds HttpRequestEncoder to send requests to the server

11.2.2 HTTP message aggregation

After the initializer has installed the handlers in the `ChannelPipeline` you can operate on the different `HttpObject` messages. But because HTTP requests and responses can be composed of many parts, you'll need to aggregate them to form complete messages. To eliminate this cumbersome task, Netty provides an aggregator that merges message parts into `FullHttpRequest` and `FullHttpResponse` messages. This way you always see the full message contents.

There's a slight cost to this operation because the message segments need to be buffered until complete messages can be forwarded to the next `ChannelInboundHandler`. The trade-off is that you don't need to worry about message fragmentation.

Introducing this automatic aggregation is a matter of adding another `ChannelHandler` to the pipeline. This listing shows how this is done.

Listing 11.3 Automatically aggregating HTTP message fragments

```
public class HttpAggregatorInitializer extends ChannelInitializer<Channel> {
    private final boolean isClient;

    public HttpAggregatorInitializer(boolean isClient) {
        this.isClient = isClient;
    }

    @Override
    protected void initChannel(Channel ch) throws Exception {
        ChannelPipeline pipeline = ch.pipeline();
        if (isClient) {
            pipeline.addLast("codec", new HttpClientCodec());
        } else {
            pipeline.addLast("codec", new HttpServerCodec());
        }
        pipeline.addLast("aggregator",
            new HttpObjectAggregator(512 * 1024));
    }
}
```

If client, adds HttpClientCodec

If server, adds HttpServerCodec

Adds HttpObjectAggregator with a max message size of 512 KB to the pipeline

11.2.3 HTTP compression

When using HTTP, it's advisable to employ compression to reduce the size of transmitted data as much as possible. Although compression does have some cost in CPU cycles, it's generally a good idea, especially for text data.

Netty provides `ChannelHandler` implementations for compression and decompression that support both `gzip` and `deflate` encodings.

> **HTTP request header**
>
> The client can indicate supported encryption modes by supplying the following header:
>
> ```
> GET /encrypted-area HTTP/1.1
> Host: www.example.com
> Accept-Encoding: gzip, deflate
> ```
>
> Note, however, that the server isn't obliged to compress the data it sends.

An example is shown in the following listing.

Listing 11.4 Automatically compressing HTTP messages

```
public class HttpCompressionInitializer extends ChannelInitializer<Channel> {
    private final boolean isClient;

    public HttpCompressionInitializer(boolean isClient) {
        this.isClient = isClient;
    }

    @Override
    protected void initChannel(Channel ch) throws Exception {
        ChannelPipeline pipeline = ch.pipeline();
        if (isClient) {
            pipeline.addLast("codec", new HttpClientCodec());
                pipeline.addLast("decompressor",
                new HttpContentDecompressor());
        } else {
            pipeline.addLast("codec", new HttpServerCodec());
            pipeline.addLast("compressor",
            new HttpContentCompressor());
        }
    }
}
```

If client, adds HttpClientCodec

If client, adds HttpContentDecompressor to handle compressed content from the server

If server, adds HttpServerCodec

If server, adds HttpContentCompressor to compress the data (if the client supports it)

Compression and dependencies

If you're using JDK 6 or earlier, you'll need to add JZlib (www.jcraft.com/jzlib/) to the CLASSPATH to support compression.

For Maven, add the following dependency:

```
<dependency>
    <groupId>com.jcraft</groupId>
    <artifactId>jzlib</artifactId>
    <version>1.1.3</version>
</dependency>
```

11.2.4 Using HTTPS

The following listing shows that enabling HTTPS is only a matter of adding an `SslHandler` to the mix.

Listing 11.5 Using HTTPS

```
public class HttpsCodecInitializer extends ChannelInitializer<Channel> {
    private final SslContext context;
    private final boolean isClient;

    public HttpsCodecInitializer(SslContext context, boolean isClient) {
        this.context = context;
        this.isClient = isClient;
    }

    @Override
    protected void initChannel(Channel ch) throws Exception {
        ChannelPipeline pipeline = ch.pipeline();
        SSLEngine engine = context.newEngine(ch.alloc());
        pipeline.addFirst("ssl", new SslHandler(engine));

        if (isClient) {
            pipeline.addLast("codec", new HttpClientCodec());
        } else {
            pipeline.addLast("codec", new HttpServerCodec());
        }
    }
}
```

Adds SslHandler to the pipeline to use HTTPS

If client, adds HttpClientCodec

If server, adds HttpServerCodec

The preceding code is a good example of how Netty's architectural approach turns reuse into leverage. Simply by adding a `ChannelHandler` to the `ChannelPipeline` you can provide a new capability, even one as significant as encryption.

11.2.5 WebSocket

Netty's extensive toolkit for HTTP-based applications includes support for some of its most advanced features. In this section we'll explore WebSocket, a protocol standardized by the Internet Engineering Task Force (IETF) in 2011.

WebSocket addresses a longstanding problem: how to publish information in real time given that the underlying protocol, HTTP, is a sequence of request-response interactions. AJAX provides some improvement, but the flow of data is still driven by requests from the client side. There have been other more-or-less clever approaches,[2] but in the end they have remained workarounds with limited scalability.

The WebSocket specification and its implementations represent an attempt at a more effective solution. Simply stated, a WebSocket provides "a single TCP connection for traffic in both directions ... Combined with the WebSocket API ... it provides an alternative to HTTP polling for two-way communication from a web page to a remote server."[3]

That is, WebSockets provide a true *bidirectional* exchange of data between client and server. We won't go into too much detail about the internals, but we should mention that though the earliest implementations were limited to text data, this is no longer the case; a WebSocket can now be used for any data, much like a normal socket.

Figure 11.4 gives a general idea of the WebSocket protocol. In this scenario the communication starts as plain HTTP and upgrades to bidirectional WebSocket.

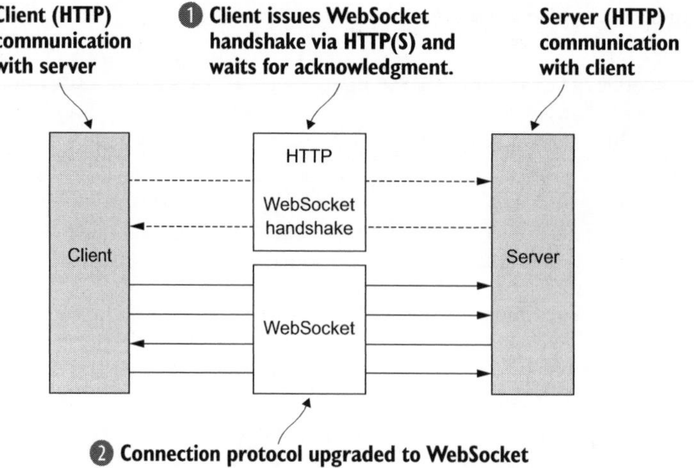

Figure 11.4 WebSocket protocol

To add WebSocket support to your application, you include the appropriate client-side or server-side WebSocket `ChannelHandler` in the pipeline. This class will handle the special message types defined by WebSocket, known as *frames*. As shown in table 11.3, `WebSocketFrames` can be classed as data or control frames.

---

[2] Comet is one example, http://en.wikipedia.org/wiki/Comet_%28programming%29.

[3] RFC 6455, The WebSocket Protocol, http://tools.ietf.org/html/rfc6455.

Table 11.3 `WebSocketFrame` types

Name	Description
`BinaryWebSocketFrame`	Data frame: binary data
`TextWebSocketFrame`	Data frame: text data
`ContinuationWebSocketFrame`	Data frame: text or binary data that belongs to a previous `BinaryWebSocketFrame` or `TextWebSocketFrame`
`CloseWebSocketFrame`	Control frame: a `CLOSE` request, close status code, and a phrase
`PingWebSocketFrame`	Control frame: requests a `PongWebSocketFrame`
`PongWebSocketFrame`	Control frame: responds to a `PingWebSocketFrame` request

Because Netty is principally a server-side technology, we'll focus here on creating a WebSocket server.[4] Listing 11.6 presents a simple example using `WebSocketServerProtocolHandler`. This class handles the protocol upgrade handshake as well as the three control frames—`Close`, `Ping`, and `Pong`. `Text` and `Binary` data frames will be passed along to the next handlers (implemented by you) for processing.

Listing 11.6 Supporting WebSocket on the server

```
public class WebSocketServerInitializer extends ChannelInitializer<Channel>{
    @Override
    protected void initChannel(Channel ch) throws Exception {
        ch.pipeline().addLast(
            new HttpServerCodec(),
            new HttpObjectAggregator(65536),
            new WebSocketServerProtocolHandler("/websocket"),
            new TextFrameHandler(),
            new BinaryFrameHandler(),
            new ContinuationFrameHandler());
    }

    public static final class TextFrameHandler extends
        SimpleChannelInboundHandler<TextWebSocketFrame> {
        @Override
        public void channelRead0(ChannelHandlerContext ctx,
            TextWebSocketFrame msg) throws Exception {
            // Handle text frame
        }
    }
```

Provides aggregated HttpRequests for the handshake

Handles the upgrade handshake if the endpoint requested is "/websocket"

TextFrameHandler handles TextWebSocketFrames

BinaryFrameHandler handles BinaryWebSocketFrames

ContinuationFrameHandler handles ContinuationWebSocketFrames

[4] For client-side examples, refer to the examples included in the Netty source code, https://github.com/netty/netty/tree/4.0/example/src/main/java/io/netty/example/http/websocketx/client.

```
    public static final class BinaryFrameHandler extends
        SimpleChannelInboundHandler<BinaryWebSocketFrame> {
        @Override
        public void channelRead0(ChannelHandlerContext ctx,
            BinaryWebSocketFrame msg) throws Exception {
            // Handle binary frame
        }
    }

    public static final class ContinuationFrameHandler extends
        SimpleChannelInboundHandler<ContinuationWebSocketFrame> {
        @Override
        public void channelRead0(ChannelHandlerContext ctx,
            ContinuationWebSocketFrame msg) throws Exception {
            // Handle continuation frame
        }
    }
}
```

Secure WebSocket

To add security to WebSocket, simply insert the `SslHandler` as the first `ChannelHandler` in the pipeline.

For a more extensive example, please see chapter 12, which explores in depth the design of a real-time WebSocket application.

11.3 Idle connections and timeouts

So far our discussion has focused on Netty's support for the HTTP variants HTTPS and WebSocket via specialized codecs and handlers. These technologies can make your web applications more effective, usable, and secure, provided that you manage your network resources efficiently. So let's talk about the primary concern, connection management.

Detecting idle connections and timeouts is essential to freeing resources in a timely manner. This is such a common task that Netty provides several `ChannelHandler` implementations just for this purpose. Table 11.4 gives an overview of these.

Table 11.4 `ChannelHandlers` for idle connections and timeouts

Name	Description
`IdleStateHandler`	Fires an `IdleStateEvent` if the connection idles too long. You can then handle the `IdleStateEvent` by overriding `userEventTriggered()` in your `ChannelInboundHandler`.
`ReadTimeoutHandler`	Throws a `ReadTimeoutException` and closes the `Channel` when no inbound data is received for a specified interval. The `ReadTimeoutException` can be detected by overriding `exceptionCaught()` in your `ChannelHandler`.

Table 11.4 `ChannelHandlers` for idle connections and timeouts

Name	Description
`WriteTimeoutHandler`	Throws a `WriteTimeoutException` and closes the `Channel` when no inbound data is received for a specified interval. The `WriteTimeoutException` can be detected by overriding `exceptionCaught()` in your `ChannelHandler`.

Let's take a closer look at `IdleStateHandler`, the one most used in practice. Listing 11.7 shows how to get notification if no data has been received or sent for 60 seconds, using the common method of sending a heartbeat message to the remote peer; if there is no response the connection is closed.

Listing 11.7 Sending heartbeats

```
public class IdleStateHandlerInitializer extends ChannelInitializer<Channel>
    {
    @Override
    protected void initChannel(Channel ch) throws Exception {
        ChannelPipeline pipeline = ch.pipeline();
        pipeline.addLast(
            new IdleStateHandler(0, 0, 60, TimeUnit.SECONDS));
        pipeline.addLast(new HeartbeatHandler());
    }

    public static final class HeartbeatHandler
        extends ChannelStateHandlerAdapter {
        private static final ByteBuf HEARTBEAT_SEQUENCE =
            Unpooled.unreleasableBuffer(Unpooled.copiedBuffer(
            "HEARTBEAT", CharsetUtil.ISO_8859_1));

        @Override
        public void userEventTriggered(ChannelHandlerContext ctx,
            Object evt) throws Exception {
            if (evt instanceof IdleStateEvent) {
                ctx.writeAndFlush(HEARTBEAT_SEQUENCE.duplicate())
                    .addListener(
                        ChannelFutureListener.CLOSE_ON_FAILURE);
            } else {
                super.userEventTriggered(ctx, evt);
            }
        }
    }
}
```

❶ IdleStateHandler sends an IdleStateEvent when triggered

Adds a HeartbeatHandler to the pipeline

Implements userEventTriggered() to send the heartbeat

The heartbeat to send to the remote peer

❷ Sends the heartbeat and closes the connection if the send fails

Not an IdleStateEvent, so pass it to the next handler

This example illustrates how to employ `IdleStateHandler` to test whether the remote peer is still alive and to free up resources by closing the connection if it is not.

`IdleStateHandler` ❶ will call `userEventTriggered()` with an `IdleStateEvent` if the connection has not received or sent data for 60 seconds. `HeartbeatHandler` implements `userEventTriggered()`. If this method detects an `IdleStateEvent` it sends the heartbeat message and adds a `ChannelFutureListener` that closes the connection if the send operation fails ❷.

11.4 Decoding delimited and length-based protocols

As you work with Netty, you'll encounter delimited and length-based protocols that require decoders. The next sections explain the implementations that Netty provides to handle these cases.

11.4.1 Delimited protocols

Delimited message protocols use defined characters to mark the beginning or end of a message or message segment, often called a *frame*. This is true of many protocols formally defined by RFC documents, such as SMTP, POP3, IMAP, and Telnet.[5] And, of course, private organizations often have their own proprietary formats. Whatever protocol you work with, the decoders listed in table 11.5 will help you to define custom decoders that can extract frames delimited by any sequence of tokens.

Table 11.5 Decoders for handling delimited and length-based protocols

Name	Description
`DelimiterBasedFrameDecoder`	A generic decoder that extracts frames using any user-provided delimiter.
`LineBasedFrameDecoder`	A decoder that extracts frames delimited by the line-endings `\n` or `\r\n`. This decoder is faster than `DelimiterBasedFrameDecoder`.

Figure 11.5 shows how frames are handled when delimited by the end-of-line sequence `\r\n` (carriage return + line feed).

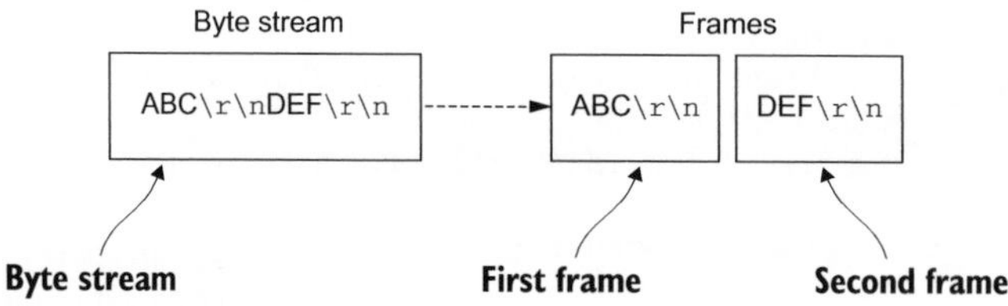

Figure 11.5 Frames delimited by line endings

[5] The RFCs for these protocols can be found on the IETF site: SMTP at www.ietf.org/rfc/rfc2821.txt, POP3 at www.ietf.org/rfc/rfc1939.txt, IMAP at http://tools.ietf.org/html/rfc3501, and Telnet at http://tools.ietf.org/search/rfc854.

The following listing shows how you can use `LineBasedFrameDecoder` to handle the case shown in figure 11.5.

Listing 11.8 Handling line-delimited frames

```
public class LineBasedHandlerInitializer extends ChannelInitializer<Channel>
    {
    @Override
    protected void initChannel(Channel ch) throws Exception {
        ChannelPipeline pipeline = ch.pipeline();
        pipeline.addLast(new LineBasedFrameDecoder(64 * 1024));
        pipeline.addLast(new FrameHandler());
    }

    public static final class FrameHandler
        extends SimpleChannelInboundHandler<ByteBuf> {
        @Override
        public void channelRead0(ChannelHandlerContext ctx,
            ByteBuf msg) throws Exception {
            // Do something with the data extracted from the frame
        }
    }
}
```

The LineBasedFrameDecoder forwards extracted frames to the next handler

Adds the FrameHandler to receive the frames

Passes in the contents of a single frame

If you're working with frames delimited by something other than line endings, you can use the `DelimiterBasedFrameDecoder` in a similar fashion, specifying the specific delimiter sequence to the constructor.

These decoders are tools for implementing your own delimited protocols. As an example, we'll use the following protocol specification:

- The incoming data stream is a series of frames, each delimited by a line feed (`\n`).
- Each frame consists of a series of items, each delimited by a single space character.
- The contents of a frame represent a command, defined as a name followed by a variable number of arguments.

Our custom decoder for this protocol will define the following classes:

- `Cmd`—Stores the contents of the frame (a command) in one `ByteBuf` for the name and another for the arguments.
- `CmdDecoder`—Retrieves a line from the overridden `decode()` method and constructs a `Cmd` instance from its contents.
- `CmdHandler`—Receives the decoded `Cmd` object from the `CmdDecoder` and performs some processing on it.
- `CmdHandlerInitializer`—For simplicity, we'll define the preceding classes as nested classes of a specialized `ChannelInitializer` that will install the handlers in the pipeline.

As you can see in the next listing, the key to this decoder is to extend `LineBasedFrameDecoder`.

Listing 11.9 Using a `ChannelInitializer` as a decoder installer

```
public class CmdHandlerInitializer extends ChannelInitializer<Channel> {
    final byte SPACE = (byte)' ';
    @Override
    protected void initChannel(Channel ch) throws Exception {
        ChannelPipeline pipeline = ch.pipeline();
        pipeline.addLast(new CmdDecoder(64 * 1024));
        pipeline.addLast(new CmdHandler());
    }

    public static final class Cmd {
        private final ByteBuf name;
        private final ByteBuf args;

        public Cmd(ByteBuf name, ByteBuf args) {
            this.name = name;
            this.args = args;
        }

        public ByteBuf name() {
            return name;
        }

        public ByteBuf args() {
            return args;
        }
    }

    public static final class CmdDecoder extends LineBasedFrameDecoder {
        public CmdDecoder(int maxLength) {
            super(maxLength);
        }

        @Override
        protected Object decode(ChannelHandlerContext ctx, ByteBuf buffer)
            throws Exception {
            ByteBuf frame = (ByteBuf) super.decode(ctx, buffer);
            if (frame == null) {
                return null;
            }
            int index = frame.indexOf(frame.readerIndex(),
                frame.writerIndex(), SPACE);
            return new Cmd(frame.slice(frame.readerIndex(), index),
                frame.slice(index + 1, frame.writerIndex()));
        }
    }

    public static final class CmdHandler
        extends SimpleChannelInboundHandler<Cmd> {
```

Adds a CmdDecoder to extract a Cmd object and forwards it to the next handler

Adds a CmdHandler to receive and process the Cmd objects

The Cmd POJO

Extracts a frame delimited by an end-of-line sequence from the ByteBuf

Null is returned if there is no frame in the input.

Finds the index of the first space character. The command name precedes it, the arguments follow.

New Cmd object instantiated with slices that hold the command name and arguments

```
        @Override
        public void channelRead0(ChannelHandlerContext ctx, Cmd msg)
            throws Exception {
            // Do something with the command     <-- Processes the Cmd object passed through the pipeline
        }
    }
}
```

11.4.2 Length-based protocols

A length-based protocol defines a frame by encoding its length in a header segment of the frame, rather than by marking its end with a special delimiter. Table 11.6 lists the two decoders Netty provides for handling this type of protocol.

Table 11.6 Decoders for length-based protocols

Name	Description
`FixedLengthFrameDecoder`	Extracts frames of a fixed size, specified when the constructor is called.
`LengthFieldBasedFrameDecoder`	Extracts frames based on a length value encoded in a field in the frame header; the offset and length of the field are specified in the constructor.

Figure 11.6 shows the operation of a `FixedLengthFrameDecoder` that has been constructed with a frame length of 8 bytes.

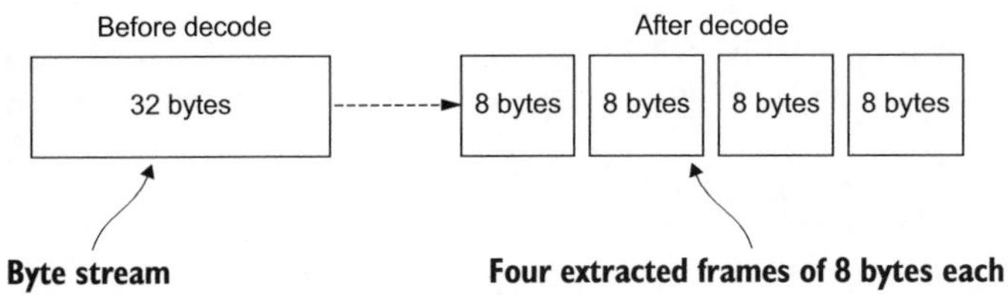

Figure 11.6 Decoding a frame length of 8 bytes

You'll frequently encounter protocols where the frame size encoded in the message header is not a fixed value. To handle such variable-length frames you'll use the `LengthFieldBasedFrameDecoder`, which determines the frame length from the header field and extracts the specified number of bytes from the data stream.

Figure 11.7 shows an example where the length field in the header is at offset 0 and has a length of 2 bytes.

The `LengthFieldBasedFrameDecoder` provides several constructors to cover a variety of header configuration cases. Listing 11.10 shows the use of a constructor whose

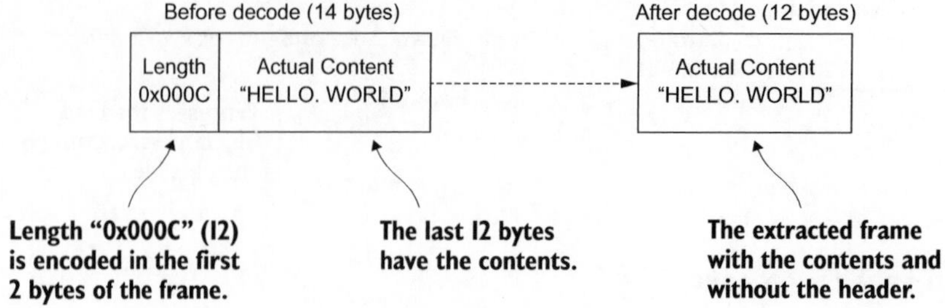

Figure 11.7 Message with variable frame size encoded in the header

three arguments are `maxFrameLength`, `lengthFieldOffset`, and `lengthFieldLength`. In this case, the length of the frame is encoded in the frame's first 8 bytes.

Listing 11.10 Decoder for the command and the handler

```
public class LengthBasedInitializer extends ChannelInitializer<Channel> {
    @Override
    protected void initChannel(Channel ch) throws Exception {
        ChannelPipeline pipeline = ch.pipeline();
        pipeline.addLast(
            new LengthFieldBasedFrameDecoder(64 * 1024, 0, 8));
        pipeline.addLast(new FrameHandler());
    }

    public static final class FrameHandler
        extends SimpleChannelInboundHandler<ByteBuf> {
        @Override
        public void channelRead0(ChannelHandlerContext ctx,
            ByteBuf msg) throws Exception {
            // Do something with the frame
        }
    }
}
```

- LengthFieldBasedFrameDecoder for messages that encode frame length in the first 8 bytes
- Adds a FrameHandler to handle each frame
- Processes the frame data

You've now seen the codecs Netty provides to support protocols that define the structure of byte streams by specifying either delimiters or the length (fixed or variable) of a protocol frame. You'll find numerous uses for these codecs, as a great many common protocols fall into one or the other categories.

11.5 Writing big data

Writing big chunks of data efficiently is a special problem in asynchronous frameworks because of the possibility of network saturation. Because the write operations are non-blocking, they return on completion and notify the `ChannelFuture` even if all the data hasn't been written out. When this occurs, if you don't stop writing you risk running out of memory. So when writing large masses of data, you need to be prepared to handle cases where a slow connection to a remote peer can cause delays in freeing memory. Let's consider the case of writing the contents of a file to the network.

In our discussion of transports (see section 4.2) we mentioned the zero-copy feature of NIO, which eliminates copying steps in moving the contents of a file from the file system to the network stack. All of this happens in Netty's core, so all that's required is that the application use an implementation of interface `FileRegion`, defined in the Netty API documentation as "a region of a file that is sent via a `Channel` that supports zero-copy file transfer."

This listing shows how you can transmit a file's contents using zero-copy by creating a `DefaultFileRegion` from a `FileInputStream` and writing it to a `Channel`.

Listing 11.11 Transferring file contents with `FileRegion`

```
FileInputStream in = new FileInputStream(file);
FileRegion region = new DefaultFileRegion(
    in.getChannel(), 0, file.length());
channel.writeAndFlush(region).addListener(
    new ChannelFutureListener() {
    @Override
    public void operationComplete(ChannelFuture future)
        throws Exception {
        if (!future.isSuccess()) {
            Throwable cause = future.cause();
            // Do something
        }
    }
});
```

- **Creates a FileInputStream**
- **Creates a new DefaultFileRegion for the full length of the file**
- **Sends the DefaultFileRegion and registers a ChannelFutureListener**
- **Handles failure**

This example applies only to the direct transmission of a file's contents, excluding any processing of the data by the application. In cases where you need to copy the data from the file system into user memory, you can use `ChunkedWriteHandler`, which provides support for writing a large data stream asynchronously without incurring high memory consumption.

The key is `interface ChunkedInput<B>`, where the parameter `B` is the type returned by the method `readChunk()`. Four implementations of this interface are provided, as listed in table 11.7. Each one represents a data stream of indefinite length to be consumed by a `ChunkedWriteHandler`.

Table 11.7 `ChunkedInput` implementations

Name	Description
`ChunkedFile`	Fetches data from a file chunk by chunk, for use when your platform doesn't support zero-copy or you need to transform the data
`ChunkedNioFile`	Similar to `ChunkedFile` except that it uses `FileChannel`
`ChunkedStream`	Transfers content chunk by chunk from an `InputStream`
`ChunkedNioStream`	Transfers content chunk by chunk from a `ReadableByteChannel`

Listing 11.12 illustrates the use of `ChunkedStream`, the implementation most often used in practice. The class shown is instantiated with a `File` and an `SslContext`. When `initChannel()` is called, it initializes the channel with the chain of handlers shown.

When the channel becomes active, the `WriteStreamHandler` will write data from the file chunk by chunk as a `ChunkedStream`. The data will be encrypted by the `SslHandler` before being transmitted.

Listing 11.12 Transferring file contents with `ChunkedStream`

```
public class ChunkedWriteHandlerInitializer
    extends ChannelInitializer<Channel> {
    private final File file;
    private final SslContext sslCtx;

    public ChunkedWriteHandlerInitializer(File file, SslContext sslCtx) {
       this.file = file;
       this.sslCtx = sslCtx;
    }

    @Override
    protected void initChannel(Channel ch) throws Exception {
        ChannelPipeline pipeline = ch.pipeline();
        pipeline.addLast(new SslHandler(sslCtx.createEngine()));
        pipeline.addLast(new ChunkedWriteHandler());
        pipeline.addLast(new WriteStreamHandler());
    }

    public final class WriteStreamHandler
        extends ChannelInboundHandlerAdapter {

        @Override
        public void channelActive(ChannelHandlerContext ctx)
            throws Exception {
            super.channelActive(ctx);
            ctx.writeAndFlush(
            new ChunkedStream(new FileInputStream(file)));
        }
    }
}
```

Adds an SslHandler to the ChannelPipeline

Adds a ChunkedWriteHandler to handle data passed in as ChunkedInput

WriteStreamHandler starts to write the file data once the connection is established.

channelActive() writes the file data using ChunkedInput when the connection is established.

CHUNKED INPUT To use your own `ChunkedInput` implementation install a `ChunkedWriteHandler` in the pipeline.

In this section we discussed how to transfer files efficiently by using the zero-copy feature and how to write large data without risking `OutOfMemoryErrors` by using `ChunkedWriteHandler`. In the next section we'll examine several approaches to serializing POJOs.

11.6 Serializing data

The JDK provides `ObjectOutputStream` and `ObjectInputStream` for serializing and deserializing primitive data types and graphs of POJOs over the network. The API isn't complex and can be applied to any object that implements `java.io.Serializable`. But it's also not terribly efficient. In this section we'll see what Netty has to offer.

11.6.1 JDK serialization

If your application has to interact with peers that use `ObjectOutputStream` and `ObjectInputStream`, and compatibility is your primary concern, then JDK serialization is the right choice.[6] Table 11.8 lists the serialization classes that Netty provides for interoperating with the JDK.

Table 11.8 JDK serialization codecs

Name	Description
`CompatibleObjectDecoder`	Decoder for interoperating with non-Netty peers that use JDK serialization.
`CompatibleObjectEncoder`	Encoder for interoperating with non-Netty peers that use JDK serialization.
`ObjectDecoder`	Decoder that uses custom serialization for decoding on top of JDK serialization; it provides a speed improvement when external dependencies are excluded. Otherwise the other serialization implementations are preferable.
`ObjectEncoder`	Encoder that uses custom serialization for encoding on top of JDK serialization; it provides a speed improvement when external dependencies are excluded. Otherwise the other serialization implementations are preferable.

11.6.2 Serialization with JBoss Marshalling

If you are free to make use of external dependencies, JBoss Marshalling is ideal: It's up to three times faster than JDK Serialization and more compact. The overview on the JBoss Marshalling homepage[7] defines it this way:

> JBoss Marshalling is an alternative serialization API that fixes many of the problems found in the JDK serialization API while remaining fully compatible with `java.io.Serializable` and its relatives, and adds several new tunable parameters and additional features, all of which are pluggable

[6] See "Java Object Serialization" in Oracle's Java SE documentation, http://docs.oracle.com/javase/8/docs/technotes/guides/serialization/.

[7] "About JBoss Marshalling," www.jboss.org/jbossmarshalling.

via factory configuration (externalizers, class/instance lookup tables, class resolution, and object replacement, to name a few).

Netty supports JBoss Marshalling with the two decoder/encoder pairs shown in table 11.9. The first set is compatible with peers that use only JDK Serialization. The second, which provides maximum performance, is for use with peers that use JBoss Marshalling.

Table 11.9 JBoss Marshalling codecs

Name	Description
`CompatibleMarshallingDecoder` `CompatibleMarshallingEncoder`	For compatibility with peers that use JDK serialization.
`MarshallingDecoder` `MarshallingEncoder`	For use with peers that use JBoss Marshalling. These classes must be used together.

The following listing shows how to use `MarshallingDecoder` and `MarshallingEncoder`. Again, it's mostly a matter of configuring the `ChannelPipeline` appropriately.

Listing 11.13 Using JBoss Marshalling

```
public class MarshallingInitializer extends ChannelInitializer<Channel> {
    private final MarshallerProvider marshallerProvider;
    private final UnmarshallerProvider unmarshallerProvider;

    public MarshallingInitializer(
        UnmarshallerProvider unmarshallerProvider,
        MarshallerProvider marshallerProvider) {
        this.marshallerProvider = marshallerProvider;
        this.unmarshallerProvider = unmarshallerProvider;
    }

    @Override
    protected void initChannel(Channel channel) throws Exception {
        ChannelPipeline pipeline = channel.pipeline();
        pipeline.addLast(new MarshallingDecoder(unmarshallerProvider));
        pipeline.addLast(new MarshallingEncoder(marshallerProvider));
        pipeline.addLast(new ObjectHandler());
    }

    public static final class ObjectHandler
        extends SimpleChannelInboundHandler<Serializable> {
        @Override
        public void channelRead0(
            ChannelHandlerContext channelHandlerContext,
            Serializable serializable) throws Exception {
            // Do something
        }
    }
}
```

Adds a MarshallingDecoder to convert ByteBufs to POJOs

Adds a MarshallingEncoder to convert POJOs to ByteBufs

Adds an ObjectHandler for normal POJOs that implement Serializable

11.6.3 Serialization via Protocol Buffers

The last of Netty's solutions for serialization is a codec that utilizes Protocol Buffers,[8] a data interchange format developed by Google and now open source. The code can be found at https://github.com/google/protobuf.

Protocol Buffers encodes and decodes structured data in a way that's compact and efficient. It has bindings for many programming languages, making it a good fit for cross-language projects. Table 11.10 shows the `ChannelHandler` implementations Netty supplies for protobuf support.

Table 11.10 Protobuf codec

Name	Description
`ProtobufDecoder`	Decodes a message using protobuf
`ProtobufEncoder`	Encodes a message using protobuf
`ProtobufVarint32FrameDecoder`	Splits received `ByteBufs` dynamically by the value of the Google Protocol "Base 128 Varints"[a] integer length field in the message

a. See Google's Protocol Buffers Encoding developer guide, https://developers.google.com/protocol-buffers/docs/encoding.

Here again, using protobuf is a matter of adding the right `ChannelHandler` to the `ChannelPipeline`, as shown in listing 11.14.

Listing 11.14 Using protobuf

```
public class ProtoBufInitializer extends ChannelInitializer<Channel> {
    private final MessageLite lite;

    public ProtoBufInitializer(MessageLite lite) {
        this.lite = lite;
    }

    @Override
    protected void initChannel(Channel ch) throws Exception {
        ChannelPipeline pipeline = ch.pipeline();
        pipeline.addLast(new ProtobufVarint32FrameDecoder());
        pipeline.addLast(new ProtobufEncoder());
        pipeline.addLast(new ProtobufDecoder(lite));
        pipeline.addLast(new ObjectHandler());
    }

    public static final class ObjectHandler
        extends SimpleChannelInboundHandler<Object> {
```

Adds ProtobufVarint32FrameDecoder to break down frames

Adds ProtobufEncoder to handle encoding of messages

Adds ProtobufDecoder to decode messages

Adds ObjectHandler to handle the decoded messages

[8] Protocol Buffers are described at https://developers.google.com/protocol-buffers/?hl=en.

```
        @Override
        public void channelRead0(ChannelHandlerContext ctx, Object msg)
            throws Exception {
            // Do something with the object
        }
    }
}
```

In this section we explored the different serialization options supported by Netty's specialized decoders and encoders: standard JDK serialization, JBoss Marshalling, and Google's Protocol Buffers.

11.7 Summary

The codecs and handlers provided by Netty can be combined and extended to implement a very broad range of processing scenarios. Furthermore, they are proven and robust components that have been employed in many large systems.

Note that we've covered only the most common examples; the API documents provide more extensive coverage.

In the next chapter we'll study another advanced protocol that has been developed to improve the performance and responsiveness of web applications: WebSocket. Netty provides the tools you'll need to quickly and easily take advantage of its powerful capabilities.

Part 3

Network protocols

WebSocket is an advanced network protocol that has been developed to improve the performance and responsiveness of web applications. We'll explore Netty's support for each of them by writing a sample application.

In chapter 12 you'll learn how to implement bidirectional data transmission using WebSocket by building a chat room server where multiple browser clients can communicate in real time. You'll also see how to switch from HTTP to the WebSocket protocol in your applications by detecting whether the client supports it.

We'll conclude part 3 with a study of Netty's support for the User Datagram Protocol (UDP) in chapter 13. Here you'll build a broadcasting server and monitor client that can be adapted to many practical uses.

12 WebSocket

This chapter covers

- The concept of a real-time web
- The WebSocket protocol
- Building a WebSocket-based chat room server with Netty

If you follow recent developments in web technologies you are likely to come across the phrase real-time web, and if you have had experience with real-time applications in engineering domains, you may be a little skeptical about what this term implies.

So let's clarify at the outset that this is not about so-called hard real-time Quality of Service (QoS), where the delivery of computation results within a specified time interval is guaranteed. The request/response design of HTTP alone makes that highly problematic, as evidenced by the fact that none of the approaches devised in the past have provided a satisfactory solution.

And while there has been some academic discussion about formally defining the semantics of *timed web services*,[1] universally accepted definitions don't appear to

[1] "Real-time Web Services Orchestration and Choreography," http://ceur-ws.org/Vol-601/EOMAS10_paper13.pdf.

be on the horizon. So for now we'll accept the following non-authoritative description from Wikipedia as adequate:

> The *real-time web* is a network web using technologies and practices that enable users to receive information as soon as it is published by its authors, rather than requiring that they or their software check a source periodically for updates.

In short, a full-blown real-time web may not be just around the corner, but the idea behind it is fueling a growing expectation of almost instantaneous access to information. The WebSocket[2] protocol we'll discuss in this chapter is a well-supported step in that direction.

12.1 Introducing WebSocket

The WebSocket protocol was designed from the ground up to provide a practical solution to the problem of bidirectional data transmission on the web, allowing client and server to transmit messages at any time and, consequently, requiring them to handle message receipt asynchronously. (Most recent browsers support WebSocket as the client-side API of HTML5.)

Netty's support for WebSocket includes all of the principal implementations in use, so adopting it in your next application is straightforward. As usual with Netty, you can make complete use of the protocol without having to worry about its internal implementation details. We'll demonstrate this by creating a real-time chat application built on WebSocket.

12.2 Our example WebSocket application

Our example application will demonstrate real-time functionality by using the WebSocket protocol to implement a browser-based chat application such as you may have encountered in the text-messaging feature of Facebook. We'll take it further by enabling multiple users to communicate with each other simultaneously.

Figure 12.1 illustrates the application logic:

1. A client sends a message.
2. The message is broadcast to all other connected clients.

This is just how you would expect a chat room to work: everyone can talk to everyone else. In our example we'll implement only the server side, the client being a browser that accesses the chat room via a web page. As you'll see in the next few pages, WebSocket makes writing this server simple.

[2] IETF RFC 6455, The WebSocket Protocol, http://tools.ietf.org/html/rfc6455.

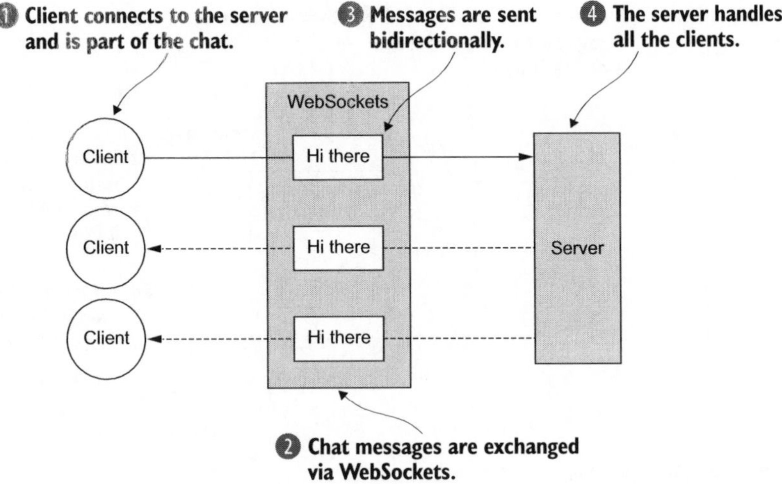

Figure 12.1 WebSocket application logic

12.3 Adding WebSocket support

A mechanism known as the *upgrade handshake*[3] is used to switch from standard HTTP or HTTPS protocol to WebSocket. Thus, an application that uses WebSocket will always start with HTTP/S and then perform the upgrade. When precisely this happens is specific to the application; it may be at startup or when a specific URL has been requested.

Our application adopts the following convention: If the URL requested ends with `/ws` we'll upgrade the protocol to WebSocket. Otherwise the server will use basic HTTP/S. After the connection has been upgraded, all data will be transmitted using WebSocket. Figure 12.2 illustrates the server logic, which, as always in Netty, will be implemented by a set of `ChannelHandlers`. We'll describe them in the next sections as we explain the techniques used to handle the HTTP and WebSocket protocols.

12.3.1 Handling HTTP requests

First we'll implement the component that handles HTTP requests. This component will serve the page that provides access to the chat room and display messages sent by

[3] Mozilla Developer Network, "Protocol upgrade mechanism," https://developer.mozilla.org/en-US/docs/HTTP/Protocol_upgrade_mechanism.

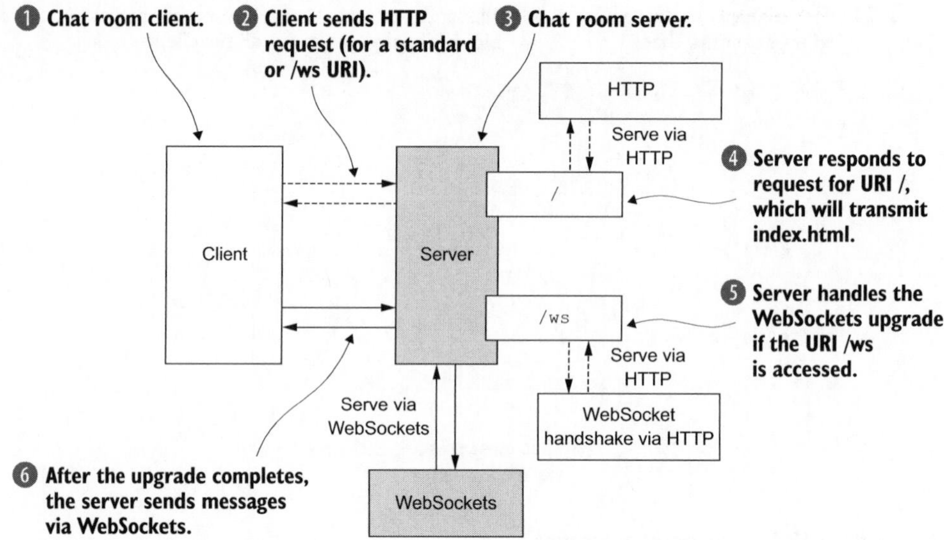

Figure 12.2 Server logic

connected clients. Listing 12.1 has the code for this `HttpRequestHandler`, which extends `SimpleChannelInboundHandler` for `FullHttpRequest` messages. Notice how the implementation of `channelRead0()` forwards any requests for the URI `/ws`.

Listing 12.1 HTTPRequestHandler

```
public class HttpRequestHandler
    extends SimpleChannelInboundHandler<FullHttpRequest> {
    private final String wsUri;
    private static final File INDEX;

    static {
        URL location = HttpRequestHandler.class
            .getProtectionDomain()
            .getCodeSource().getLocation();
        try {
            String path = location.toURI() + "index.html";
            path = !path.contains("file:") ? path : path.substring(5);
            INDEX = new File(path);
        } catch (URISyntaxException e) {
            throw new IllegalStateException(
                "Unable to locate index.html", e);
        }
    }

    public HttpRequestHandler(String wsUri) {
        this.wsUri = wsUri;
    }
```

Extends SimpleChannelInboundHandler to handle FullHttpRequest messages

```
    @Override
    public void channelRead0(ChannelHandlerContext ctx,
        FullHttpRequest request) throws Exception {
        if (wsUri.equalsIgnoreCase(request.getUri())) {
            ctx.fireChannelRead(request.retain());
        } else {
            if (HttpHeaders.is100ContinueExpected(request)) {
                send100Continue(ctx);
            }
            RandomAccessFile file = new RandomAccessFile(INDEX, "r");
            HttpResponse response = new DefaultHttpResponse(
                request.getProtocolVersion(), HttpResponseStatus.OK);
            response.headers().set(
                HttpHeaders.Names.CONTENT_TYPE,
                "text/plain; charset=UTF-8");
            boolean keepAlive = HttpHeaders.isKeepAlive(request);
            if (keepAlive) {
                response.headers().set(
                    HttpHeaders.Names.CONTENT_LENGTH, file.length());
                response.headers().set( HttpHeaders.Names.CONNECTION,
                    HttpHeaders.Values.KEEP_ALIVE);
            }
            ctx.write(response);
            if (ctx.pipeline().get(SslHandler.class) == null) {
               ctx.write(new DefaultFileRegion(
                   file.getChannel(), 0, file.length()));
            } else {
                ctx.write(new ChunkedNioFile(file.getChannel()));
            }
            ChannelFuture future = ctx.writeAndFlush(
                LastHttpContent.EMPTY_LAST_CONTENT);
            if (!keepAlive) {
                future.addListener(ChannelFutureListener.CLOSE);
            }
        }
    }

    private static void send100Continue(ChannelHandlerContext ctx) {
        FullHttpResponse response = new DefaultFullHttpResponse(
            HttpVersion.HTTP_1_1, HttpResponseStatus.CONTINUE);
        ctx.writeAndFlush(response);
    }

    @Override
    public void exceptionCaught(ChannelHandlerContext ctx, Throwable cause)
        throws Exception {
        cause.printStackTrace();
        ctx.close();
    }
}
```

1. If a WebSocket upgrade is requested, increments the reference count (retain) and passes it to the next ChannelInboundHandler
2. Handles 100 Continue requests in conformity with HTTP 1.1
- Reads index.html
- If keepalive is requested, adds the required headers
3. Writes the HttpResponse to the client
4. Writes index.html to the client
5. Writes and flushes the LastHttpContent to the client
6. If keepalive is not requested, closes the Channel after the write completes

If the HTTP request references the URI /ws, `HttpRequestHandler` calls `retain()` on the `FullHttpRequest` and forwards it to the next `ChannelInboundHandler` (1) by calling `fireChannelRead(msg)`. The call to `retain()` is needed because after `channelRead()`

completes, it will call `release()` on the `FullHttpRequest` to release its resources. (Please refer to our discussion of `SimpleChannelInboundHandler` in chapter 6.)

If the client sends the HTTP 1.1 header `Expect: 100-continue`, `HttpRequestHandler` sends a `100 Continue` ❷ response. `HttpRequestHandler` writes an `HttpResponse` ❸ back to the client after the headers are set. This is not a `FullHttpResponse` as it's only the first part of the response. Also, `writeAndFlush()` is not called here. This is done at the end.

If neither encryption nor compression is required, the greatest efficiency can be achieved by storing the contents of index.html ❹ in a `DefaultFileRegion`. This will utilize zero-copy to perform the transmission. For this reason you check to see if there is an `SslHandler` in the `ChannelPipeline`. Alternatively, you use `ChunkedNioFile`.

`HttpRequestHandler` writes a `LastHttpContent` ❺ to mark the end of the response. If `keepalive` isn't requested ❻, `HttpRequestHandler` adds a `ChannelFutureListener` to the `ChannelFuture` of the last write and closes the connection. This is where you call `writeAndFlush()` to flush all previously written messages.

This represents the first part of the chat server, which manages pure HTTP requests and responses. Next we'll handle the WebSocket frames, which transmit the actual chat messages.

WEBSOCKET FRAMES WebSockets transmit data in frames, each of which represents a part of a message. A complete message may consist of many frames.

12.3.2 Handling WebSocket frames

The WebSocket RFC, published by the IETF, defines six frames; Netty provides a POJO implementation for each of them. Table 12.1 lists the frame types and describes their use.

Table 12.1 `WebSocketFrame` types

Frame type	Description
`BinaryWebSocketFrame`	Contains binary data
`TextWebSocketFrame`	Contains text data
`ContinuationWebSocketFrame`	Contains text or binary data that belongs to a previous `BinaryWebSocketFrame` or `TextWebSocketFrame`
`CloseWebSocketFrame`	Represents a `CLOSE` request and contains a close status code and a phrase
`PingWebSocketFrame`	Requests the transmission of a `PongWebSocketFrame`
`PongWebSocketFrame`	Sent as a response to a `PingWebSocketFrame`

Our chat application will use the following frame types:

- `CloseWebSocketFrame`
- `PingWebSocketFrame`

- PongWebSocketFrame
- TextWebSocketFrame

TextWebSocketFrame is the only one we actually need to handle. In conformity with the WebSocket RFC, Netty provides a WebSocketServerProtocolHandler to manage the others.

The following listing shows our ChannelInboundHandler for TextWebSocketFrames, which will also track all the active WebSocket connections in its ChannelGroup.

Listing 12.2 Handling text frames

```
public class TextWebSocketFrameHandler
    extends SimpleChannelInboundHandler<TextWebSocketFrame> {
    private final ChannelGroup group;

    public TextWebSocketFrameHandler(ChannelGroup group) {
        this.group = group;
    }

    @Override
    public void userEventTriggered(ChannelHandlerContext ctx,
        Object evt) throws Exception {
        if (evt == WebSocketServerProtocolHandler
            .ServerHandshakeStateEvent.HANDSHAKE_COMPLETE) {
            ctx.pipeline().remove(HttpRequestHandler.class);
            group.writeAndFlush(new TextWebSocketFrame(
                "Client " + ctx.channel() + " joined"));
            group.add(ctx.channel());
        } else {
            super.userEventTriggered(ctx, evt);
        }
    }

    @Override
    public void channelRead0(ChannelHandlerContext ctx,
        TextWebSocketFrame msg) throws Exception {
        group.writeAndFlush(msg.retain());
    }
}
```

Extends SimpleChannelInboundHandler and handle TextWebSocketFrame messages

Overrides userEventTriggered() to handle custom events

If the event indicates that the handshake was successful, removes the HttpRequestHandler from the ChannelPipeline because no further HTTP messages will be received.

❶ Notifies all connected WebSocket clients that new Client has connected

❷ Adds the new WebSocket Channel to the ChannelGroup so it will receive all messages

❸ Increments the reference count of the message and writes it to all connected clients in the ChannelGroup

The TextWebSocketFrameHandler has a very small set of responsibilities. When the WebSocket handshake with the new client has completed successfully ❶, it notifies all connected clients by writing to all the Channels in the ChannelGroup, then it adds the new Channel to the ChannelGroup ❷.

If a TextWebSocketFrame is received ❸, it calls retain() on it and uses writeAndFlush() to transmit it to the ChannelGroup so that all connected WebSocket Channels will receive it.

As before, calling `retain()` is required because the reference count of `TextWebSocketFrame` will be decremented when `channelRead0()` returns. Because all operations are asynchronous, `writeAndFlush()` might complete later and it must not access a reference that has become invalid.

Because Netty handles most of the remaining functionality internally, the only thing left to do now is to initialize the `ChannelPipeline` for each new `Channel` that is created. For this we'll need a `ChannelInitializer`.

12.3.3 Initializing the ChannelPipeline

As you have learned, to install `ChannelHandlers` in the `ChannelPipeline` you extend `ChannelInitializer` and implement `initChannel()`. The following listing shows the code for the resulting `ChatServerInitializer`.

Listing 12.3 Initializing the `ChannelPipeline`

```
public class ChatServerInitializer extends ChannelInitializer<Channel> {
    private final ChannelGroup group;

    public ChatServerInitializer(ChannelGroup group) {
        this.group = group;
    }

    @Override
    protected void initChannel(Channel ch) throws Exception {
        ChannelPipeline pipeline = ch.pipeline();
        pipeline.addLast(new HttpServerCodec());
        pipeline.addLast(new ChunkedWriteHandler());
        pipeline.addLast(new HttpObjectAggregator(64 * 1024));
        pipeline.addLast(new HttpRequestHandler("/ws"));
        pipeline.addLast(new WebSocketServerProtocolHandler("/ws"));
        pipeline.addLast(new TextWebSocketFrameHandler(group));
    }
}
```

Extends ChannelInitializer

Adds all needed ChannelHandlers to the ChannelPipeline

The call to `initChannel()` sets up the `ChannelPipeline` of the newly registered `Channel` by installing all the required `ChannelHandlers`. These are summarized in table 12.2, along with their individual responsibilities.

Table 12.2 `ChannelHandlers` for the WebSocket chat server

ChannelHandler	Responsibility
`HttpServerCodec`	Decodes bytes to `HttpRequest`, `HttpContent`, and `LastHttpContent`. Encodes `HttpRequest`, `HttpContent`, and `LastHttpContent` to bytes.
`ChunkedWriteHandler`	Writes the contents of a file.

Table 12.2 `ChannelHandlers` for the WebSocket chat server *(continued)*

ChannelHandler	Responsibility
`HttpObjectAggregator`	Aggregates an `HttpMessage` and its following `HttpContents` into a single `FullHttpRequest` or `FullHttpResponse` (depending on whether it's being used to handle requests or responses). With this installed, the next `ChannelHandler` in the pipeline will receive only full HTTP requests.
`HttpRequestHandler`	Handles `FullHttpRequests` (those not sent to a `/ws` URI).
`WebSocketServerProtocolHandler`	As required by the WebSocket specification, handles the WebSocket upgrade handshake, `PingWebSocketFrames`, `PongWebSocketFrames`, and `CloseWebSocketFrames`.
`TextWebSocketFrameHandler`	Handles `TextWebSocketFrames` and handshake-completion events

Netty's `WebSocketServerProtocolHandler` handles all mandated WebSocket frame types and the upgrade handshake itself. If the handshake is successful, the required `ChannelHandlers` are added to the pipeline, and those that are no longer needed are removed.

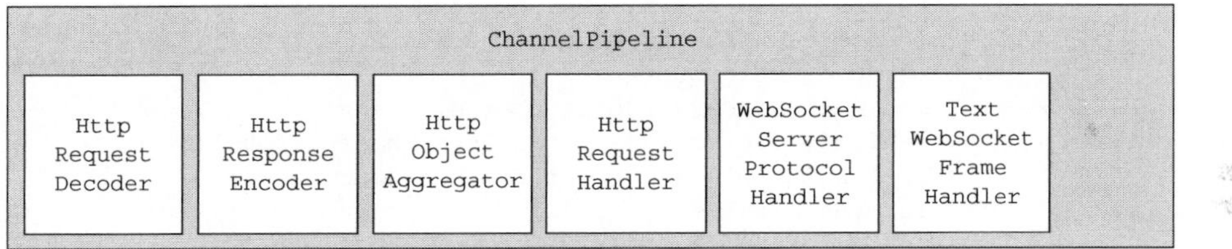

Figure 12.3 `ChannelPipeline` before WebSocket upgrade

The state of the pipeline before the upgrade is illustrated in figure 12.3. This represents the `ChannelPipeline` just after it has been initialized by the `ChatServerInitializer`.

When the upgrade is completed, the `WebSocketServerProtocolHandler` replaces the `HttpRequestDecoder` with a `WebSocketFrameDecoder` and the `HttpResponseEncoder` with a `WebSocketFrameEncoder`. To maximize performance it will then remove any `ChannelHandlers` that aren't required for WebSocket connections. These would include the `HttpObjectAggregator` and `HttpRequestHandler` shown in figure 12.3.

Figure 12.4 shows the `ChannelPipeline` after these operations have completed. Note that Netty currently supports four versions of the WebSocket protocol, each with its own implementation classes. The selection of the correct version of `WebSocket-`

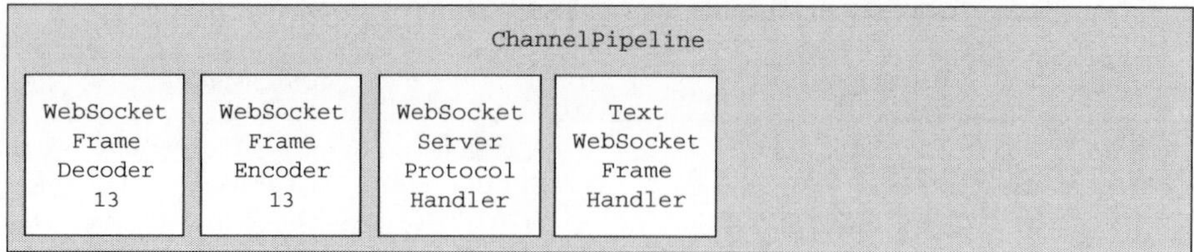

Figure 12.4 `ChannelPipeline` **after WebSocket upgrade**

`FrameDecoder` and `WebSocketFrameEncoder` are performed automatically, depending on what the client (here the browser) supports.[4]

12.3.4 Bootstrapping

The final piece of the picture is the code that bootstraps the server and installs the `ChatServerInitializer`. This will be handled by the `ChatServer` class, as shown here.

Listing 12.4 Bootstrapping the server

```
public class ChatServer {
    private final ChannelGroup channelGroup =
        new DefaultChannelGroup(ImmediateEventExecutor.INSTANCE);   <-- Creates DefaultChannelGroup that will hold all connected WebSocket channels
    private final EventLoopGroup group = new NioEventLoopGroup();
    private Channel channel;

    public ChannelFuture start(InetSocketAddress address) {
        ServerBootstrap bootstrap = new ServerBootstrap();   <-- Bootstraps the server
        bootstrap.group(group)
            .channel(NioServerSocketChannel.class)
            .childHandler(createInitializer(channelGroup));
        ChannelFuture future = bootstrap.bind(address);
        future.syncUninterruptibly();
        channel = future.channel();
        return future;
    }

    protected ChannelInitializer<Channel> createInitializer(   <-- Creates the ChatServerInitializer
        ChannelGroup group) {
        return new ChatServerInitializer(group);
    }

    public void destroy() {   <-- Handles server shutdown and releases all resources
        if (channel != null) {
            channel.close();
        }
        channelGroup.close();
        group.shutdownGracefully();
    }
```

[4] In this example we assume that version 13 of the WebSockets protocol is used, so `WebSocketFrameDecoder13` and `WebSocketFrameEncoder13` are shown in the figure.

```
    public static void main(String[] args) throws Exception {
        if (args.length != 1) {
            System.err.println("Please give port as argument");
            System.exit(1);
        }
        int port = Integer.parseInt(args[0]);
        final ChatServer endpoint = new ChatServer();
        ChannelFuture future = endpoint.start(
            new InetSocketAddress(port));
        Runtime.getRuntime().addShutdownHook(new Thread() {
            @Override
            public void run() {
                endpoint.destroy();
            }
        });
        future.channel().closeFuture().syncUninterruptibly();
    }
}
```

That completes the application itself. Now let's test it.

12.4 Testing the application

The example code in the chapter12 directory has everything you need to build and run the server. (If you haven't yet set up your development environment including Apache Maven, please refer to the instructions in chapter 2.)

We'll use the following Maven command to build and start the server:

```
mvn -PChatServer clean package exec:exec
```

The project file pom.xml is configured to start the server on port 9999. To use a different port, you can either edit the value in the file or override it with a `System` property:

```
mvn -PChatServer -Dport=1111 clean package exec:exec
```

The following listing shows the main output of the command (inessential lines have been deleted).

Listing 12.5 Compile and start the `ChatServer`

```
$ mvn -PChatServer clean package exec:exec
[INFO] Scanning for projects...
[INFO]
[INFO] ----------------------------------------------------------------
[INFO] Building ChatServer 1.0-SNAPSHOT
[INFO] ----------------------------------------------------------------
...
[INFO]
[INFO] --- maven-jar-plugin:2.4:jar (default-jar) @ netty-in-action ---
[INFO] Building jar: target/chat-server-1.0-SNAPSHOT.jar
[INFO]
[INFO] --- exec-maven-plugin:1.2.1:exec (default-cli) @ chat-server ---
Starting ChatServer on port 9999
```

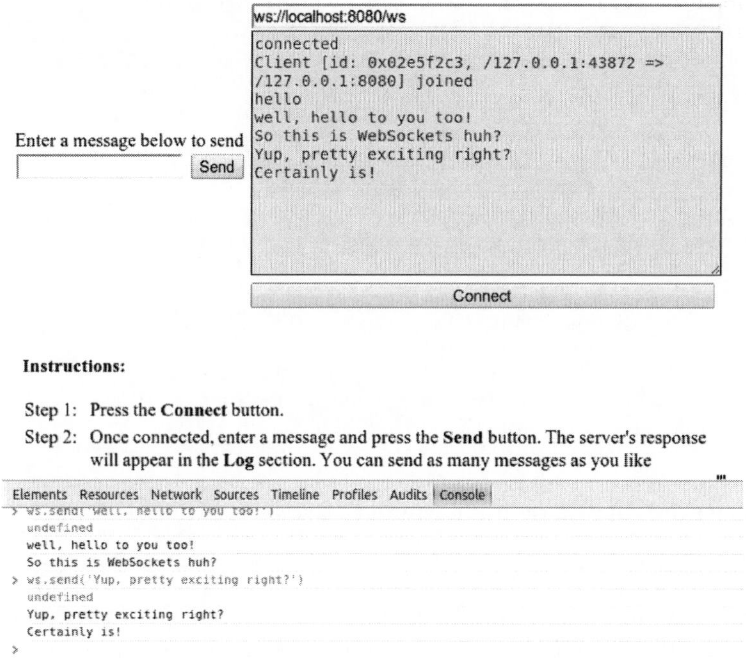

ws://localhost:8080/ws

```
connected
Client [id: 0x02e5f2c3, /127.0.0.1:43872 =>
/127.0.0.1:8080] joined
hello
well, hello to you too!
So this is WebSockets huh?
Yup, pretty exciting right?
Certainly is!
```

Enter a message below to send

Send

Connect

Instructions:

Step 1: Press the **Connect** button.

Step 2: Once connected, enter a message and press the **Send** button. The server's response will appear in the **Log** section. You can send as many messages as you like

Elements Resources Network Sources Timeline Profiles Audits Console

```
> ws.send('well, hello to you too!')
  undefined
  well, hello to you too!
  So this is WebSockets huh?
> ws.send('Yup, pretty exciting right?')
  undefined
  Yup, pretty exciting right?
  Certainly is!
>
```

Figure 12.5 WebSocket `ChatServer` demonstration

You can access the application by pointing your browser to http://localhost:9999. Figure 12.5 shows the UI in the Chrome browser.

The figure shows two connected clients. The first is connected using the interface at the top. The second client is connected via the Chrome browser's command line at the bottom. You'll notice that there are messages sent from both clients, and each message is displayed to both.

This is a very simple demonstration of how WebSocket enables real-time communication in a browser.

12.4.1 What about encryption?

In a real-life scenario, you'd soon be asked to add encryption to this server. With Netty this is just a matter of adding an `SslHandler` to the `ChannelPipeline` and configuring it. The following listing shows how this can be done by extending our `ChatServerInitializer` to create a `SecureChatServerInitializer`.

Listing 12.6 Adding encryption to the `ChannelPipeline`

```
public class SecureChatServerInitializer extends ChatServerInitializer {
    private final SslContext context;

    public SecureChatServerInitializer(ChannelGroup group,
        SslContext context) {
```

Extends ChatServerInitializer to add encryption

```
        super(group);
        this.context = context;
    }

    @Override
    protected void initChannel(Channel ch) throws Exception {
        super.initChannel(ch);                                         <-- Calls the parent's initChannel()
        SSLEngine engine = context.newEngine(ch.alloc());
        ch.pipeline().addFirst(new SslHandler(engine));             <-- Adds the SslHandler to the ChannelPipeline
    }
}
```

The final step is to adapt the ChatServer to use the SecureChatServerInitializer so as to install the SslHandler in the pipeline. This gives us the SecureChatServer shown here.

Listing 12.7 Adding encryption to the ChatServer

```
public class SecureChatServer extends ChatServer {       <-- SecureChatServer extends ChatServer to support encryption
    private final SslContext context;

    public SecureChatServer(SslContext context) {
        this.context = context;
    }

    @Override
    protected ChannelInitializer<Channel> createInitializer(
        ChannelGroup group) {
        return new SecureChatServerInitializer(group, context);    <-- Returns the previously created SecureChat-ServerInitializer to enable encryption
    }

    public static void main(String[] args) throws Exception {
        if (args.length != 1) {
            System.err.println("Please give port as argument");
            System.exit(1);
        }
        int port = Integer.parseInt(args[0]);
        SelfSignedCertificate cert = new SelfSignedCertificate();
        SslContext context = SslContext.newServerContext(
        cert.certificate(), cert.privateKey());

        final SecureChatServer endpoint = new SecureChatServer(context);
        ChannelFuture future = endpoint.start(new InetSocketAddress(port));
        Runtime.getRuntime().addShutdownHook(new Thread() {
            @Override
            public void run() {
                endpoint.destroy();
            }
        });
        future.channel().closeFuture().syncUninterruptibly();
    }
}
```

That's all that's needed to enable SSL/TLS encryption of all communications. As before, you can use Apache Maven to run the application. It will also retrieve any needed dependencies.

Listing 12.8 Starting the `SecureChatServer`

```
$ mvn -PSecureChatServer clean package exec:exec
[INFO] Scanning for projects...
[INFO]
[INFO] ----------------------------------------------------------------
[INFO] Building ChatServer 1.0-SNAPSHOT
[INFO] ----------------------------------------------------------------
...
[INFO]
[INFO] --- maven-jar-plugin:2.4:jar (default-jar) @ netty-in-action ---
[INFO] Building jar: target/chat-server-1.0-SNAPSHOT.jar
[INFO]
[INFO] --- exec-maven-plugin:1.2.1:exec (default-cli) @ chat-server ---
Starting SecureChatServer on port 9999
```

Now you can access the `SecureChatServer` from its HTTPS URL: https://localhost:9999.

12.5 Summary

In this chapter you learned how to use Netty's WebSocket implementation to manage real-time data in a web application. We covered the supported data types and discussed the limitations you may encounter. Although it may not be possible to use WebSocket in all cases, it should be clear that it represents an important advance in technologies for the web.

13 Broadcasting events with UDP

This chapter covers

- An overview of UDP
- A sample broadcasting application

Most of the examples you've seen so far have used connection-based protocols such as TCP. In this chapter we'll focus on a connectionless protocol, User Datagram Protocol (UDP), which is often used when performance is critical and some packet loss can be tolerated.[1]

We'll start with an overview of UDP, its characteristics and limitations. Following that we'll describe this chapter's sample application, which will demonstrate how to use the broadcasting capabilities of UDP. We'll also make use of an encoder and a decoder to handle a POJO as the broadcast message format. By the end of the chapter, you'll be ready to make use of UDP in your own applications.

[1] One of the best-known UDP-based protocols is the Domain Name Service (DNS), which maps fully qualified names to numeric IP addresses.

13.1 UDP basics

Connection-oriented transports (like TCP) manage the establishment of a connection between two network endpoints, the ordering and reliable transmission of messages sent during the lifetime of the connection, and finally, orderly termination of the connection. By contrast, in a connectionless protocol like UDP, there's no concept of a durable connection and each message (a UDP datagram) is an independent transmission.

Furthermore, UDP doesn't have the error-correcting mechanism of TCP, where each peer acknowledges the packets it receives and unacknowledged packets are retransmitted by the sender.

By analogy, a TCP connection is like a telephone conversation, where a series of ordered messages flows in both directions. UDP, conversely, resembles dropping a bunch of postcards in a mailbox. You can't know the order in which they will arrive at their destination, or even if they all will arrive.

These aspects of UDP may strike you as serious limitations, but they also explain why it's so much faster than TCP: all overhead of handshaking and message management has been eliminated. Clearly, UDP is a good fit for applications that can handle or tolerate lost messages, unlike those that handle financial transactions.

13.2 UDP broadcast

All of our examples so far have utilized a transmission mode called *unicast*,[2] defined as the sending of messages to a single network destination identified by a unique address. This mode is supported by both connected and connectionless protocols.

UDP provides additional transmission modes for sending a message to multiple recipients:

- *Multicast*—Transmission to a defined group of hosts
- *Broadcast*—Transmission to all of the hosts on a network (or a subnet)

The example application in this chapter will demonstrate the use of UDP broadcast by sending messages that can be received by all the hosts on the same network. For this purpose we'll use the special limited broadcast or *zero network* address 255.255.255.255. Messages sent to this address are destined for all the hosts on the local network (0.0.0.0) and are never forwarded to other networks by routers.

Next we'll discuss the design of the application.

13.3 The UDP sample application

Our example application will open a file and broadcast each line as a message to a specified port via UDP. If you're familiar with UNIX-like OSes, you may recognize this as a very simplified version of the standard *syslog* utility. UDP is a perfect fit for such an application because the occasional loss of a line of a log file can be tolerated, given

---

[2] See http://en.wikipedia.org/wiki/Unicast.

that the file itself is stored in the file system. Furthermore, the application provides the very valuable capability of effectively handling a large volume of data.

What about the receiver? With UDP broadcast, you can create an event monitor to receive the log messages simply by starting up a listener program on a specified port. Note that this ease of access raises a potential security concern, which is one reason why UDP broadcast tends not to be used in insecure environments. For the same reason, routers often block broadcast messages, restricting them to the network where they originate.

> **PUBLISH/SUBSCRIBE** Applications like *syslog* are typically classified as publish/subscribe: a producer or service publishes the events, and multiple clients subscribe to receive them.

Figure 14.1 presents a high-level view of the overall system, which consists of a broadcaster and one or more event monitors. The broadcaster listens for new content to appear, and when it does, transmits it as a broadcast message via UDP.

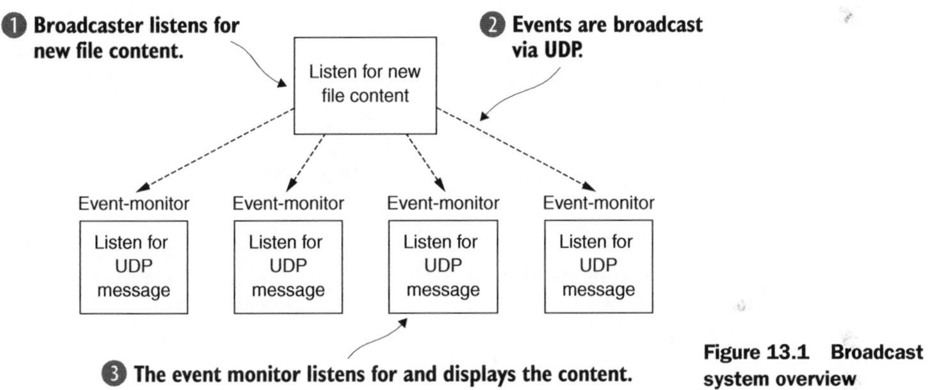

Figure 13.1 Broadcast system overview

All event monitors listening on the UDP port receive the broadcast messages.

To keep things simple, we won't be adding authentication, verification, or encryption to our sample application. But it would not be difficult to incorporate these features to make this a robust, usable utility.

In the next section we'll start to explore the design and implementation details of the broadcaster component.

13.4 The message POJO: LogEvent

In messaging applications, data is often represented by a POJO, which may hold configuration or processing information in addition to the actual message content. In this application we'll handle a message as an event, and because the data comes from a log file, we'll call it `LogEvent`. Listing 14.1 shows the details of this simple POJO.

Listing 13.1 LogEvent message

```
public final class LogEvent {
    public static final byte SEPARATOR = (byte) ':';
    private final InetSocketAddress source;
    private final String logfile;
    private final String msg;
    private final long received;

    public LogEvent(String logfile, String msg) {
        this(null, -1, logfile, msg);
    }

    public LogEvent(InetSocketAddress source, long received,
        String logfile, String msg) {
        this.source = source;
        this.logfile = logfile;
        this.msg = msg;
        this.received = received;
    }

    public InetSocketAddress getSource() {
        return source;
    }

    public String getLogfile() {
        return logfile;
    }

    public String getMsg() {
        return msg;
    }

    public long getReceivedTimestamp() {
       return received;
    }
}
```

Constructor for an outgoing message

Constructor for an incoming message

Returns the InetSocket-Address of the source that sent the LogEvent

Returns the name of the log file for which the LogEvent was sent

Returns the message contents

Returns the time at which the LogEvent was received

With the message component defined, we can implement the application's broadcasting logic. In the next section we'll examine the Netty framework classes that are used to encode and transmit `LogEvent` messages.

13.5 Writing the broadcaster

Netty provides a number of classes to support the writing of UDP applications. The primary ones we'll be using are the message containers and `Channel` types listed in table 14.1.

Table 13.1 Netty UDP classes used in broadcaster

Name	Description
`interface AddressedEnvelope <M, A extends SocketAddress> extends ReferenceCounted`	Defines a message that wraps another message with sender and recipient addresses. `M` is the message type; `A` is the address type.

Table 13.1 Netty UDP classes used in broadcaster *(continued)*

Name	Description
class DefaultAddressedEnvelope <M, A extends SocketAddress> implements AddressedEnvelope<M,A>	Provides a default implementation of interface AddressedEnvelope.
class DatagramPacket extendsDefaultAddressedEnvelope <ByteBuf, InetSocketAddress> implements ByteBufHolder	Extends DefaultAddressedEnvelope to use ByteBuf as the message data container.
interface DatagramChannel extends Channel	Extends Netty's Channel abstraction to support UDP multicast group management.
class NioDatagramChannnel extends AbstractNioMessageChannel implements DatagramChannel	Defines a Channel type that can send and receive AddressedEnvelope messages.

Netty's DatagramPacket is a simple message container used by DatagramChannel implementations to communicate with remote peers. Like the postcards we referred to in our earlier analogy, it carries the address of the recipient (and optionally, the sender) as well as the message payload itself.

To convert EventLog messages to DatagramPackets, we'll need an encoder. But there's no need to write our own from scratch. We'll extend Netty's MessageToMessageEncoder, which we used in chapters 9 and 10.

Figure 14.2 shows the broadcasting of three log entries, each one via a dedicated DatagramPacket.

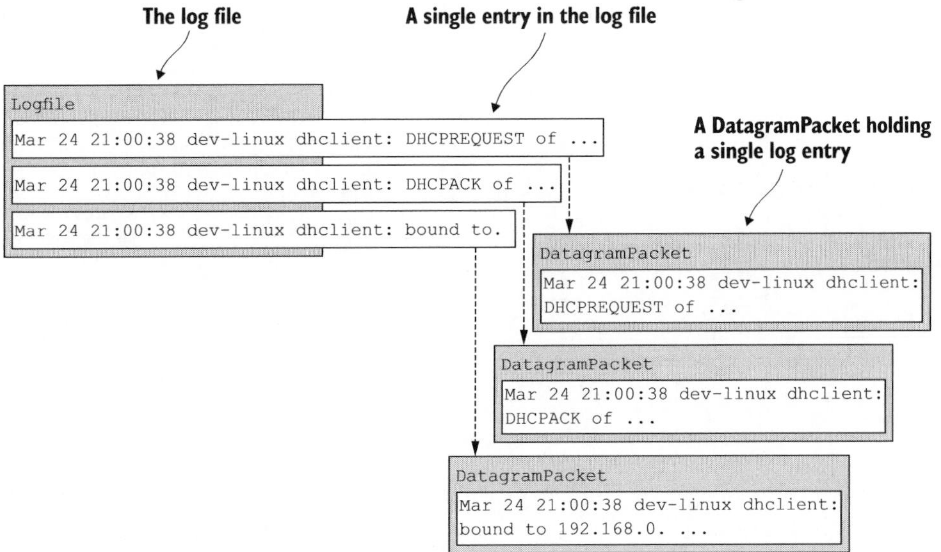

Figure 13.2 Log entries sent via DatagramPackets

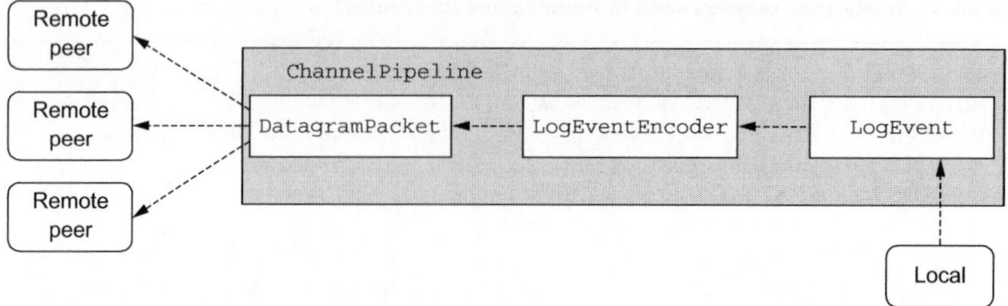

Figure 13.3 `LogEventBroadcaster`: `ChannelPipeline` and `LogEvent` flow

Figure 14.3 represents a high-level view of the `ChannelPipeline` of the `LogEventBroadcaster`, showing how `LogEvents` flow through it.

As you've seen, all data to be transmitted is encapsulated in `LogEvent` messages. The `LogEventBroadcaster` writes these to the channel, sending them through the `ChannelPipeline` where they're converted (encoded) into `DatagramPacket` messages. Finally, they are broadcast via UDP and picked up by remote peers (monitors).

The next listing shows our customized version of `MessageToMessageEncoder`, which performs the conversion just described.

Listing 13.2 `LogEventEncoder`

```
public class LogEventEncoder extends MessageToMessageEncoder<LogEvent> {
    private final InetSocketAddress remoteAddress;

    public LogEventEncoder(InetSocketAddress remoteAddress) {
        this.remoteAddress = remoteAddress;
    }

    @Override
    protected void encode(ChannelHandlerContext channelHandlerContext,
        LogEvent logEvent, List<Object> out) throws Exception {
        byte[] file = logEvent.getLogfile().getBytes(CharsetUtil.UTF_8);
        byte[] msg = logEvent.getMsg().getBytes(CharsetUtil.UTF_8);
        ByteBuf buf = channelHandlerContext.alloc()
            .buffer(file.length + msg.length + 1);
        buf.writeBytes(file);
        buf.writeByte(LogEvent.SEPARATOR);
        buf.writeBytes(msg);
        out.add(new DatagramPacket(buf, remoteAddress));
    }
}
```

LogEventEncoder creates DatagramPacket messages to be sent to the specified InetSocketAddress

Writes the filename to the ByteBuf

Adds a SEPARATOR

Writes the log message to the ByteBuf

Adds a new DatagramPacket with the data and destination address to the list of outbound messages

With `LogEventEncoder` implemented, we're ready to bootstrap the server, which includes setting various `ChannelOptions` and installing the needed `ChannelHandlers` in the pipeline. This will be done by the main class, `LogEventBroadcaster`, shown next.

Listing 13.3 LogEventBroadcaster

```
public class LogEventBroadcaster {
    private final EventLoopGroup group;
    private final Bootstrap bootstrap;
    private final File file;

    public LogEventBroadcaster(InetSocketAddress address, File file) {
        group = new NioEventLoopGroup();
        bootstrap = new Bootstrap();
        bootstrap.group(group).channel(NioDatagramChannel.class)
            .option(ChannelOption.SO_BROADCAST, true)
            .handler(new LogEventEncoder(address));
        this.file = file;
    }

    public void run() throws Exception {
        Channel ch = bootstrap.bind(0).sync().channel();
        long pointer = 0;
        for (;;) {
            long len = file.length();
            if (len < pointer) {
                // file was reset
                pointer = len;
            } else if (len > pointer) {
                // Content was added
                RandomAccessFile raf = new RandomAccessFile(file, "r");
                raf.seek(pointer);
                String line;
                while ((line = raf.readLine()) != null) {
                    ch.writeAndFlush(new LogEvent(null, -1,
                    file.getAbsolutePath(), line));
                }
                pointer = raf.getFilePointer();
                raf.close();
            }
            try {
                Thread.sleep(1000);
            } catch (InterruptedException e) {
                Thread.interrupted();
                break;
            }
        }
    }

    public void stop() {
        group.shutdownGracefully();
    }

    public static void main(String[] args) throws Exception {
        if (args.length != 2) {
            throw new IllegalArgumentException();
        }
```

Bootstraps the NioDatagram-Channel (connectionless)

Sets the SO_BROADCAST socket option

Binds the channel

Starts the main processing loop

If necessary, sets the file pointer to the last byte of the file

Sets the current file pointer so nothing old is sent

For each log entry, writes a LogEvent to the channel

Stores the current position within the file

Sleeps for 1 second. If interrupted, exits the loop; else restarts it.

```
        LogEventBroadcaster broadcaster = new LogEventBroadcaster(
            new InetSocketAddress("255.255.255.255",
                Integer.parseInt(args[0])), new File(args[1]));
        try {
            broadcaster.run();
        }
        finally {
            broadcaster.stop();
        }
    }
}
```

Creates and starts a new LogEventBroadcaster instance

This completes the broadcaster component of the application. For initial testing you can use the *netcat* program. On UNIX/Linux systems you should find it installed as *nc*. A version for Windows is available at http://nmap.org/ncat.

netcat is perfect for basic testing of this application; it just listens on a specified port and prints all data received to standard output. Set it to listen for UDP data on port 9999 as follows:

```
$ nc -l -u 9999
```

Now we need to start our `LogEventBroadcaster`. Listing 14.4 shows how to compile and run the broadcaster using `mvn`. The configuration in pom.xml points to a file that is frequently updated, /var/log/messages (assuming a UNIX/Linux environment), and sets the port to 9999. The entries in the file will be broadcast to that port via UDP and printed to the console on which you started netcat.

Listing 13.4 Compile and start the `LogEventBroadcaster`

```
$ chapter14> mvn clean package exec:exec LogEventBroadcaster
[INFO] Scanning for projects...
[INFO]
[INFO] --------------------------------------------------------------------
[INFO] Building UDP Broadcast 1.0-SNAPSHOT
[INFO] --------------------------------------------------------------------
...
...
[INFO]
[INFO] --- maven-jar-plugin:2.4:jar (default-jar) @ netty-in-action ---
[INFO] Building jar: target/chapter14-1.0-SNAPSHOT.jar
[INFO]
[INFO] --- exec-maven-plugin:1.2.1:exec (default-cli) @ netty-in-action -
 LogEventBroadcaster running
```

To change the file and port values, specify them as `System` properties when invoking `mvn`. The next listing shows how to set the logfile to /var/log/mail.log and the port to 8888.

Listing 13.5 Compile and start the `LogEventBroadcaster`

```
$ chapter14> mvn clean package exec:exec -PLogEventBroadcaster /
-Dlogfile=/var/log/mail.log -Dport=8888 -....
....
[INFO]
[INFO] --- exec-maven-plugin:1.2.1:exec (default-cli) @ netty-in-action -
 LogEventBroadcaster running
```

When you see `LogEventBroadcaster running`, you'll know it started up successfully. If there are errors, an exception message will be printed. Once the process is running, it will broadcast any new log messages that are added to the logfile.

Using netcat is adequate for testing purposes but it would not be suitable for a production system. This brings us to the second part of our application—the broadcast monitor we'll implement in the next section.

13.6 Writing the monitor

Our goal is to replace netcat with a more complete event consumer, which we'll call `EventLogMonitor`. This program will

1. Receive UDP `DatagramPackets` broadcast by the `LogEventBroadcaster`
2. Decode them to `LogEvent` messages
3. Write the `LogEvent` messages to `System.out`

As before, the logic will be implemented by custom `ChannelHandlers`—for our decoder we'll extend `MessageToMessageDecoder`. Figure 14.4 depicts the `ChannelPipeline` of the `LogEventMonitor` and shows how `LogEvents` will flow through it.

Figure 13.4 `LogEventMonitor`

The first decoder in the pipeline, `LogEventDecoder`, is responsible for decoding incoming `DatagramPackets` to `LogEvent` messages (a typical setup for any Netty application that transforms inbound data). The following listing shows the implementation.

Listing 13.6 `LogEventDecoder`

```
public class LogEventDecoder extends MessageToMessageDecoder<DatagramPacket> {

    @Override
    protected void decode(ChannelHandlerContext ctx,
        DatagramPacket datagramPacket, List<Object> out) throws Exception {
```

```
        ByteBuf data = datagramPacket.data();
        int idx = data.indexOf(0, data.readableBytes(),
            LogEvent.SEPARATOR);
        String filename = data.slice(0, idx)
            .toString(CharsetUtil.UTF_8);
        String logMsg =  data.slice(idx + 1,
            data.readableBytes()).toString(CharsetUtil.UTF_8);

        LogEvent event = new LogEvent(datagramPacket.remoteAddress(),
            System.currentTimeMillis(), filename, logMsg);
        out.add(event);
    }
}
```

Gets a reference to the data in the DatagramPacket (a ByteBuf)

Gets the index of the SEPARATOR

Extracts the filename

Extracts the log message

Constructs a new LogEvent object and adds it to the list

The job of the second ChannelHandler is to perform some processing on the LogEvent messages created by the first. In this case, it will simply write them to System.out. In a real-world application you might aggregate them with events originating from a different log file or post them to a database. This listing, which shows the LogEventHandler, illustrates the basic steps to follow.

Listing 13.7 LogEventHandler

```
public class LogEventHandler
    extends SimpleChannelInboundHandler<LogEvent> {

    @Override
    public void exceptionCaught(ChannelHandlerContext ctx,
        Throwable cause) throws Exception {
        cause.printStackTrace();
        ctx.close();
    }

    @Override
    public void channelRead0(ChannelHandlerContext ctx,
        LogEvent event) throws Exception {
        StringBuilder builder = new StringBuilder();
        builder.append(event.getReceivedTimestamp());
        builder.append(" [");
        builder.append(event.getSource().toString());
        builder.append("] [");
        builder.append(event.getLogfile());
        builder.append("] : ");
        builder.append(event.getMsg());
        System.out.println(builder.toString());
    }
}
```

Extends SimpleChannelInboundHandler to handle LogEvent messages

On exception, prints the stack trace and closes the channel

Creates a StringBuilder and builds up the output

Prints out the LogEvent data

The LogEventHandler prints the LogEvents in an easy-to-read format that consists of the following:

- The received timestamp in milliseconds
- The InetSocketAddress of the sender, which consists of the IP address and port

- The absolute name of the file the `LogEvent` was generated from
- The actual log message, which represents one line in the log file

Now we need to install our handlers in the `ChannelPipeline`, as seen in figure 14.4. This listing shows how it is done by the `LogEventMonitor` main class.

Listing 13.8 LogEventMonitor

```
public class LogEventMonitor {
    private final EventLoopGroup group;
    private final Bootstrap bootstrap;

    public LogEventMonitor(InetSocketAddress address) {
        group = new NioEventLoopGroup();
        bootstrap = new Bootstrap();
        bootstrap.group(group)
            .channel(NioDatagramChannel.class)
            .option(ChannelOption.SO_BROADCAST, true)
            .handler( new ChannelInitializer<Channel>() {
                @Override
                protected void initChannel(Channel channel)
                    throws Exception {
                    ChannelPipeline pipeline = channel.pipeline();
                    pipeline.addLast(new LogEventDecoder());
                    pipeline.addLast(new LogEventHandler());
                }
            } )
            .localAddress(address);
    }

    public Channel bind() {
        return bootstrap.bind().sync().channel();
    }

    public void stop() {
        group.shutdownGracefully();
    }

    public static void main(String[] main) throws Exception {
        if (args.length != 1) {
            throw new IllegalArgumentException(
            "Usage: LogEventMonitor <port>");
        }
        LogEventMonitor monitor = new LogEventMonitor(
            new InetSocketAddress(args[0]));
        try {
            Channel channel = monitor.bind();
            System.out.println("LogEventMonitor running");
            channel.closeFuture().sync();
        } finally {
            monitor.stop();
        }
    }
}
```

Bootstraps the NioDatagramChannel

Sets the SO_BROADCAST socket option

Adds the ChannelHandlers to the ChannelPipeline

Binds the channel. Note that DatagramChannel is connectionless.

Constructs a new LogEventMonitor

13.7 Running the LogEventBroadcaster and LogEventMonitor

As before, we'll use Maven to run the application. This time you'll need to open two console windows, one for each of the programs. Each will keep running until you stop it with Ctrl-C.

First you need to start the `LogEventBroadcaster`. Because you've already built the project, the following command will suffice (using the default values):

```
$ chapter14> mvn exec:exec -PLogEventBroadcaster
```

As before, this will broadcast the log messages via UDP.

Now, in a new window, build and start the `LogEventMonitor` to receive and display the broadcast messages.

Listing 13.9 Compiling and starting the `LogEventBroadcaster`

```
$ chapter13> mvn clean package exec:exec -PLogEventMonitor
[INFO] Scanning for projects...
[INFO]
[INFO] --------------------------------------------------------------------
[INFO] Building UDP Broadcast 1.0-SNAPSHOT
[INFO] --------------------------------------------------------------------
[INFO]
[INFO] --- maven-jar-plugin:2.4:jar (default-jar) @ netty-in-action ---
[INFO] Building jar: target/chapter14-1.0-SNAPSHOT.jar
[INFO]
[INFO] --- exec-maven-plugin:1.2.1:exec (default-cli) @ netty-in-action ---
LogEventMonitor running
```

When you see `LogEventMonitor running`, you'll know it started up successfully. If there is an error, an exception message will be printed.

The console will display any events as they are added to the log file, as shown next. The format of the messages is that created by the `LogEventHandler`.

Listing 13.10 `LogEventMonitor` output

```
1364217299382 [/192.168.0.38:63182] [/var/log/messages] : Mar 25 13:55:08
    dev-linux dhclient: DHCPREQUEST of 192.168.0.50 on eth2 to 192.168.0.254
    port 67
1364217299382 [/192.168.0.38:63182] [/var/log/messages] : Mar 25 13:55:08
    dev-linux dhclient: DHCPACK of 192.168.0.50 from 192.168.0.254
1364217299382 [/192.168.0.38:63182] [/var/log/messages] : Mar 25 13:55:08
    dev-linux dhclient: bound to 192.168.0.50 -- renewal in 270 seconds.
1364217299382 [/192.168.0.38:63182] [[/var/log/messages] : Mar 25 13:59:38
    dev-linux dhclient: DHCPREQUEST of 192.168.0.50 on eth2 to 192.168.0.254
    port 67
1364217299382 [/192.168.0.38:63182] [/[/var/log/messages] : Mar 25 13:59:38
    dev-linux dhclient: DHCPACK of 192.168.0.50 from 192.168.0.254
1364217299382 [/192.168.0.38:63182] [/var/log/messages] : Mar 25 13:59:38
    dev-linux dhclient: bound to 192.168.0.50 -- renewal in 259 seconds.
```

```
1364217299383 [/192.168.0.38:63182] [/var/log/messages] : Mar 25 14:03:57
     dev-linux dhclient: DHCPREQUEST of 192.168.0.50 on eth2 to 192.168.0.254
     port 67
1364217299383 [/192.168.0.38:63182] [/var/log/messages] : Mar 25 14:03:57
     dev-linux dhclient: DHCPACK of 192.168.0.50 from 192.168.0.254
1364217299383 [/192.168.0.38:63182] [/var/log/messages] : Mar 25 14:03:57
     dev-linux dhclient: bound to 192.168.0.50 -- renewal in 285 seconds.
```

If you don't have access to a UNIX syslog, you can create a custom file and supply content manually to see the application in action. The steps shown next use UNIX commands, starting with `touch` to create an empty file.

```
$ touch ~/mylog.log
```

Now start up the `LogEventBroadcaster` again and point it to the file by setting the system property:

```
$ chapter14> mvn exec:exec -PLogEventBroadcaster -Dlogfile=~/mylog.log
```

Once the `LogEventBroadcaster` is running, you can manually add messages to the file to see the broadcast output in the `LogEventMonitor` console. Use `echo` and redirect the output to the file as shown here:

```
$ echo 'Test log entry' >> ~/mylog.log
```

You can start as many instances of the monitor as you like; each will receive and display the same messages.

13.8 Summary

In this chapter we provided an introduction to connectionless protocols using UDP as an example. We built a sample application that converts log entries to UDP datagrams and broadcasts them to be picked up by subscribed monitor clients. Our implementation made use of a POJO to represent the log data and a custom encoder to convert from this message format to Netty's `DatagramPacket`. The example illustrates the ease with which a Netty UDP application can be developed and extended to support specialized uses.

In the next two chapters we'll look at case studies presented by users from well-known companies who have built industrial-strength applications with Netty.

Part 4

Case studies

This final part of the book presents case studies of mission-critical systems that five well-known companies have implemented with Netty. Chapter 14 is about projects at Droplr, Firebase, and Urban Airship. Chapter 15 discusses work done at Facebook and Twitter.

The projects described range from core infrastructure components to mobile services and new network protocols, including two for executing remote procedure calls (RPC). In all cases, you'll see that these organizations have adopted Netty to achieve the same performance and architectural benefits that you've studied throughout the book.

14 Case studies, part 1

This chapter covers

- Droplr
- Firebase
- Urban Airship

In this chapter we'll present the first of two sets of case studies contributed by companies that have used Netty extensively in their internal infrastructure. We hope that these examples of how others have utilized the framework to solve real-world problems will broaden your understanding of what you can accomplish with Netty.

NOTE The author or authors of each study were directly involved in the project they discuss.

14.1 Droplr—building mobile services

Bruno de Carvalho, Lead Architect

At Droplr we use Netty at the heart of our infrastructure, in everything from our API servers to auxiliary services.

This is a case study on how we moved from a monolithic and sluggish LAMP[1] application to a modern, high-performance and horizontally distributed infrastructure, implemented atop Netty.

14.1.1 How it all started

When I joined the team, we were running a LAMP application that served both as the front end for users and as an API for the client applications—among which, my reverse-engineered, third-party Windows client, *windroplr.*

Windroplr went on to become *Droplr for Windows,* and I, being mostly an infrastructure guy, eventually got a new challenge: completely rethink Droplr's infrastructure.

By then Droplr had established itself as a working concept, so the goals were pretty standard for a 2.0 version:

- Break the monolithic stack into multiple horizontally scalable components
- Add redundancy to avoid downtime
- Create a clean API for clients
- Make it all run on HTTPS

Josh and Levi, the founders, asked me to "make it fast, whatever it takes."

I knew those words meant more than making it *slightly faster* or even *a lot faster.* "Whatever it takes" meant *a full order of magnitude faster.* And I knew then that Netty would eventually play an important role in this endeavor.

14.1.2 How Droplr works

Droplr has an extremely simple workflow: drag a file to the app's menu bar icon and Droplr uploads the file. When the upload completes, Droplr copies a short URL to the file—the *drop*—to the clipboard.

That's it. Frictionless, instant sharing.

Behind the scenes, *drop* metadata is stored in a database—creation date, name, number of downloads, and so on—and the files are stored on Amazon S3.

14.1.3 Creating a faster upload experience

The upload flow for Droplr's first version was woefully naïve:

1. Receive upload
2. Upload to S3
3. Create thumbnails if it's an image
4. Reply to client applications

A closer look at this flow quickly reveals two choke points on steps 2 and 3. No matter how fast the upload from the client to our servers, the creation of a drop would always

[1] An acronym for a typical application technology stack; originally Linux, Apache Web Server, MySQL, and PHP.

go through an annoying hiatus after the actual upload completed, until the successful response was received—because the file would still need to be uploaded to S3 and have its thumbnails generated.

The larger the file, the longer the hiatus. For very large files the connection would eventually time out waiting for the okay from the server. Back then Droplr could offer uploads of only up to 32 MB per file because of this very problem.

There were two distinct approaches to cut down upload times:

- Approach A, optimistic and apparently simpler (figure 15.1):
  - Fully receive the file
  - Save to the local filesystem and immediately return success to client
  - Schedule an upload to S3 some time in the future

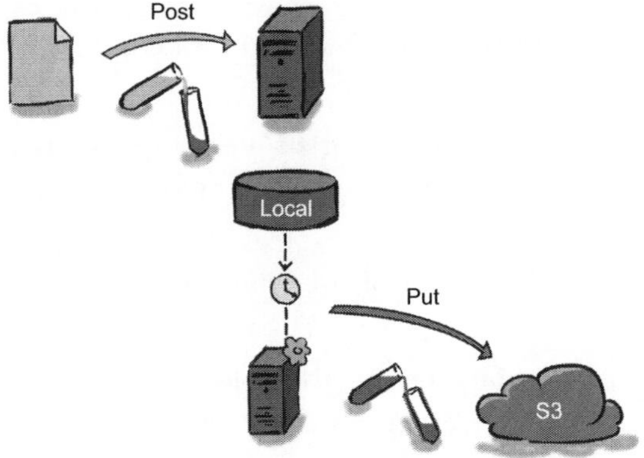

Figure 14.1 Approach A, optimistic and apparently simpler

- Approach B, safe but complex (figure 15.2):
  - Pipe the upload from the client directly to S3, in real time (streaming)

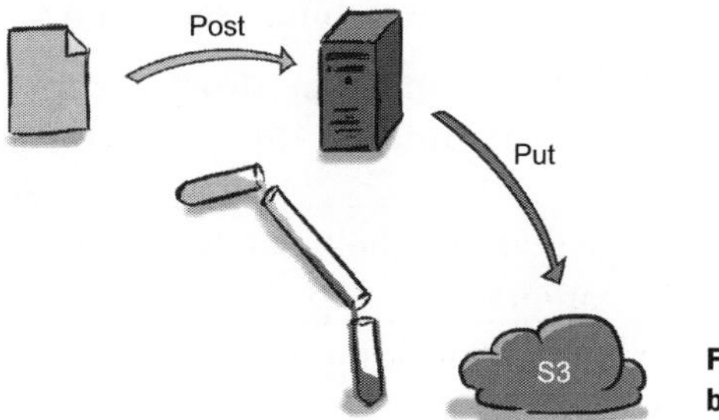

Figure 14.2 Approach B, safe but complex

THE OPTIMISTIC AND APPARENTLY SIMPLER APPROACH

Returning a short URL after receiving the file creates an expectation—one could even go as far as calling it *an implicit contract*—that the file is immediately available at that

URL. But there is no guarantee that the second stage of the upload (actually pushing the file to S3) will ultimately succeed, and the user could end up with a broken link that might get posted on Twitter or sent to an important client. This is unacceptable, even if it happens on one in every hundred thousand uploads.

Our current numbers show that we have an upload failure rate slightly below 0.01% (1 in every 10,000), the vast majority being connection timeouts between client and server before the upload actually completes.

We could try to work around it by serving the file from the machine that received it until it is finally pushed to S3, but this approach is in itself a can of worms:

- If the machine fails before a batch of files is completely uploaded to S3, the files would be forever lost.
- There would be synchronization issues across the cluster ("Where is the file for this drop?").
- Extra, complex logic would be required to deal with edge cases, and this keeps creating more edge cases.

Thinking through all the pitfalls with every workaround, I quickly realized that it's a classic hydra problem—for each head you chop off, two more appear in its place.

THE SAFE BUT COMPLEX APPROACH

The other option required low-level control over the whole process. In essence, we had to be able to

- Open a connection to S3 while receiving the upload from the client.
- Pipe data from the client connection to the S3 connection.
- Buffer and throttle both connections:
  - Buffering is required to keep a steady flow between both client-to-server and server-to-S3 legs of the upload.
  - Throttling is required to prevent explosive memory consumption in case the server-to-S3 leg of the upload becomes slower than the client-to-server leg.
- Cleanly roll everything back on both ends if things went wrong.

It seems conceptually simple, but it's hardly something your average webserver can offer. Especially when you consider that in order to throttle a TCP connection, you need low-level access to its socket.

It also introduced a new challenge that would ultimately end up shaping our final architecture: deferred thumbnail creation.

This meant that whichever technology stack the platform ended up being built upon, it had to offer not only a few basic things like incredible performance and stability but also the flexibility to go *bare metal* (read: *down to the bytes*) if required.

14.1.4 The technology stack

When kick-starting a new project for a webserver, you'll end up asking yourself, "Okay, so what frameworks are the cool kids using these days?" I did too.

Going with Netty wasn't a *no-brainer*; I explored plenty of frameworks, having in mind three factors that I considered to be paramount:

- *It had to be fast.* I wasn't about to replace a low-performance stack with another low-performance stack.
- *It had to scale.* Whether it had 1 or 10,000 connections, each server instance would have to be able to sustain throughput without crashing or leaking memory over time.
- *It had to offer low-level data control.* Byte-level reads, TCP congestion control, the works.

Factors 1 and 2 pretty much excluded any noncompiled language. I'm a sucker for Ruby and love lightweight frameworks like Sinatra and Padrino, but I knew the kind of performance I was looking for couldn't be achieved by building on these blocks.

Factor 2, on its own, meant that whatever the solution, it couldn't rely on blocking I/O. By this point in the book, you certainly understand why non-blocking I/O was the only option.

Factor 3 was trickier. It meant finding the perfect balance between a framework that would offer low-level control of the data it received, but at the same time would be fast to develop with and build upon. This is where language, documentation, community, and other success stories come into play.

At this point I had a strong feeling Netty was my weapon of choice.

THE BASICS: A SERVER AND A PIPELINE

The server is merely a `ServerBootstrap` built with an `NioServerSocketChannelFactory`, configured with a few common handlers and an HTTP `RequestController` at the end, as shown here.

Listing 14.1 Setting up the `ChannelPipeline`

```
pipelineFactory = new ChannelPipelineFactory() {
    @Override
    public ChannelPipeline getPipeline() throws Exception {
        ChannelPipeline pipeline = Channels.pipeline();
        pipeline.addLast("idleStateHandler", new IdleStateHandler(...));
        pipeline.addLast("httpServerCodec", new HttpServerCodec());
        pipeline.addLast("requestController",
            new RequestController(...));
        return pipeline;
    }
};
```

IdleStateHandler shuts down inactive connections

HttpServerCodec converts incoming bytes to HttpRequests and outgoing HttpResponses to bytes

Adds a RequestController to the pipeline

The `RequestController` is the only custom Droplr code in the pipeline and is probably the most complex part of the whole webserver. Its role is to handle initial request validations and, if all is well, route the request to the appropriate request handler. A new instance is created for every established client connection and lives for as long as that connection remains active.

The request controller is responsible for

- Handling load peaks
- HTTP pipeline management
- Setting up a context for request handling
- Spawning new request handlers
- Feeding request handlers
- Handling internal and external errors

Here is a quick rundown of the relevant parts of the `RequestController`.

Listing 14.2 The `RequestController`

```
public class RequestController
    extends IdleStateAwareChannelUpstreamHandler {

    @Override
    public void channelIdle(ChannelHandlerContext ctx,
        IdleStateEvent e) throws Exception {
        // Shut down connection to client and roll everything back.
    }

    @Override public void channelConnected(ChannelHandlerContext ctx,
        ChannelStateEvent e) throws Exception {
        if (!acquireConnectionSlot()) {
            // Maximum number of allowed server connections reached,
            // respond with 503 service unavailable
            // and shutdown connection.
        } else {
            // Set up the connection's request pipeline.
        }
    }

    @Override public void messageReceived(ChannelHandlerContext ctx,
        MessageEvent e) throws Exception {
        if (isDone()) return;

        if (e.getMessage() instanceof HttpRequest) {
            handleHttpRequest((HttpRequest) e.getMessage());
        } else if (e.getMessage() instanceof HttpChunk) {
            handleHttpChunk((HttpChunk)e.getMessage());
        }
    }
}
```

The gist of Droplr's server request validation

If there's an active handler for the current request and it accepts chunks, it then passes on the chunk.

As explained previously in this book, you should never execute non-CPU-bound code on Netty's I/O threads—you'll be stealing away precious resources from Netty and thus affecting the server's throughput.

For this reason, both the `HttpRequest` and `HttpChunk` may hand off the execution to the request handler by switching over to a different thread. This happens when the request handlers aren't CPU-bound, whether because they access the database or perform logic that's not confined to local memory or CPU.

When thread-switching occurs, it's imperative that all the blocks of code execute in serial fashion; otherwise we'd risk, for an upload, having `HttpChunk` *n-1* being processed after `HttpChunk` *n* and thus corrupting the body of the file. (We'd be swapping how bytes were laid out in the uploaded file.) To cope with this, I created a custom thread-pool executor that ensures all tasks sharing a common identifier will be executed serially.

From here on, the data (requests and chunks) ventures out of the realms of Netty and Droplr.

I'll explain briefly how the request handlers are built for the sake of shedding some light on the bridge between the `RequestController`—which lives in Netty-land—and the handlers—Droplr-land. Who knows, maybe this will help you architect your own server!

THE REQUEST HANDLERS

Request handlers provide Droplr's functionality. They're the endpoints behind URIs such as /account or /drops. They're the logic cores—the server's interpreters of clients' requests.

Request handler implementations are where the framework actually becomes Droplr's API server.

THE PARENT INTERFACE

Each request handler, whether directly or through a subclass hierarchy, is a realization of the interface `RequestHandler`.

In its essence, the `RequestHandler` interface represents a stateless handler for requests (instances of `HttpRequest`) and chunks (instances of `HttpChunk`). It's an extremely simple interface with a couple of methods to help the request controller perform and/or decide how to perform its duties, such as:

- Is the request handler stateful or stateless? Does it need to be cloned from a prototype or can the prototype be used to handle the request?
- Is the request handler CPU or non-CPU bound? Can it execute on Netty's worker threads or should it be executed in a separate thread pool?
- Roll back current changes.
- Clean up any used resources.

This interface is all the `RequestController` knows about actions. Through its very clear and concise interface, the controller can interact with stateful and stateless, CPU-bound and non-CPU-bound handlers (or combinations of these) in an isolated and implementation-agnostic fashion.

HANDLER IMPLEMENTATIONS

The simplest realization of `RequestHandler` is `AbstractRequestHandler`, which represents the root of a subclass hierarchy that becomes ever more specific until it reaches the actual handlers that provide all of Droplr's functionality. Eventually it leads to the stateful implementation `SimpleHandler`, which executes in a non-IO-worker thread and is therefore not CPU-bound. `SimpleHandler` is ideal for quickly implementing endpoints that do the typical tasks of reading in JSON, hitting the database, and then writing out some JSON.

THE UPLOAD REQUEST HANDLER

The upload request handler is the crux of the whole Droplr API server. It was the action that shaped the design of the `webserver` module—the *frameworky* part of the server—and it's by far the most complex and tuned piece of code in the whole stack.

During uploads, the server has dual behaviors:

- On one side, it acts as a server for the API clients that are uploading the files.
- On the other side, it acts as client to S3 to push the data it receives from the API clients.

To act as a client, the server uses an HTTP client library that is also built with Netty.[2] This asynchronous library exposes an interface that perfectly matches the needs of the server. It begins executing an HTTP request and allows data to be fed to it as it becomes available, and this greatly reduces the complexity of the client facade of the upload request handler.

14.1.5 Performance

After the initial version of the server was complete, I ran a batch of performance tests. The results were nothing short of mind blowing. After continuously increasing the load in disbelief, I saw the new server peak at 10~12x faster uploads over the old LAMP stack—a full order of magnitude faster—and it could handle over 1000x more concurrent uploads, for a total of nearly 10 k concurrent uploads (running on a single EC2 large instance).

The following factors contributed to this:

- It was running in a tuned JVM.
- It was running in a highly tuned custom stack, created specifically to address this problem, instead of an all-purpose web framework.
- The custom stack was built with Netty using NIO (selector-based model), which meant it could scale to tens or even hundreds of thousands of concurrent connections, unlike the one-process-per-client LAMP stack.
- There was no longer the overhead of receiving a full file and then uploading it to S3 in two separate phases. The file was now streamed directly to S3.

---

[2] You can find the HTTP client library at https://github.com/brunodecarvalho/http-client.

- Because the server was now streaming files,
  - It was not spending time on I/O operations, writing to temporary files and later reading them in the second stage of the upload.
  - It was using less memory for each upload, which meant more parallel uploads could take place.
- Thumbnail generation became an asynchronous post-process.

14.1.6 Summary—standing on the shoulders of giants

All of this was possible thanks to Netty's incredibly well-designed API and performant nonblocking I/O architecture.

Since the launch of Droplr 2.0 in December 2011, we've had virtually zero downtime at the API level. A couple of months ago we interrupted a year-and-a-half clean run of 100% infrastructure uptime due to a scheduled full-stack upgrade (databases, OS, major server and daemons codebase upgrade) that took just under an hour.

The servers soldier on, day after day, taking hundreds—sometimes thousands—of concurrent requests per second, all the while keeping both memory and CPU use to levels so low it's hard to believe they're actually doing such an incredible amount of work:

- CPU use rarely ever goes above 5%.
- Memory footprint can't be accurately described as the process starts with 1 GB of preallocated memory, with the JVM configured to grow up to 2 GB if necessary, and not a single time in the past two years has this happened.

Anyone can throw more machines at any given problem, but Netty helped Droplr scale intelligently, and keep the server bills pretty low.

14.2 Firebase—a real-time data synchronization service

Sara Robinson, VP of Developer Happiness

Greg Soltis, VP of Cloud Architecture

Real-time updates are an integral part of the user experience in modern applications. As users come to expect this behavior, more and more applications are pushing data changes to users in real time. Real-time data synchronization is difficult to achieve with the traditional three-tiered architecture, which requires developers to manage their own ops, servers, and scaling. By maintaining real-time, bidirectional communication with the client, Firebase provides an immediately intuitive experience allowing developers to synchronize application data across diverse clients in a few minutes—all without any backend work, servers, ops, or scaling required.

Implementing this presented a difficult technical challenge, and Netty was the optimal solution in building the underlying framework for all network communications in Firebase. This study will provide an overview of Firebase's architecture, and then examine three ways Firebase uses Netty to power its real-time synchronization service:

- Long polling
- HTTP 1.1 keep-alive and pipelining
- Control of SSL handler

14.2.1 The Firebase architecture

Firebase allows developers to get an application up and running using a two-tiered architecture. Developers simply include the Firebase library and write client-side code. The data is exposed to the developer's code as JSON and is cached locally. The library handles synchronizing this local cache with the master copy, which is stored on Firebase's servers. Changes made to any data are synchronized in real time to potentially hundreds of thousands of clients connected to Firebase. The interaction between multiple clients across platforms and devices and Firebase is depicted in figure 15.3.

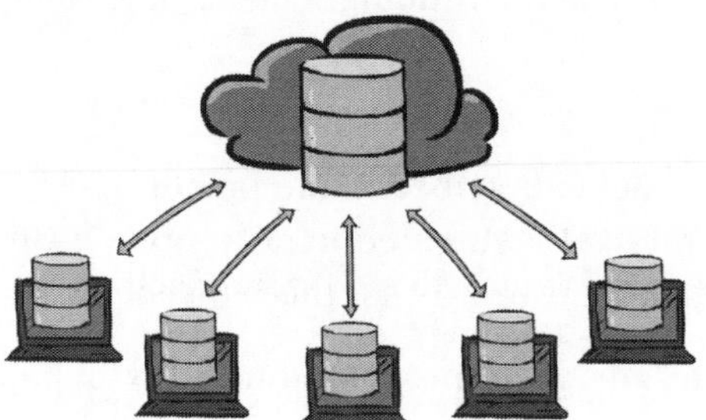

Figure 14.3 Firebase architecture

Firebase servers take incoming data updates and immediately synchronize them to all of the connected clients that have registered interest in the changed data. To enable real-time notification of state changes, clients maintain an active connection to Firebase at all times. This connection may range from an abstraction over a single Netty channel to an abstraction over multiple channels or even multiple, concurrent abstractions if the client is in the middle of switching transport types.

Because clients can connect to Firebase in a variety of ways, it's important to keep the connection code modular. Netty's `Channel` abstraction is a fantastic building block for integrating new transports into Firebase. In addition, the pipeline-and-handler pattern makes it simple to keep transport-specific details isolated and provide a common message stream abstraction to the application code. Similarly, this greatly simplifies adding support for new protocols. Firebase added support for a binary transport simply by adding a few new handlers to the pipeline. Netty's speed, level of abstraction, and fine-grained control made it an excellent framework for implementing real-time connections between the client and server.

14.2.2 Long polling

Firebase uses both long polling and WebSocket transports. The long-polling transport is highly reliable across all browsers, networks, and carriers; the WebSocket-based transport is faster but not always available due to limitations of browsers/clients. Initially, Firebase connects using long polling and then upgrades to WebSockets if possible. For the minority of Firebase traffic that doesn't support WebSockets, Firebase uses Netty to implement a custom library for long polling tuned to be highly performant and responsive.

The Firebase library logic deals with bidirectional streams of messages with notifications when either side closes the stream. Although this is relatively simple to implement on top of TCP or WebSockets, it presents a challenge when dealing with a long-polling transport. The two properties that must be enforced for the long-polling case are

- Guaranteed in-order delivery of messages
- Close notifications

GUARANTEED IN-ORDER DELIVERY OF MESSAGES

In-order delivery for long polling can be achieved by having only a single request outstanding at a given time. Because the client won't send another request until it receives a response from its last request, it can guarantee that its previous messages were received and that it's safe to send more. Similarly, on the server side, there won't be a new request outstanding until the client has received the previous response. Therefore, it's always safe to send everything that's buffered up in between requests. However, this leads to a major drawback. Using the single-request technique, both the client and server spend a significant amount of time buffering up messages. If the client has new data to send but already has an outstanding request, for example, it must wait for the server to respond before sending the new request. This could take a long time if there's no data available on the server.

A more performant solution is to tolerate more requests being in flight concurrently. In practice, this can be achieved by swapping the single-request pattern for the at-most-two-requests pattern. This algorithm has two parts:

- Whenever a client has new data to send, it sends a new request unless two are already in flight.
- Whenever the server receives a request from a client, if it already has an open request from the client, it immediately responds to the first even if there is no data.

This provides an important improvement over the single-request pattern: both the client's and server's buffer time are bound to at most a single network round-trip.

Of course, this increase in performance doesn't come without a price; it results in a commensurate increase in code complexity. The long-polling algorithm no longer guarantees in-order delivery, but a few ideas from TCP can ensure that messages are delivered in order. Each request sent by the client includes a serial number, incremented for each request. In addition, each request includes metadata about the number of messages in the payload. If a message spans multiple requests, the portion of the message contained in this payload is included in the metadata.

The server maintains a ring buffer of incoming message segments and processes them as soon as they're complete and no incomplete messages are ahead of them. Downstream is easier because the long-polling transport responds to an HTTP GET request and doesn't have the same restrictions on payload size. In this case, a serial number is included and is incremented once for each response. The client can process all messages in the list as long as it has received all responses up to the given serial number. If it hasn't, it buffers the list until it receives the outstanding responses.

CLOSE NOTIFICATIONS

The second property enforced in the long-polling transport is close notification. In this case, having the server be aware that the transport has closed is significantly more important than having the client recognize the close. The Firebase library used by clients queues up operations to be run when a disconnect occurs, and those operations can have an impact on other still-connected clients. So it's important to know when a client has actually gone away. Implementing a server-initiated close is relatively simple and can be achieved by responding to the next request with a special protocol-level close message.

Implementing client-side close notifications is trickier. The same close notification can be used, but there are two things that can cause this to fail: the user can close the browser tab, or the network connection could disappear. The tab-closure case is handled with an `iframe` that fires a request containing the close message on page unload. The second case is dealt with via a server-side timeout. It's important to pick your timeout values carefully, because the server is unable to distinguish a slow network from a disconnected client. That is to say, there's no way for the server to know that a request was actually delayed for a minute, rather than the client losing its network connection. It's important to choose an appropriate timeout that balances the cost of false positives (closing transports for clients on slow networks) against how quickly the application needs to be aware of disconnected clients.

Figure 15.4 demonstrates how the Firebase long-polling transport handles different types of requests.

In this diagram, each long-poll request indicates different types of scenarios. Initially, the client sends a poll (poll 0) to the server. Some time later, the server receives data from elsewhere in the system that is destined for this client, so it responds to poll 0 with the data. As soon as the poll returns, the client sends a new poll (poll 1), because it currently has none outstanding. A short time later, the client needs to send data to the server. Since it only has a single poll outstanding, it sends a new one (poll 2) that includes the data to be delivered. Per the protocol, as soon as the server has two simultaneous polls from the same client, it responds to the first one. In this case, the server has no data available for the client, so it sends back an empty response. The client also maintains a timeout and will send a second poll when it fires, even if it has no

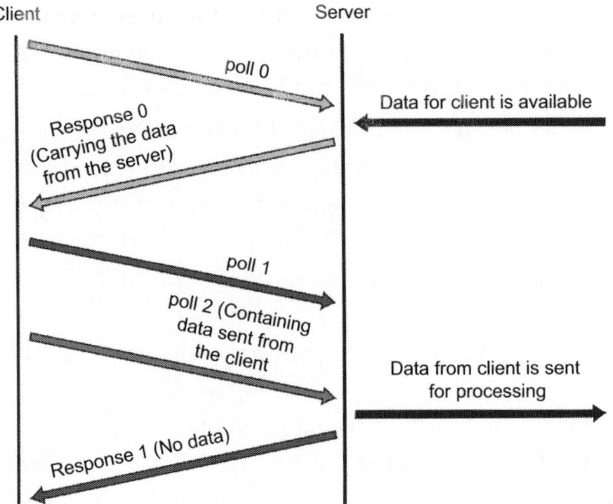

Figure 14.4 Long polling

additional data to send. This insulates the system from failures due to browsers timing out slow requests.

14.2.3 HTTP 1.1 keep-alive and pipelining

With HTTP 1.1 keep-alive, multiple requests can be sent on one connection to a server. This allows for pipelining—new requests can be sent without waiting for a response from the server. Implementing support for pipelining and keep-alive is typically straightforward, but it gets significantly more complex when mixed with long polling.

If a long-polling request is immediately followed by a REST (Representational State Transfer) request, there are some considerations that need to be taken into account to ensure the browser performs properly. A channel may mix asynchronous messages (long-poll requests) with synchronous messages (REST requests). When a synchronous request comes in on one channel, Firebase must synchronously respond to all preceding requests in that channel in order. For example, if there's an outstanding long-poll request, the long-polling transport needs to respond with a no-op before handling the REST request.

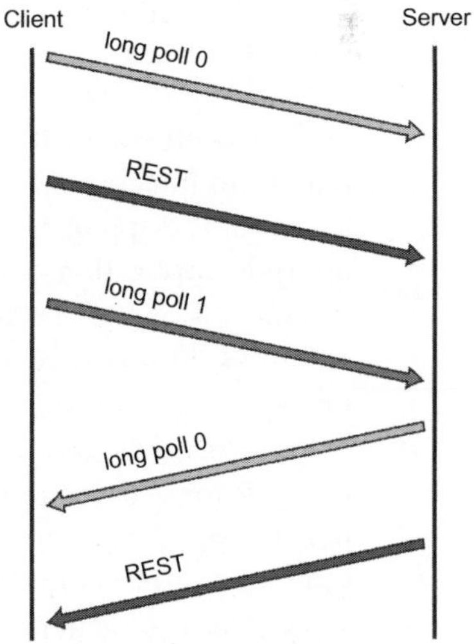

Figure 14.5 Network diagram

Figure 15.5 illustrates how Netty lets Firebase respond to multiple request types in one socket.

If the browser has more than one connection open and is using long polling, it will reuse the connection for messages from both of those open tabs. Given long-polling requests, this is difficult and requires proper management of a queue of HTTP requests. Long-polling requests can be interrupted, but proxied requests can't. Netty made serving multiple request types easy:

- *Static HTML pages*—Cached content that can be returned with no processing; examples include a single-page HTML app, robots.txt, and crossdomain.xml.
- *REST requests*—Firebase supports traditional `GET`, `POST`, `PUT`, `DELETE`, `PATCH`, and `OPTIONS` requests.
- *WebSocket*—A bidirectional connection between a browser and a Firebase server with its own framing protocol.
- *Long polling*—These are similar to HTTP `GET` requests but are treated differently by the application.
- *Proxied requests*—Some requests can't be handled by the server that receives them. In that case, Firebase proxies the request to the correct server in its cluster, so that end users don't have to worry about where data is located. These are like the REST requests, but the proxying server treats them differently.
- *Raw bytes over SSL*—A simple TCP socket running Firebase's own framing protocol and optimized handshaking.

Firebase uses Netty to set up its pipeline to decode an incoming request and then reconfigure the remainder of the pipeline appropriately. In some cases, like WebSockets and raw bytes, once a particular type of request has been assigned a channel, it will stay that way for its entire duration. In other cases, like the various HTTP requests, the assignment must be made on a per-message basis. The same channel could handle REST requests, long-polling requests, and proxied requests.

14.2.4 Control of SslHandler

Netty's `SslHandler` class is an example of how Firebase uses Netty for fine-grained control of its network communications. When a traditional web stack uses an HTTP server like Apache or Nginx to pass requests to the app, incoming SSL requests have already been decoded when they're received by the application code. With a multitenant architecture, it's difficult to assign portions of the encrypted traffic to the tenant of the application using a specific service. This is complicated by the fact that multiple applications could use the same encrypted channel to talk to Firebase (for instance, the user might have two Firebase applications open in different tabs). To solve this, Firebase needs enough control in handling SSL requests before they are decoded.

Firebase charges customers based on bandwidth. However, the account to be charged for a message is typically not available before the SSL decryption has been performed, because it's contained in the encrypted payload. Netty allows Firebase to intercept traffic at multiple points in the pipeline, so the counting of bytes can start as soon as byes come in off the wire. After the message has been decrypted and processed by Firebase's server-side logic, the byte count can be assigned to the appropriate account.

In building this feature, Netty provided control for handling network communications at every layer of the protocol stack, and also allowed for very accurate billing, throttling, and rate limiting, all of which had significant business implications.

Netty made it possible to intercept all inbound and outbound messages and to count bytes with a small amount of Scala code.

Listing 14.3 Setting up the `ChannelPipeline`

```
case class NamespaceTag(namespace: String)

class NamespaceBandwidthHandler extends ChannelDuplexHandler {
    private var rxBytes: Long = 0
    private var txBytes: Long = 0
    private var nsStats: Option[NamespaceStats] = None

    override def channelRead(ctx: ChannelHandlerContext, msg: Object) {
        msg match {
            case buf: ByteBuf => {
                rxBytes += buf.readableBytes(                  <-- When a message
                                      tryFlush(ctx)                comes in, counts the
            }                                                      number of bytes
            case _ => { }
        }
        super.channelRead(ctx, msg)
    }

    override def write(ctx: ChannelHandlerContext, msg: Object,
            promise: ChannelPromise) {
        msg match {
            case buf: ByteBuf => {                         <-- When there is an
                txBytes += buf.readableBytes()                 outbound message,
                tryFlush(ctx)                                  counts those bytes as well
                super.write(ctx, msg, promise)
            }
            case tag: NamespaceTag => {                    <-- If a tag is received, ties
                updateTag(tag.namespace, ctx)                  this channel to an
            }                                                  account, remembers the
            case _ => {                                        account, and assigns the
                super.write(ctx, msg, promise)                 current byte counts to it.
            }
        }
    }

    private def tryFlush(ctx: ChannelHandlerContext) {
        nsStats match {
            case Some(stats: NamespaceStats) => {          <-- If there's already a tag
                stats.logOutgoingBytes(txBytes.toInt)          for the namespace the
                txBytes = 0                                    channel belongs to,
                stats.logIncomingBytes(rxBytes.toInt)          assigns the bytes to
                rxBytes = 0                                    that account and
            }                                                  resets the counters
            case None => {
                // no-op, we don't have a namespace
            }
        }
    }
```

```
    private def updateTag(ns: String, ctx: ChannelHandlerContext) {
        val (_, isLocalNamespace) = NamespaceOwnershipManager.getOwner(ns)
        if (isLocalNamespace) {
            nsStats = NamespaceStatsListManager.get(ns)
            tryFlush(ctx)
        } else {
            // Non-local namespace, just flush the bytes
            txBytes = 0
            rxBytes = 0
        }
    }
}
```

If the count isn't applicable to this machine, ignores it and resets the counters

14.2.5 Firebase summary

Netty plays an indispensable role in the server architecture of Firebase's real-time data synchronization service. It allows support for a heterogeneous client ecosystem, which includes a variety of browsers, along with clients that are completely controlled by Firebase. With Netty, Firebase can handle tens of thousands of messages per second on each server. Netty is especially awesome for several reasons:

- *It's fast.* It took only a few days to develop a prototype, and was never a production bottleneck.
- *It's positioned well in the abstraction layer.* Netty provides fine-grained control where necessary and allows for customization at every step of the control flow.
- *It supports multiple protocols over the same port.* HTTP, WebSockets, long polling, and standalone TCP.
- *Its GitHub repo is top-notch.* Well-written javadocs make it frictionless to develop against.
- *It has a highly active community.* The community is very responsive on issue maintenance and seriously considers all feedback and pull requests. In addition, the team provides great and up-to-date example code. Netty is an excellent, well-maintained framework and it has been essential in building and scaling Firebase's infrastructure. Real-time data synchronization in Firebase wouldn't be possible without Netty's speed, control, abstraction, and extraordinary team.

14.3 Urban Airship—building mobile services

Erik Onnen, Vice President of Architecture

As smartphone use grows across the globe at unprecedented rates, a number of service providers have emerged to assist developers and marketers toward the end of providing amazing end-user experiences. Unlike their feature phone predecessors, smartphones crave IP connectivity and seek it across a number of channels (3G, 4G, WiFi, WiMAX, and Bluetooth). As more and more of these devices access public networks via IP-based protocols, the challenges of scale, latency, and throughput become more and more daunting for back-end service providers.

Thankfully, Netty is well suited to many of the concerns faced by this thundering herd of always-connected mobile devices. This chapter will detail several practical applications of Netty in scaling a mobile developer and marketer platform, Urban Airship.

14.3.1 Basics of mobile messaging

Although marketers have long used SMS as a channel to reach mobile devices, a more recent functionality called *push notifications* is rapidly becoming the preferred mechanism for messaging smartphones. Push notifications commonly use the less expensive data channel and the price per message is a fraction of the cost of SMS. The throughput of push notifications is commonly two to three orders of magnitude higher than SMS, making it an ideal channel for breaking news. Most importantly, push notifications give users device-driven control of the channel. If a user dislikes the messaging from an application, the user can disable notifications for an application or outright delete the application.

At a very high level, the interaction between a device and push notification behavior is similar to the depiction in figure 15.6.

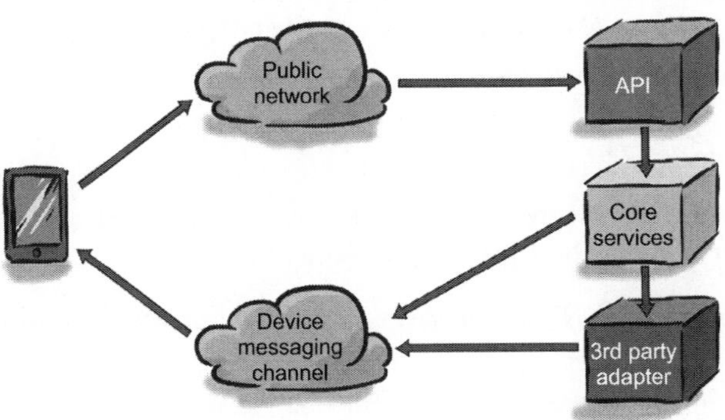

Figure 14.6 High-level mobile messaging platform integration

At a high level, when an application developer wants to send push notifications to a device, the developer must plan to store information about the device and its application installation.[3] Commonly, an application installation will execute code to retrieve a platform-specific identifier and report that identifier back to a centralized service where the identifier is persisted. Later, logic external to the application installation will initiate a request to deliver a message to the device.

Once an application installation has registered its identifier with a back-end service, the delivery of a push message can in turn take two paths. In the first path, a message can be delivered directly to the application itself, with the application maintaining a direct connection to a back-end service. In the second and more common

[3] Some mobile OSes allow a form of push notifications called local notifications that would not follow this approach.

approach, an application will rely on a third party to deliver the message to the application on behalf of a back-end service. At Urban Airship, both approaches to delivering push notifications are used, and both leverage Netty extensively.

14.3.2 Third-party delivery

In the case of third-party push delivery, every push notification platform provides a different API for developers to deliver messages to application installations. These APIs differ in terms of their protocol (binary vs. text), authentication (OAuth, X.509, and so on), and capabilities. Each approach has its own unique challenges for integration as well as for achieving optimal throughput.

Despite the fact that the fundamental purpose of each of these providers is to deliver a notification to an application, each takes a different approach with significant implications for system integrators. For example, Apple Push Notification Service (APNS) defines a strictly binary protocol; other providers base their service on some form of HTTP, all with subtle variations that affect how to best achieve maximum throughput. Thankfully, Netty is an amazingly flexible tool and it significantly helps smoothing over the differences between the various protocols.

The following sections will provide examples of how Urban Airship uses Netty to integrate with two of the listed providers.

14.3.3 Binary protocol example

Apple's APNS is a binary protocol with a specific, network byte-ordered payload. Sending an APNS notification involves the following sequence of events:

1. Connect a TCP socket to APNS servers over an SSLv3 connection, authenticated with an X.509 certificate.
2. Format a binary representation of a push message structured according to the format defined by Apple.[4]
3. Write the message to the socket.
4. Read from the socket if you're ready to determine any error codes associated with a sent message.
5. In the case of an error, reconnect the socket and continue from step 2.

As part of formatting the binary message, the producer of the message is required to generate an identifier that's opaque to the APNS system. In the event of an invalid message (incorrect formatting, size, or device information, for example), the identifier will be returned to the client in the error response message of step 4.

[4] For information on APNS: http://docs.aws.amazon.com/sns/latest/dg/mobile-push-apns.html, http://bit.ly/189mmpG.

At face value the protocol seems straightforward, but there are nuances to successfully addressing all of the preceding concerns, in particular on the JVM:

- The APNS specification dictates that certain payload values should be sent in big-endian ordering (for example, token length).
- Step 3 in the previous sequence requires one of two solutions. Because the JVM will not allow reading from a closed socket even if data exists in the output buffer, you have two options:
  - After a write, perform a blocking read with a timeout on the socket. This has multiple disadvantages:
    - The amount of time to block waiting for an error is non-deterministic. An error may occur in milliseconds or seconds.
    - As socket objects can't be shared across multiple threads, writes to the socket must immediately block while waiting for errors. This has dramatic implications for throughput. If a single message is delivered in a socket write, no additional messages can go out on that socket until the read timeout has occurred. When you're delivering tens of millions of messages, a three-second delay between messages isn't acceptable.
    - Relying on a socket timeout is an expensive operation. It results in an exception being thrown and several unnecessary system calls.
  - Use asynchronous I/O. In this model, neither reads nor writes block. This allows writers to continue sending messages to APNS while at the same time allowing the OS to inform user code when data is ready to be read.

Netty makes addressing all of these concerns trivial while at the same time delivering amazing throughput.

First, let's see how Netty simplifies packing a binary APNS message with correct endian ordering.

Listing 14.4 `ApnsMessage` implementation

```
public final class ApnsMessage {
    private static final byte COMMAND = (byte) 1;
    public ByteBuf toBuffer() {
        short size = (short) (1 + // Command
            4 + // Identifier
            4 + // Expiry
            2 + // DT length header
            32 + //DS length
            2 + // body length header
            body.length);

        ByteBuf buf = Unpooled.buffer(size).order(ByteOrder.BIG_ENDIAN);
        buf.writeByte(COMMAND);
        buf.writeInt(identifier);
        buf.writeInt(expiryTime);
```

An APNS message always starts with a command 1 byte in size, so that value is coded as a constant.

Messages size varies, so for efficiency it is calculated before the ByteBuf is created.

At creation the ByteBuf is sized exactly and the endianness for APNS is specified.

Various values are inserted into the buffer from state maintained elsewhere in the class.

```
        buf.writeShort((short) deviceToken.length);
        buf.writeBytes(deviceToken);
        buf.writeShort((short) body.length);
        buf.writeBytes(body);
        return buf;
    }
}
```

❶ The deviceToken field in this class (not shown) is a Java byte[].

❷ When the buffer is ready, it is simply returned.

Some important notes on the implementation:

❶ The length property of a Java array is always an integer. However, the APNS protocol requires a 2-byte value. In this case, the length of the payload has been validated elsewhere, so casting to a `short` is safe at this location. Note that without explicitly constructing the `ByteBuf` to be big endian, subtle bugs could occur with values of types `short` and `int`.

❷ Unlike the standard `java.nio.ByteBuffer`, it's not necessary to flip the buffer and worry about its position—Netty's `ByteBuf` handles read and write position management automatically.

In a small amount of code, Netty has made trivial the act of creating a properly formatted APNS message. Because this message is now packed into a `ByteBuf`, it can easily be written directly to a `Channel` connected to APNS when the message is ready for sending.

Connecting to APNS can be accomplished via multiple mechanisms, but at its most basic, a `ChannelInitializer` that populates the `ChannelPipeline` with an `SslHandler` and a decoder is required.

Listing 14.5 Setting up the `ChannelPipeline`

```
public final class ApnsClientPipelineInitializer
    extends ChannelInitializer<Channel> {
    private final SSLEngine clientEngine;

    public ApnsClientPipelineFactory(SSLEngine engine) {
        this.clientEngine = engine;
    }

    @Override
    public void initChannel(Channel channel) throws Exception {
        final ChannelPipeline pipeline = channel.pipeline();
        final SslHandler handler = new SslHandler(clientEngine);
        handler.setEnableRenegotiation(true);
        pipeline.addLast("ssl", handler);
        pipeline.addLast("decoder", new ApnsResponseDecoder());
    }
}
```

An X.509 authenticated request requires a javax.net.ssl.SSLEngine instance.

Constructs a Netty SslHandler

APNS will attempt to renegotiate SSL shortly after connection, need to allow renegotiation.

This class extends Netty's ByteToMessageDecoder and handles cases where APNS returns an error code and disconnects.

It's worth noting how easy Netty makes negotiating an X.509 authenticated connection in conjunction with asynchronous I/O. In early prototypes of APNS code at Urban Airship without Netty, negotiating an asynchronous X.509 authenticated connection required over 80 lines of code and a thread pool simply to connect. Netty hides all the complexity of the SSL handshake, the authentication, and most importantly the encryption of cleartext bytes to cipher text and the key renegotiation that comes along with using SSL. These incredibly tedious, error prone, and poorly documented APIs in the JDK are hidden behind three lines of Netty code.

At Urban Airship, Netty plays a role in all connectivity to numerous third-party push notification services including APNS and Google's GCM. In every case, Netty is flexible enough to allow explicit control over exactly how integration takes place from higher-level HTTP connectivity behavior down to basic socket-level settings such as TCP keep-alive and socket buffer sizing.

14.3.4 Direct to device delivery

The previous section provides insight into how Urban Airship integrates with a third party for message delivery. In referring to figure 15.1, note that two paths exist for delivering messages to a device. In addition to delivering messages through a third party, Urban Airship has experience serving directly as a channel for message delivery. In this capacity, individual devices connect directly to Urban Airship's infrastructure, bypassing third-party providers. This approach brings a distinctly different set of challenges:

- *Socket connections from mobile devices are often short-lived.* Mobile devices frequently switch between different types of networks depending on various conditions. To back-end providers of mobile services, devices constantly reconnect and experience short but frequent periods of connectivity.
- *Connectivity across platforms is irregular.* From a network perspective, tablet devices tend to behave differently than mobile phones, and mobile phones behave differently than desktop computers.
- *Frequency of mobile phone updates to back-end providers is certain to increase.* Mobile phones are increasingly used for daily tasks, producing significant amounts of general network traffic but also analytics data for back-end providers.
- *Battery and bandwidth can't be ignored.* Unlike a traditional desktop environment, mobile phones tend to operate on limited data plans. Service providers must honor the fact that end users have limited battery life and they use expensive, limited bandwidth. Abuse of either will frequently result in the uninstallation of an application, the worst possible outcome for a mobile developer.
- *All aspects of infrastructure will need to scale massively.* As mobile device popularity increases, more application installations result in more connections to a mobile services infrastructure. Each of the previous elements in this list are further complicated by the sheer scale and growth of mobile devices.

Over time, Urban Airship learned several critical lessons as connections from mobile devices continued to grow:

- The diversity of mobile carriers can have a dramatic effect on device connectivity.
- Many carriers don't allow TCP keep-alive functionality. Given that, many carriers will aggressively cull idle TCP sessions.
- UDP isn't a viable channel for messaging to mobile devices because many carriers disallow it.
- The overhead of SSLv3 is an acute pain for short-lived connections.

Given the challenges of mobile growth and the lessons learned by Urban Airship, Netty was a natural fit for implementing a mobile messaging platform for reasons highlighted in the following sections.

14.3.5 Netty excels at managing large numbers of concurrent connections

As mentioned in the previous section, Netty makes supporting asynchronous I/O on the JVM trivial. Because Netty operates on the JVM, and because the JVM on Linux ultimately uses the Linux epoll facility to manage interest in socket file descriptors, Netty makes it possible to accommodate the rapid growth of mobile by allowing developers to easily accept large numbers of open sockets—close to 1 million TCP connections per single Linux process. At numbers of this scale, service providers can keep costs low, allowing a large number of devices to connect to a single process on a physical server.[5]

In controlled testing and with configuration options optimized to use small amounts of memory, a Netty-based service was able to accommodate slightly less than 1 million connections (approximately 998,000). In this case, the limit was fundamentally the Linux kernel imposing a hard-coded limit of 1 million file handles per process. Had the JVM itself not held a number of sockets and file descriptors for JAR files, the server would likely have been capable of handling even more connections, all on a 4 GB heap. Leveraging this efficiency, Urban Airship has successfully sustained over 20 million persistent TCP socket connections to its infrastructure for message delivery, all on a handful of servers.

It's worth noting that while in practice a single Netty-based service is capable of handling nearly a million inbound TCP socket connections, doing so is not necessarily pragmatic or advisable. As with all things in distributed computing, hosts will fail, processes will need to be restarted, and unexpected behavior will occur. As a result of these realities, proper capacity planning means considering the consequences of a single process failing.

---

[5] Note the distinction of a *physical server* in this case. Although virtualization offers many benefits, leading cloud providers were regularly unable to accommodate more than 200,000–300,000 concurrent TCP connections to a single virtual host. With connections at or above this scale, expect to use bare metal servers and expect to pay close attention to the NIC (Network Interface Card) vendor.

14.3.6 Summary—Beyond the perimeter of the firewall

We've demonstrated two everyday uses of Netty at the perimeter of the Urban Airship network. Netty works exceptionally well for these purposes, but it has also found a home as scaffolding for many other components inside Urban Airship.

INTERNAL RPC FRAMEWORK

Netty has been the centerpiece of an internal RPC framework that has consistently evolved inside Urban Airship. Today, this framework processes hundreds of thousands of requests per second with very low latency and exceptional throughput. Nearly every API request fielded by Urban Airship processes through multiple back-end services with Netty at the core of all of those services.

LOAD AND PERFORMANCE TESTING

Netty has been used at Urban Airship for several different load- and performance-testing frameworks. For example, to simulate millions of device connections in testing the previously described device-messaging service, Netty was used in conjunction with a Redis (http://redis.io/) instance to test end-to-end message throughput with a minimal client-side footprint.

ASYNCHRONOUS CLIENTS FOR COMMONLY SYNCHRONOUS PROTOCOLS

For some internal uses, Urban Airship has been experimenting with Netty to create asynchronous clients for typically synchronous protocols, including services like Apache Kafka (http://kafka.apache.org/) and Memcached (http://memcached.org/). Netty's flexibility easily allows us to craft clients that are asynchronous in nature but that can be converted back and forth between truly asynchronous or synchronous implementations without requiring upstream code changes.

All in all, Netty has been a cornerstone of Urban Airship as a service. The authors and community are fantastic and have produced a truly first-class framework for anything requiring networking on the JVM.

14.4 Summary

This chapter aimed at providing insight into real-world use of Netty and how it has helped companies to solve significant networking problems. It's worth noting how in all cases Netty was leveraged not only as a code framework, but also as an essential component of development and architectural best practices.

In the next chapter we'll present case studies contributed by Facebook and Twitter describing open source projects that evolved from Netty-based code originally developed to address internal needs.

15 Case studies, part 2

This chapter covers

- Facebook case study
- Twitter case study

In this chapter we'll see how Facebook and Twitter, two of the most popular social networks, are using Netty. Each has exploited Netty's flexible and generic design to build frameworks and services that meet requirements for extreme scalability and extensibility.

The case studies presented here were written by the engineers responsible for the design and implementation of the solutions described.

15.1 Netty at Facebook: Nifty and Swift[1]

Andrew Cox, Software Engineer at Facebook

At Facebook we use Netty in several of our back-end services (for handling messaging traffic from mobile phone apps, for HTTP clients, and so on), but our fastest-growing

[1] The views expressed in this section are those of the author and do not necessarily reflect the views of the author's employer.

usage is via two new frameworks we've developed for building Thrift services in Java: Nifty and Swift.

15.1.1 What is Thrift?

Thrift is a framework for building services and clients that communicate via remote procedure calls (RPC). It was originally developed at Facebook[2] to meet our requirements for building services that can handle certain types of interface mismatches between client and server. This comes in very handy because services and their clients usually can't all be upgraded simultaneously.

Another important feature of Thrift is that it's available for a wide variety of languages. This enables teams at Facebook to choose the right language for the job, without worrying about whether they'll be able to find client code for interacting with other services. Thrift has grown to become one of the primary means by which our back-end services at Facebook communicate with one another, and it's also used for non-RPC serialization tasks, because it provides a common, compact storage format that can be read from a wide selection of languages for later processing.

Since its development at Facebook, Thrift has been open sourced as an Apache project (http://thrift.apache.org/), where it continues to grow to fill the needs of service developers, not only at Facebook but also at other companies, including Evernote and last.fm,[3] and on major open source projects such as Apache Cassandra and HBase.

These are the major components of Thrift:

- *Thrift Interface Definition Language (IDL)*—Used to define your services and compose any custom types that your services will send and receive
- *Protocols*—Used to control encoding/decoding elements of data into a common binary format (such as Thrift binary protocol or JSON)
- *Transports*—Provides a common interface for reading/writing to different media (such as TCP socket, pipe, memory buffer)
- *Thrift compiler*—Parses Thrift IDL files to generate stub code for the server and client interfaces, and serialization/deserialization code for the custom types defined in IDL
- *Server implementation*—Handles accepting connections, reading requests from those connections, dispatching calls to an object that implements the interface, and sending the responses back to clients
- *Client implementation*—Translates method calls into requests and sends them to the server

2 A now-ancient whitepaper from the original Thrift developers can be found at http://thrift.apache.org/static/files/thrift-20070401.pdf.

3 Find more examples at http://thrift.apache.org.

15.1.2 Improving the state of Java Thrift using Netty

The Apache distribution of Thrift has been ported to about twenty different languages, and there are also separate frameworks compatible with Thrift built for other languages (Twitter's Finagle for Scala is a great example). Several of these languages receive at least some use at Facebook, but the most common ones used for writing Thrift services here at Facebook are C++ and Java.

When I arrived at Facebook, we were already well underway with the development of a solid, high-performance, asynchronous Thrift implementation in C++, built around libevent. From libevent, we get cross-platform abstractions over the OS APIs for asynchronous I/O, but libevent isn't any easier to use than, say, raw Java NIO. So we've also built abstractions on top of that, such as asynchronous message channels, and we make use of chained buffers from Folly[4] to avoid copies as much as possible. This framework also has a client implementation that supports asynchronous calls with multiplexing, and a server implementation that supports asynchronous request handling. (The server can start an asynchronous task to handle a request and return immediately, then invoke a callback or set a `Future` later when the response is ready.)

Meanwhile, our Java Thrift framework received a lot less attention, and our load-testing tools showed that Java performance lagged well behind C++. There were already Java Thrift frameworks built on NIO, and asynchronous NIO-based clients were available as well. But the clients didn't support pipelining or multiplexing requests, and the servers didn't support asynchronous request handling. Because of these missing features, Java Thrift service developers here at Facebook were running into problems that had been already solved in C++, and it became a source of frustration.

We could have built a similar custom framework on top of NIO and based our new Java Thrift implementation on that, as we had done for C++. But experience showed us that this was a *ton* of work to get right, and as it happened, the framework we needed was already out there, just waiting for us to make use of it: Netty.

We quickly put together a server implementation and mashed the names "Netty" and "Thrift" together to come up with "Nifty," the name for the new server. It was immediately impressive how much less code was needed to get Nifty working, compared to everything we needed to achieve the same results in C++.

Next we put together a simple load-tester Thrift server using Nifty and used our load-testing tools to compare it to existing servers. The results were clear: Nifty outperformed the other NIO servers, and it was in the same ballpark as our newest C++ Thrift server. Using Netty was going to improve performance!

15.1.3 Nifty server design

Nifty (https://github.com/facebook/nifty) is an open source, Apache-licensed Thrift client/server implementation built on top of the Apache Thrift library. It's designed

[4] Folly is Facebook's open-source C++ common library: https://www.facebook.com/notes/facebook-engineering/folly-the-facebook-open-source-library/10150864656793920.

so that moving from any other Java Thrift server implementation should be painless: you can reuse the same Thrift IDL files, the same Thrift code generator (packaged with the Apache Thrift library), and the same service interface implementation. The only thing that really needs to change is your server startup code (Nifty setup follows a slightly different style from that of the traditional Thrift server implementations in Apache Thrift).

NIFTY ENCODER/DECODER

The default Nifty server handles either plain messages or framed messages (with a 4-byte prefix). It does this by using a custom Netty frame decoder that looks at the first few bytes to determine how to decode the rest. Then, when a complete message is found, the decoder wraps the message content along with a field that indicates the type of message. The server later refers to this field to encode the response in the same format.

Nifty also supports plugging in your own custom codec. For example, some of our services use a custom codec to read extra information from headers that clients insert before each message (containing optional metadata, client capabilities, and so on). The decoder could also easily be extended to handle other types of message transports, such as HTTP.

ORDERING RESPONSES ON THE SERVER

Initial versions of Java Thrift used OIO sockets, and servers maintained one thread per active connection. With this setup, each request was read, processed, and answered, all on the same thread, before the next response was read. This guaranteed that responses would always be returned in the order in which the corresponding requests arrived.

Newer asynchronous I/O server implementations were built that didn't need one thread per connection, and these servers could handle more simultaneous connections, but clients still mainly used synchronous I/O, so the server could count on not receiving the next request until after it had sent the current response. This request/execution flow is shown in figure 16.1.

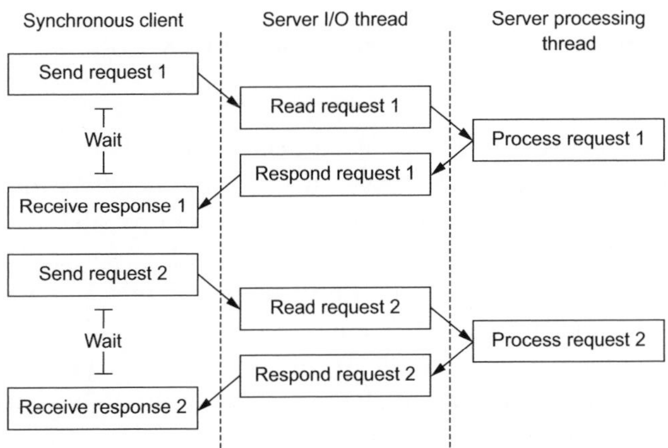

Figure 15.1 Synchronous request/response flow

Initial pseudo-asynchronous usages of clients started happening when a few Thrift users took advantage of the fact that for a generated client method `foo()`, methods `send_foo()` and `recv_foo()` were also exposed separately. This allows Thrift users to send several requests (whether on several clients, or on the same client) and then call the corresponding receive methods to start waiting for and collecting the results.

In this new scenario, the server may read multiple requests from a single client before it has finished processing the first. In an ideal world, we could assure all asynchronous Thrift clients that pipeline requests can handle the responses to those requests in whatever order they arrive. In the world we live in, though, newer clients *can* handle this, whereas older asynchronous Thrift clients may write multiple requests but must receive the responses in order.

This kind of problem is solved by using the Netty 4 `EventExecutor` or `OrderedMemoryAwareThreadPoolExcecutor` in Netty 3.x, which guarantee sequential processing for all incoming messages on a connection, without forcing all of those messages to run on the same executor thread.

Figure 16.2 shows how pipelined requests are handled in the correct order, which means the response for the first request will be returned, and then the response for the second, and so on.

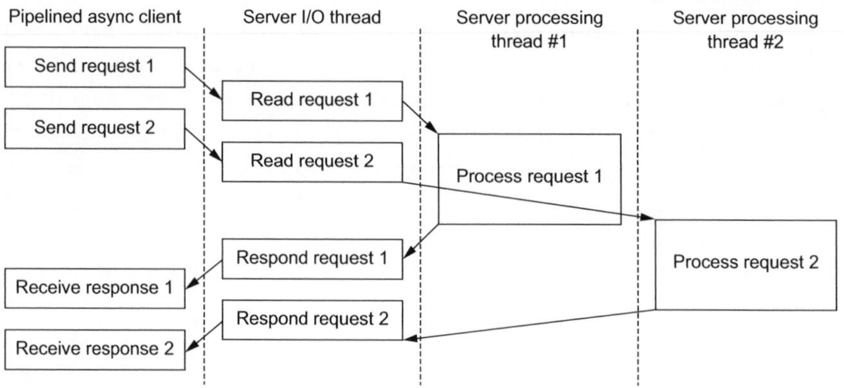

Figure 15.2 Request/response flow for sequential processing of pipelined requests

Nifty has special requirements though: we aim to serve each client with the best response ordering that it can handle. We'd like to allow the handlers for multiple pipelined requests from a single connection to be processed in parallel, but then we couldn't control the order in which these handlers would finish.

Instead we use a solution that involves buffering responses; if the client requires in-order responses, we'll buffer later responses until all the earlier ones are also available, and then we'll send them together, in the required order. See figure 16.3.

Of course, Nifty includes asynchronous channels (usable through Swift) that *do* support out-of-order responses. When using a custom transport that allows the client

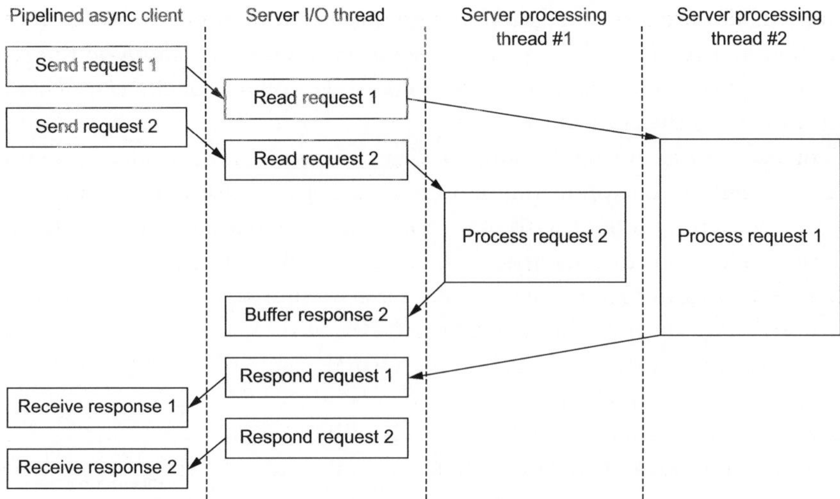

Figure 15.3 Request/response flow for parallel processing of pipelined requests

to notify the server of this client capability, the server is relieved of the burden of buffering responses, and it will send them back in whatever order the requests finish.

15.1.4 *Nifty asynchronous client design*

Nifty client development is mostly focused on asynchronous clients. Nifty actually does provide a Netty implementation of Thrift's synchronous transport interface, but its use is pretty limited because it doesn't provide much win over a standard socket transport from Thrift. Because of this, the user should use the asynchronous clients whenever possible.

PIPELINING

The Thrift library has its own NIO-based asynchronous client implementation, but one feature we wanted was request pipelining. Pipelining is the ability to send multiple requests on the same connection without waiting for a response. If the server has idle worker threads, it can process these requests in parallel, but even if all worker threads are busy, pipelining can still help in other ways. The server will spend less time waiting for something to read, and the client may be able to send multiple small requests together in a single TCP packet, thus better utilizing network bandwidth.

With Netty, pipelining just works. Netty does all the hard work of managing the state of the various NIO selection keys, and Nifty can focus on encoding requests and decoding responses.

MULTIPLEXING

As our infrastructure has grown, we've started to see a *lot* of connections building up on our servers. Multiplexing—sharing connections for all the Thrift clients connecting from a single source—can help to mitigate this. But multiplexing over a client connection that requires ordered responses presents a problem: one client on the connection may incur extra latency because its response must come after the responses for other requests sharing the connection.

The basic solution is pretty simple: Thrift already sends a sequence identifier with every message, so to support out-of-order responses we just need the client channels to keep a map from sequence ID to response handler, instead of using a queue.

The catch is that in standard synchronous Thrift clients, the protocol is responsible for extracting the sequence identifier from the message, and the protocol calls the transport, but never the other way around.

That simple flow (shown in figure 16.4) works fine for a synchronous client, where the protocol can wait on the transport to actually receive the response, but for an asynchronous client the control flow gets a bit more complicated. The client call is dispatched to the Swift library, which first asks the protocol to encode the request into a buffer, and then passes that encoded request buffer to the Nifty channel to be written out. When the channel receives a response from the server, it notifies the Swift library, which again uses the protocol to decode the response buffer. This is the flow shown in figure 16.5.

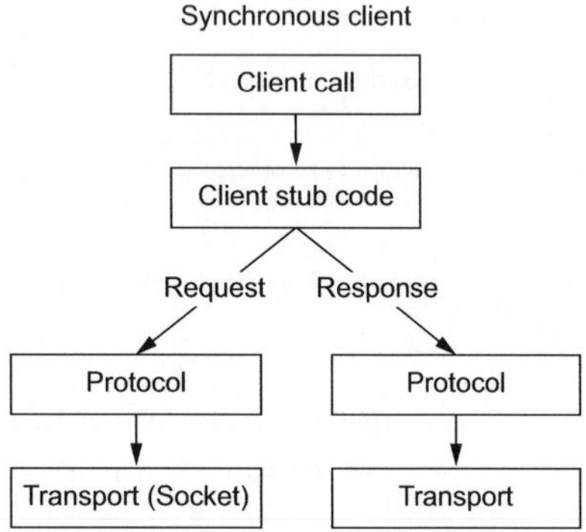

Figure 15.4 Multiplexing/transport layers

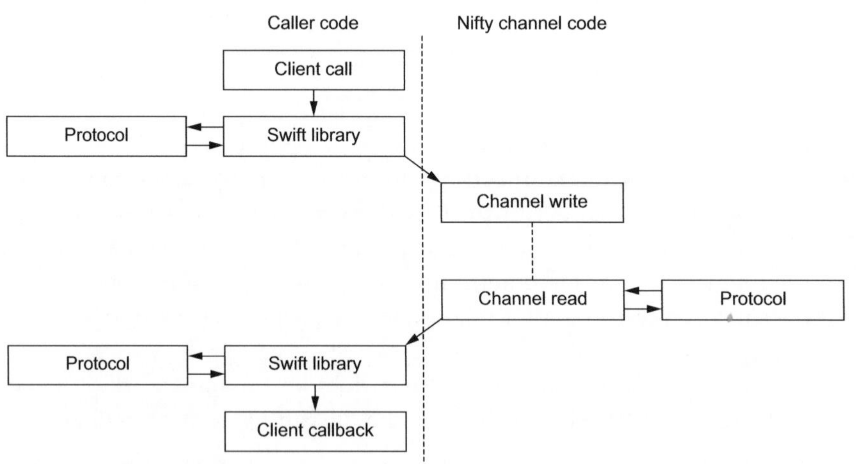

Figure 15.5 Dispatching

15.1.5 Swift: a faster way to build Java Thrift service

The other key part of our new Java Thrift framework is called Swift. It uses Nifty as its I/O engine, but the service specifications can be represented directly in Java using annotations, giving Thrift service developers the ability to work purely in Java. When your service starts up, the Swift runtime gathers information about all the services and types via a combination of reflection and interpreting Swift annotations. From that information, it can build the same kind of model that the Thrift compiler builds when parsing Thrift IDL files. Then it uses this model to run the server and client directly (without any generated server or client stub code) by generating new classes from byte code used for serializing/deserializing the custom types.

Skipping the normal Thrift code generation also makes it easier to add new features without having to change the IDL compiler, so a lot of our new features (such as asynchronous clients) are supported in Swift first. If you're interested, take a look at the introductory information on Swift's GitHub page (https://github.com/facebook/swift).

15.1.6 Results

In the following sections we'll quantify some of the outcomes we've seen from our work with Netty.

PERFORMANCE COMPARISONS

One measurement of Thrift server performance is a benchmark of no-ops. This benchmark uses long-running clients that continuously make Thrift calls to a server that sends back an empty response. Although this measurement isn't a realistic performance estimation of most actual Thrift services, it's a good measure of the maximum potential of a Thrift service, and improving this benchmark does generally mean a reduction in the amount of CPU used by the framework itself.

As shown in table 16.1, Nifty outperforms all of the other NIO Thrift server implementations (TNonblockingServer, TThreadedSelectorServer, and TThreadPoolServer) on this benchmark. It even easily beats our previous Java server implementation (a pre-Nifty server implementation we used internally, based on plain NIO and direct buffers).

Table 15.1 Benchmark results for different implementations

Thrift server implementation	No-op requests/second
TNonblockingServer	~68,000
TThreadedSelectorServer	188,000
TThreadPoolServer	867,000
Older Java server (using NIO and direct buffers)	367,000
Nifty	963,000
Older libevent-based C++ server	895,000
Next-gen libevent-based C++ server	1,150,000

The only Java server we tested that can compete with Nifty is TThreadPoolServer. This server uses raw OIO and runs each connection on a dedicated thread. This gives it an edge when handling a lower number of connections; however, you can easily run into scaling problems with OIO when your server needs to handle a very large number of simultaneous connections.

Nifty even beats the previous C++ server implementation that was most prominent when we started development on Nifty, and although it falls a bit short compared to our next-gen C++ server framework, it's at least in the same ballpark.

EXAMPLE STABILITY ISSUES

Before Nifty, many of our major Java services at Facebook used an older, custom NIO-based Thrift server implementation that works similarly to Nifty. That implementation is an older codebase that had more time to mature, but because its asynchronous I/O handling code was built from scratch, and because Nifty is built on the solid foundation of Netty's asynchronous I/O framework, it has had many fewer problems.

One of our custom message queuing services had been built using the older framework, and it started to suffer from a kind of socket leak. A lot of connections were sitting around in `CLOSE_WAIT` state, meaning the server had received a notification that the client had closed the socket, but the server never reciprocated by making its own call to close the socket. This left the sockets in a kind of `CLOSE_WAIT` limbo.

The problem happened very slowly; across the entire pool of machines handling this service, there might be millions of requests per second, but usually only one socket on one server would enter this state in an hour. It wasn't an urgent issue because it took a long time before a server needed a restart at that rate, but it also complicated tracking down the cause. Extensive digging through the code didn't help much either: initially several places looked suspicious, but everything ultimately checked out and we didn't locate the problem.

Eventually we migrated the service onto Nifty. The conversion—including testing in a staging environment—took less than a day and the problem has since disappeared. We haven't really seen any such problems in Nifty.

This is just one example of the kind of subtle bug that can show up when using NIO directly, and it's similar to bugs we've had to solve in our C++ Thrift framework time and time again to stabilize it. But I think it's a great example of how using Netty has helped us take advantage of the years of stability fixes it has received.

IMPROVING TIMEOUT HANDLING FOR C++

Netty has also helped us indirectly by lending suggestions for improvements to our C++ framework. An example of this is the hashed wheel timer. Our C++ framework uses timeout events from libevent to drive client and server timeouts, but adding separate timeouts for every request proves to be prohibitively expensive, so we'd been using what we called timeout sets. The idea here was that a client connection to a particular service usually has the same receive timeout for every call made from that client, so we'd maintain only one real timer event for a set of timeouts that share the same duration. Every new timeout was guaranteed to fire after existing timeouts scheduled for that set, so when each timeout expired or was canceled, we'd schedule only the next timeout.

However, our users occasionally wanted to supply per-call timeouts, with different timeout values for different requests on the same connection. In this scenario, the benefits of using a timeout set are lost, so we tried using individual timer events. We started to see performance problems when many timeouts were scheduled at once. We knew that Nifty doesn't run into this problem, despite the fact that it doesn't use timeout sets—Netty solves this problem with its `HashedWheelTimer`.[5] So with inspiration from Netty, we put together a hashed wheel timer for our C++ Thrift framework as well, and it has resolved the performance issue with variable per-request timeouts.

FUTURE IMPROVEMENTS ON NETTY 4

Nifty is currently running on Netty 3, which has been great for us so far, but we have a Netty 4 port ready that we'll be moving to very soon, now that v4 has been finalized. We are eagerly looking forward to some of the benefits the Netty 4 API will offer us.

One example of how we plan to make better use of Netty 4 is achieving better control over which thread manages a given connection. We hope to use this feature to allow server handler methods to start asynchronous client calls from the same I/O thread the server call is running on. This is something that specialized C++ servers are already able to take advantage of (for example, a Thrift request router).

Extending from that example, we also look forward to being able to build better client connection pools that are able to migrate existing pooled connections to the desired I/O worker thread, which wasn't possible in v3.

15.1.7 Facebook summary

With the help of Netty, we've been able to build a better Java server framework that nearly matches the performance of our fastest C++ Thrift server framework. We've migrated several of our existing major Java services onto Nifty already, solving some pesky stability and performance problems, and we've even started to feed back some ideas from Netty, and from the development of Nifty and Swift, into improving aspects of C++ Thrift.

On top of that, Netty has been a pleasure to work with and has made a lot of new features, like built-in SOCKS support for Thrift clients, simple to add.

But we're not done yet. We've got plenty of performance tuning work to do, as well as plenty of other improvements planned for the future. If you're interested in Thrift development using Java, be sure to keep an eye out!

---

[5] For more information about class `HashedWheelTimer` see http://netty.io/4.0/api/io/netty/util/HashedWheelTimer.html.

15.2 Netty at Twitter: Finagle

Jeff Smick, Software engineer at Twitter

Finagle is Twitter's fault-tolerant, protocol-agnostic RPC framework built atop Netty. All of the core services that make up Twitter's architecture are built on Finagle, from back ends serving user information, tweets, and timelines to front-end API endpoints handling HTTP requests.

15.2.1 Twitter's growing pains

Twitter was originally built as a monolithic Ruby on Rails application, semi-affectionately called The Monorail. As Twitter started to experience massive growth, the Ruby runtime and Rails framework started to become a bottleneck. From a compute standpoint, Ruby was relatively inefficient with resources. From a development standpoint, The Monorail was becoming difficult to maintain. Modifications to code in one area would opaquely affect another area. Ownership of different aspects of the code was unclear. Small changes unrelated to core business objects required a full deploy. Core business objects didn't expose clear APIs, which increased the brittleness of internal structures and the likelihood of incidents.

We decided to split The Monorail into distinct services with clear owners and clear APIs allowing for faster iteration and easier maintenance. Each core business object would be maintained by a specific team and be served by its own service. There was precedent within the company for developing on the JVM—a few core services had already been moved out of The Monorail and had been rebuilt in Scala. Our operations teams had a background in JVM services and knew how to operationalize them. Given that, we decided to build all new services on the JVM using either Java or Scala. Most services decided on Scala as their JVM language of choice.

15.2.2 The birth of Finagle

In order to build out this new architecture, we needed a performant, fault-tolerant, protocol-agnostic, asynchronous RPC framework. Within a service-oriented architecture, services spend most of their time waiting for responses from other upstream services. Using an asynchronous library allows services to concurrently process requests and take full advantage of the hardware. Although Finagle could have been built directly on top of NIO, Netty had already solved many of the problems we would have encountered, and it provided a clean, clear API.

Twitter is built atop several open source protocols, primarily HTTP, Thrift, Memcached, MySQL, and Redis. Our network stack would need to be flexible enough that it could speak any of these protocols and extensible enough that we could easily add more. Netty isn't tied to any particular protocol. Adding to it is as simple as creating the appropriate `ChannelHandlers`. This extensibility has led to many community-driven protocol implementations including SPDY,[6] PostrgreSQL, WebSockets, IRC, and AWS.

Netty's connection management and protocol agnosticism provided an excellent base from which Finagle could be built. But we had a few other requirements Netty couldn't satisfy out of the box, as those requirements were more high-level. Clients needed to connect and load balance across a cluster of servers. All services needed to export metrics (request rates, latencies, and so on) that provide valuable data for debugging service behavior. With a service-oriented architecture, a single request may go through dozens of services, making debugging performance issues nearly impossible without a Dapper-inspired tracing framework.[7] Finagle was built to solve these problems.

15.2.3 How Finagle works

Internally Finagle is very modular. Components are written independently and then stacked together. Each component can be swapped in or out, depending on the provided configuration. For instance, tracers all implement the same interface, so a tracer can be created to send tracing data to a local file, hold it in memory and expose a read endpoint, or write it out to the network.

At the bottom of a Finagle stack is a `Transport`. This class is a representation of a stream of objects that can be asynchronously read from and written to. `Transports` are implemented as Netty `ChannelHandlers` and inserted into the end of a `ChannelPipeline`. Messages come in from the wire where Netty picks them up, runs them through the `ChannelPipeline` where they're interpreted by a codec, and then sent to the Finagle `Transport`. From there Finagle reads the message off the `Transport` and sends it through its own stack.

For client connections, Finagle maintains a pool of transports across which it can load-balance. Depending on the semantics of the provided connection pool, Finagle will either request a new connection from Netty or reuse an existing one. When a new connection is requested, a Netty `ChannelPipeline` is created based on the client's codec. Extra `ChannelHandlers` are added to the `ChannelPipeline` for stats, logging, and SSL. The connection is then handed to a channel transport that Finagle can write to and read from.

On the server side, a Netty server is created and then given a `ChannelPipelineFactory` that manages the codec, stats, timeouts, and logging. The last `ChannelHandler` in a server's `ChannelPipeline` is a Finagle bridge. The bridge will watch for new incoming connections and create a new `Transport` for each one. The `Transport`

---

6 For more information about SPDY see https://github.com/twitter/finagle/tree/master/finagle-spdy. About PostgreSQL: https://github.com/mairbek/finagle-postgres. About WebSockets: https://github.com/sprsquish/finagle-websocket. About IRC: https://github.com/sprsquish/finagle-irc. About AWS: https://github.com/sclasen/finagle-aws.

7 Info on Dapper can be found at http://research.google.com/pubs/pub36356.html. The tracing framework is Zipkin, found at https://github.com/twitter/zipkin.

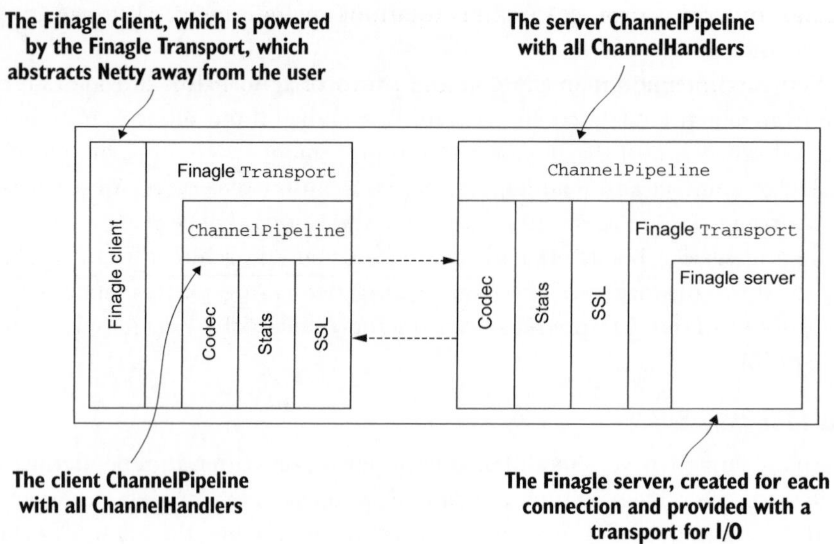
The Finagle client, which is powered by the Finagle Transport, which abstracts Netty away from the user
The server ChannelPipeline with all ChannelHandlers
Finagle client
Finagle Transport
ChannelPipeline
Codec
Stats
SSL
ChannelPipeline
Codec
Stats
SSL
Finagle Transport
Finagle server
The client ChannelPipeline with all ChannelHandlers
The Finagle server, created for each connection and provided with a transport for I/O

Figure 15.6 Netty use

wraps the new channel before it's handed to a server implementation. Messages are then read out of the `ChannelPipeline` and sent to the implemented server instance.

Figure 16.6 shows the relationship between the Finagle client and server.

NETTY/FINAGLE BRIDGE

This listing shows a static `ChannelFactory` with default options.

Listing 15.1 Setting up the `ChannelFactory`

```
object Netty3Transporter {
    val channelFactory: ChannelFactory =
        new NioClientSocketChannelFactory(
            Executor, 1 /*# boss threads*/, WorkerPool, DefaultTimer
        ){
             // no-op; unreleasable
             override def releaseExternalResources() = ()
        }
    val defaultChannelOptions: Map[String, Object] = Map(
        "tcpNoDelay" -> java.lang.Boolean.TRUE,
        "reuseAddress" -> java.lang.Boolean.TRUE
    )
}
```

Creates a ChannelFactory instance

Sets options used for new Channels

This `ChannelFactory` bridges a Netty channel with a Finagle `Transport` (stats code has been removed here for brevity). When invoked via `apply`, this will create a new

Channel and Transport. A Future is returned that is fulfilled when the Channel has either connected or failed to connect.

The next listing shows the ChannelConnector, which connects a Channel to a remote host.

Listing 15.2 Connecting to a remote host

```
private[netty3] class ChannelConnector[In, Out](
    newChannel: () => Channel,
    newTransport: Channel => Transport[In, Out]
) extends (SocketAddress => Future[Transport[In, Out]]) {
    def apply(addr: SocketAddress): Future[Transport[In, Out]] = {
        require(addr != null)
        val ch = try newChannel() catch {
            case NonFatal(exc) => return Future.exception(exc)
        }
        // Transport is now bound to the channel; this is done prior to
        // it being connected so we don't lose any messages.
        val transport = newTransport(ch)
        val connectFuture = ch.connect(addr)
        val promise = new Promise[Transport[In, Out]]
        promise setInterruptHandler { case _cause =>
           // Propagate cancellations onto the netty future.
           connectFuture.cancel()
        }
        connectFuture.addListener(new ChannelFutureListener {
            def operationComplete(f: ChannelFuture) {
                if (f.isSuccess) {
                    promise.setValue(transport)
                } else if (f.isCancelled) {
                    promise.setException(
                    WriteException(new CancelledConnectionException))
                } else {
                    promise.setException(WriteException(f.getCause))
                }
            }
        })
        promise onFailure { _ => Channels.close(ch)
        }
    }
}
```

If Channel creation fails, the exception is wrapped in a Future and returned.

Creates a new Transport with the Channel.

Connects the remote host asynchronously.

Creates a new Promise to be notified once the connect attempt is finished.

Handles the completion of the connect-Future by fulfilling the created promise.

This factory is provided a ChannelPipelineFactory, which is a channel factory and transport factory. The factory is invoked via the apply method. Once invoked, a new ChannelPipeline is created (newPipeline). That pipeline is used by the Channel-Factory to create a new Channel, which is then configured with the provided options (newConfiguredChannel). The configured channel is passed to a ChannelConnector as an anonymous factory. The connector is invoked and Future[Transport] is returned.

The following listing shows the details.[8]

Listing 15.3 Netty3-based transport

```
case class Netty3Transporter[In, Out](
    pipelineFactory: ChannelPipelineFactory,
    newChannel: ChannelPipeline => Channel =
        Netty3Transporter.channelFactory.newChannel(_),
    newTransport: Channel => Transport[In, Out] =
        new ChannelTransport[In, Out](_),
    // various timeout/ssl options
) extends (
    (SocketAddress, StatsReceiver) => Future[Transport[In, Out]]
){
    private def newPipeline(
        addr: SocketAddress,
        statsReceiver: StatsReceiver
    )={
        val pipeline = pipelineFactory.getPipeline()
        // add stats, timeouts, and ssl handlers
        pipeline
    }
    private def newConfiguredChannel(
        addr: SocketAddress,
        statsReceiver: StatsReceiver
    )={
        val ch = newChannel(newPipeline(addr, statsReceiver))
        ch.getConfig.setOptions(channelOptions.asJava)
        ch
    }
    def apply(
        addr: SocketAddress,
        statsReceiver: StatsReceiver
    ): Future[Transport[In, Out]] = {
        val conn = new ChannelConnector[In, Out](
            () => newConfiguredChannel(addr, statsReceiver),
            newTransport, statsReceiver)
        conn(addr)
    }
}
```

Creates a ChannelPipeline and adds the needed handlers

Creates a ChannelConnector, which is used internally

Finagle servers use `Listeners` to bind themselves to a given address. In this case the listener is provided a `ChannelPipelineFactory`, a `ChannelFactory`, and various options (excluded here for brevity). `Listener` is invoked with an address to bind to and a `Transport` to communicate over. A Netty `ServerBootstrap` is created and configured. Then an anonymous `ServerBridge` factory is created and passed to a `ChannelPipelineFactory`, which is given to the bootstrapped server. Finally the server is bound to the given address.

[8] Finagle source code is at https://github.com/twitter/finagle.

Now let's look at the Netty-based implementation of the `Listener`.

Listing 15.4 Netty-based `Listener`

```
case class Netty3Listener[In, Out](
    pipelineFactory: ChannelPipelineFactory,
    channelFactory: ServerChannelFactory
    bootstrapOptions: Map[String, Object], ... // stats/timeouts/ssl config
) extends Listener[In, Out] {
    def newServerPipelineFactory(
        statsReceiver: StatsReceiver, newBridge: () => ChannelHandler
    ) = new ChannelPipelineFactory {
        def getPipeline() = {
            val pipeline = pipelineFactory.getPipeline()
            ... // add stats/timeouts/ssl
            pipeline.addLast("finagleBridge", newBridge())
            pipeline
        }
    }
    def listen(addr: SocketAddress)(
        serveTransport: Transport[In, Out] => Unit
    ): ListeningServer =
        new ListeningServer with CloseAwaitably {
            val newBridge = () => new ServerBridge(serveTransport, ...)
            val bootstrap = new ServerBootstrap(channelFactory)
            bootstrap.setOptions(bootstrapOptions.asJava)
            bootstrap.setPipelineFactory(
                newServerPipelineFactory(scopedStatsReceiver, newBridge))
            val ch = bootstrap.bind(addr)
        }
}   }
```

Annotations: **Creates a ChannelPipelineFactory** (at `) = new ChannelPipelineFactory {`); **Adds the Bridge into the ChannelPipeline** (at `pipeline.addLast("finagleBridge", newBridge())`).

When a new channel is opened, the bridge creates a new `ChannelTransport` and hands it back to the Finagle server. This listing shows the code needed.[9]

Listing 15.5 Bridging Netty and Finagle

```
class ServerBridge[In, Out](
    serveTransport: Transport[In, Out] => Unit,
) extends SimpleChannelHandler {
    override def channelOpen(
        ctx: ChannelHandlerContext,
        e: ChannelStateEvent
    ){
        val channel = e.getChannel
        val transport = new ChannelTransport[In, Out](channel)
        serveTransport(transport)
        super.channelOpen(ctx, e)
    }
```

Annotation: **Creates a ChannelTransport to bridge to Finagle when a new Channel is opened** (at `val transport = new ChannelTransport[In, Out](channel)`).

[9] The complete source is at https://github.com/twitter/finagle.

```
    override def exceptionCaught(
        ctx: ChannelHandlerContext,
        e: ExceptionEvent
    ) { // log exception and close channel }
}
```

15.2.4 Finagle's abstraction

Finagle's core concept is a simple function (functional programming is the key here) from `Request` to `Future` of `Response`.

```
type Service[Req, Rep] = Req => Future[Rep]
```

This simplicity allows for very powerful composition. `Service` is a symmetric API representing both the client and the server. Servers implement the service interface. The server can be used concretely for testing, or Finagle can expose it on a network interface. Clients are provided an implemented service that's either virtual or a concrete representation of a remote server.

For example, we can create a simple HTTP server by implementing a service that takes an `HttpReq` and returns a `Future[HttpRep]` representing an eventual response.

```
val s: Service[HttpReq, HttpRep] = new Service[HttpReq, HttpRep] {
    def apply(req: HttpReq): Future[HttpRep] =
        Future.value(HttpRep(Status.OK, req.body))
}
Http.serve(":80", s)
```

A client is then provided a symmetric representation of that service.

```
val client: Service[HttpReq, HttpRep] =  Http.newService("twitter.com:80")?
val f: Future[HttpRep] = client(HttpReq("/"))?
f map { rep => processResponse(rep) }
```

This example exposes the server on port 80 of all interfaces and consumes from twitter.com port 80.

We can also choose not to expose the server and instead use it directly.

```
server(HttpReq("/")) map { rep => processResponse(rep) }
```

Here the client code behaves the same way but doesn't require a network connection. This makes testing clients and servers very simple and straightforward.

Clients and servers provide application-specific functionality. But there's a need for application-agnostic functionality as well. Timeouts, authentication, and statics are a few examples. `Filters` provide an abstraction for implementing application-agnostic functionality.

Filters receive a request and a service with which it is composed:

```
type Filter[Req, Rep] = (Req, Service[Req, Rep]) => Future[Rep]
```

Filters can be chained together before being applied to a service:

```
recordHandletime andThen
traceRequest andThen
collectJvmStats andThen
myService
```

This allows for clean abstractions of logic and good separation of concerns. Internally, Finagle heavily uses filters, which help to enhance modularity and reusability. They've proved valuable for testing as they can be unit-tested in isolation with minimal mocking.

Filters can modify both the data and type of requests and responses. Figure 16.7 shows a request making its way through a filter chain into a service and back out.

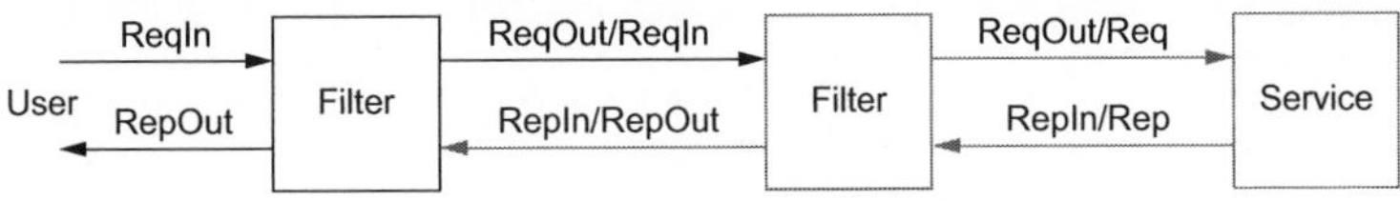

Figure 15.7 Request/response flow

We might use type modification for implementing authentication.

```
val auth: Filter[HttpReq, AuthHttpReq, HttpRes, HttpRes] =?
    { (req, svc) => authReq(req) flatMap { authReq => svc(authReq) } }

val authedService: Service[AuthHttpReq, HttpRes] = ...
val service: Service[HttpReq, HttpRes] =?
    auth andThen authedService
```

Here we have a service that requires an `AuthHttpReq`. To satisfy the requirement, a filter is created that can receive an `HttpReq` and authenticate it. The filter is then composed with the service yielding a new service that can take an `HttpReq` and produce an `HttpRes`. This allows us to test the authenticating filter in isolation from the service.

15.2.5 Failure management

We operate under the assumption of failure; hardware will fail, networks will become congested, network links fail. Libraries capable of extremely high throughput and extremely low latency are meaningless if the systems they're running on or are communicating with fail. To that end, Finagle is set up to manage failures in a principled way. It trades some throughput and latency for better failure management.

Finagle can balance load across a cluster of hosts implicitly using latency as a heuristic. Finagle clients locally track load on every host it knows about by counting the number of outstanding requests being dispatched to a single host. Given that, Finagle will dispatch new requests to hosts with the lowest load and, implicitly, the lowest latency.

Failed requests will cause Finagle to close the connection to the failing host and remove it from the load balancer. In the background, Finagle will continuously try to reconnect. The host will be re-added to the load balancer only after Finagle can reestablish a connection. Service owners are then free to shut down individual hosts without negatively impacting downstream clients.

15.2.6 Composing services

Finagle's service-as-a-function philosophy allows for simple but expressive code. For example, a user making a request for their home timeline touches a number of services, the core of which are the authentication service, timeline service, and tweet service. These relationships can be expressed succinctly.

Listing 15.6 Composing services via Finagle

```
val timelineSvc = Thrift.newIface[TimelineService](...)
val tweetSvc = Thrift.newIface[TweetService](...)
val authSvc = Thrift.newIface[AuthService](...)

val authFilter = Filter.mk[Req, AuthReq, Res, Res] { (req, svc) =>
    authSvc.authenticate(req) flatMap svc(_)
}

val apiService = Service.mk[AuthReq, Res] { req =>
    timelineSvc(req.userId) flatMap {tl =>
        val tweets = tl map tweetSvc.getById(_)
        Future.collect(tweets) map tweetsToJson(_)
    }
}

Http.serve(":80", authFilter andThen apiService)
```

Creates a client for each service

Creates new Filter to authenticate incoming requests

Creates a service to convert an authenticated timeline request to a JSON response

Starts a new HTTP server on port 80 using the authenticating filter and our service

Here we create clients for the timeline service, tweet service, and authentication service. A filter is created for authenticating raw requests. Finally our service is implemented, combined with the auth filter, and exposed on port 80.

When a request is received, the auth filter will attempt to authenticate it. A failure will be returned immediately without ever affecting the core service. Upon successful authentication, the `AuthReq` will be sent to the API service. The service will use the attached `userId` to look up the user's timeline via the timeline service. A list of tweet IDs is returned and then iterated over. Each ID is then used to request the associated tweet. Finally, the list of tweet requests is collected and converted into a JSON response.

As you can see, the flow of data is defined, and we leave the concurrency to Finagle. We don't have to manage thread pools or worry about race conditions. The code is clear and safe.

15.2.7 The future: Netty

We've been working closely with the Netty maintainers to improve on parts of Netty from which both Finagle and the wider community can benefit.[10] Recently, the internal structure of Finagle has been updated to be more modular, paving the way for an upgrade to Netty 4.

15.2.8 Twitter summary

Finagle has yielded excellent results. We've managed to dramatically increase the amount of traffic we can serve while reducing latencies and hardware requirements. For instance, after moving our API endpoints from the Ruby stack onto Finagle, we saw latencies drop from hundreds of milliseconds to tens while reducing the number of machines required from triple to single digits. Our new stack has enabled us to reach new records in throughput. As of this writing, our record tweets per second is 143,199.[11] That number would have been unthinkable on our old architecture.

Finagle was born out of a need to set Twitter up to scale out to billions of users across the entire globe at a time when keeping the service up for just a few million was a daunting task. Using Netty as a base, we were able to quickly design and build Finagle to manage our scaling challenges. Finagle and Netty handle every request Twitter sees.

15.3 Summary

This chapter provides insight into how large companies such as Facebook and Twitter build software using Netty to guarantee the highest levels of performance and flexibility.

- Facebook's Nifty project shows how Netty was used to replace an existing Thrift implementation by providing custom protocol encoders and decoders.
- Twitter's Finagle shows how you can build your own high-performance framework on top of Netty and enhance it with features such as load-balancing and failover.

We hope the case studies presented here will serve as sources of information and also inspiration as you build your next-generation masterpiece.

---

[10] "Netty 4 at Twitter: Reduced GC Overhead," https://blog.twitter.com/2013/netty-4-at-twitter-reduced-gc-overhead.

[11] "New Tweets per second record, and how!" https://blog.twitter.com/2013/new-tweets-per-second-record-and-how.

appendix *Introduction to Maven*

This appendix provides a basic introduction to Apache Maven (http://maven.apache.org/what-is-maven.html). After reading it, you should be able to jumpstart your own projects by reusing configurations from the book's samples.

Maven is a powerful tool and amply repays study. If you wish to learn more, you'll find the official documentation at http://maven.apache.org and an excellent set of freely available books in PDF format at www.sonatype.com/resources/books.

The first section presents basic Maven concepts. In the second, we'll illustrate these concepts using examples from the book's sample projects.

A.1 What is Maven?

Maven is a tool for managing Java projects, but not the kind used for resource planning and scheduling. Rather, it handles the tasks involved in managing a *physical* project, such as compilation, testing, packaging, documentation, and distribution.

Maven consists of the following:

- *A set of conventions addressing dependency management, directory layouts, and build workflows.* Standardizing on these conventions can greatly simplify development. For example, a common directory layout makes it much easier for developers to come up to speed on an unfamiliar project.
- *An XML schema for project configuration: the Project Object Model or POM.*[1] Every Maven project has a POM file,[2] named pom.xml by default, containing all the configuration information needed by Maven to manage the project.
- *A plugin architecture that delegates the execution of project tasks to external components.* This simplifies the update and extension of Maven's capabilities.

---

[1] The Maven Project, "What is a POM?," http://maven.apache.org/guides/introduction/introduction-to-the-pom.html.

[2] http://maven.apache.org/ref/3.2.5/maven-model/maven.html has a detailed descrption of the POM.

Building and testing our sample projects requires the use of only a subset of Maven's features. These are the ones we'll discuss in this appendix, leaving aside some that would certainly be required by projects intended for production deployment. The topics we'll cover include the following:

- Basic concepts: artifacts, coordinates, and dependencies
- Key elements and uses of the Maven project descriptor (pom.xml)
- The Maven build lifecycle and plugins

A.1.1 Installing and configuring Maven

You can download the appropriate Maven tar.gz or zip file for your system from http://maven.apache.org/download.cgi. Installation is simple: extract the contents of the archive to any folder of your choice (we'll call this <install_dir>). This will create the directory <install_dir>\apache-maven-3.3.3.[3]

Then,

- Set the environment variable `M2_HOME` to point to <install_dir>\apache-maven-3.3.3. This environment variable tells Maven where to find its configuration file, conf\settings.xml.
- Add `%M2_HOME%\bin` (or `${M2_HOME}/bin` on Linux) to your execution path, after which you can run Maven by executing `mvn` on the command line.

You shouldn't need to modify the default settings to compile and run the sample projects. The first time you execute `mvn`, it will create your local repository[4] and download numerous JAR files needed for basic operation from the central Maven repository. Finally, it will download the dependencies needed to build the current project (including the Netty JARs). Details on customizing settings.xml can be found at http://maven.apache.org/settings.html.

A.1.2 Basic Maven concepts

In the following sections we'll explain the most important concepts of Maven. Familiarity with these will enable you to understand the main elements of a POM file.

STANDARD DIRECTORY LAYOUTS

Maven defines a standard project directory layout.[5] Not all of its elements are required in every type of project and many can be overridden in the POM file if necessary. Table A.1 shows a basic WAR project, which differs from that of a JAR project by the presence of the directory src/main/webapp. When Maven builds the project, the contents of this directory (which contains the WEB-INF directory) will be placed at the

[3] At the time of this book's publication, the current Maven version was 3.3.3.

[4] By default this is the directory .m2/repository under your HOME directory on the current OS.

[5] Advantages of the Standard Directory Layout, http://maven.apache.org/guides/introduction/introduction-to-the-standard-directory-layout.html

root of the WAR file. The placeholder at the base of this tree, `${project.basedir}`, is a standard Maven property that identifies the root directory of the current project.

Table A.1 Basic project directory layout

<table>
<tr><th>Folder</th><th>Description</th></tr>
<tr><td>${project.basedir}</td><td>Project root</td></tr>
<tr><td>|---\src</td><td>Source root</td></tr>
<tr><td> |---\main</td><td>Program source</td></tr>
<tr><td> |---\java</td><td>Java sources</td></tr>
<tr><td> |---\resources</td><td>Properties files, XML schema, etc.</td></tr>
<tr><td> |---\webapp</td><td>Web application resources</td></tr>
<tr><td> |---\test</td><td>Test source root</td></tr>
<tr><td> |---\java</td><td>Java sources, such as JUnit test classes</td></tr>
<tr><td> |---\resources</td><td>Properties files, XML schema, etc.</td></tr>
<tr><td>|---\target</td><td>Files created by the build process</td></tr>
</table>

POM OUTLINE

This listing is an outline of a POM file from one of our sample projects. Only the top-level schema elements used are shown. Several of these are containers for other elements.

Listing A.1 POM outline

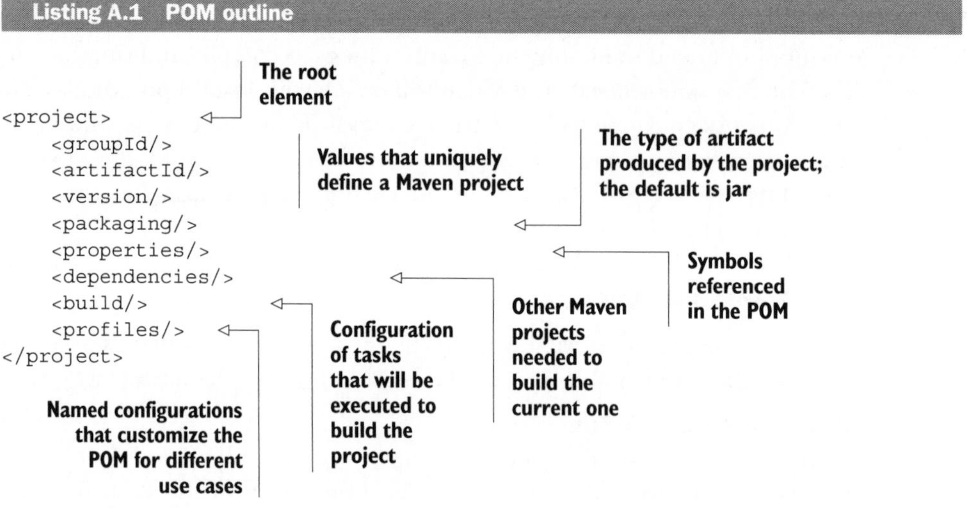

We'll discuss these elements in more detail in the remainder of this section.

ARTIFACT

Any object that can be uniquely identified by Maven's coordinate system (see the discussion of GAV coordinates that follows) is a Maven artifact. Mostly, artifacts are the files produced by building a Maven project; for example, a JAR. But a POM file that contains only definitions used by other POMs (which does not itself produce an artifact) is also a Maven artifact.

The type of a Maven artifact is specified by the `<packaging>` element of its POM file. The most frequently used values are `pom`, `jar`, `ear`, `war`, and `maven-plugin`.

POM FILE USE CASES

A POM file can be used in the following ways:

- *Default*—To build an artifact
- *Parent*—To provide a single source of configuration information to be inherited by child projects —projects that declare this POM file as their `<parent>`
- *Aggregator*—To build a group of projects, declared as `<modules>`, residing in directories after the current one, each with its own POM

A POM file serving as a parent or aggregator will have a `<packaging>` value of `pom`. Note that a single POM file may serve both functions.

GAV COORDINATES

The POM defines five elements, referred to as *coordinates*, that identify Maven artifacts. The acronym GAV refers to the initials of the three coordinates that must always be specified: `<groupId>`, `<artifactId>`, and `<version>`.

The coordinates which follow are listed in the order in which they would appear in a full coordinate expression.

1. `<groupId>` is a universally unique identifier for a project or group of projects. This is often the fully qualified Java package name used in the Java source code. Examples: io.netty, com.google.
2. `<artifactId>` identifies an artifact that is distinct with respect to a `<groupId>`. Examples: `netty-all`, `netty-handler`.
3. `<type>` refers to the type of the primary artifact associated with the project (corresponding to the `<packaging>` value in the artifact's POM). Its default value is `jar`. Examples: `pom`, `jar`, `war`, `ear`.
4. `<version>` identifies a version of an artifact. Examples: 1.1, 2.0-SNAPSHOT,[6] 4.0.31.Final.
5. `<classifier>` is used to distinguish artifacts that belong to the same POM but that were built differently from one another. Examples: javadoc, sources, jdk16, jdk17.

A full coordinate expression has the following format:

```
artifactId:groupId:packaging:version:classifier
```

The following GAV coordinates identify the JAR containing all of Netty's components.

```
io.netty:netty-all:4.0.31.Final
```

[6] See the "Snapshots and releases" discussion later in this section for more information about SNAPSHOT artifacts.

A POM file must declare the coordinates of the artifact it manages. A project with the following coordinates,

```
<groupId>io.netty</groupId>
<artifactId>netty-all</artifactId>
<version>4.0.31.Final</version>
<packaging>jar</packaging>
```

will produce an artifact whose name has the following format:

```
<artifactId>-<version>.<packaging>
```

In this case, it would produce this artifact:

```
netty-all-4.0.31.Final.jar
```

DEPENDENCIES

A project's dependencies are the external artifacts required to compile and execute it. In most cases, a dependency of your project will have its own dependencies. We refer to these as *transitive dependencies* of your project. A complex project can have a deep tree of dependencies; Maven provides a variety of facilities for understanding and managing it.[7]

A Maven `<dependency>`[8] is declared in the `<dependencies>` element of the POM.

```
<dependencies>
    <dependency>
        <groupId/>
        <artifactId/>
        <version/>
        <type/>
        <scope/>
        <systemPath/>
    </dependency>
    ...
</dependencies>
```

The GAV coordinates are always required in a `<dependency>` declaration.[9] The `<type>` and `<scope>` elements are required for values other than the defaults `jar` and `compile`, respectively.

The next code example is an extract from the top-level POM for our sample projects. Note the first entry, which declares a dependency on the Netty JAR referenced earlier.

---

[7] For example, on the command-line, execute "mvn dependency:tree" inside one of the project directories that has a POM file.

[8] Managing dependencies, http://maven.apache.org/guides/introduction/introduction-to-dependency-mechanism.html.

[9] See the following "Dependency management" section.

```
<dependencies>
    <dependency>
        <groupId>io.netty<groupId>
        <artifactId>netty-all</artifactId>
        <version>4.0.31.Final</version>
    </dependency>
    <dependency>
        <groupId>nia</groupId>
        <artifactId>util</artifactId>
        <version>1.0-SNAPSHOT</version>
    </dependency>
    <dependency>
        <groupId>com.google.protobuf</groupId>
        <artifactId>protobuf-java</artifactId>
        <version>2.5.0</version>
    </dependency>
    <dependency>
        <groupId>org.eclipse.jetty.npn</groupId>
        <artifactId>npn-api</artifactId>=
        <version>1.1.0.v20120525</version>
    </dependency>
    <dependency>
        <groupId>junit</groupId>
        <artifactId>junit</artifactId>
        <version>4.11</version>
        <scope>test</scope>
    </dependency>
</dependencies>
```

The `<scope>` element can have the following values:

- `compile`—Needed for compilation and execution (default)
- `runtime`—Needed for execution only
- `optional`—Not seen as a transitive dependency by other projects that reference the artifact produced by this project
- `provided`—Not to be included in the WEB-INF/lib directory of the WAR file produced by this POM
- `test`—Needed for compilation and execution of tests only
- `import`—This is discussed in the following "Dependency Management" section

The `<systemPath>` element is used to refer to an absolute location in the filesystem.

Maven's approach to managing project dependencies, which includes a repository protocol for storing and retrieving them, has revolutionized the way in which JAR files are shared across projects, effectively eliminating the problems that often arise when each developer on a project maintains a private lib directory.

DEPENDENCY MANAGEMENT

The `<dependencyManagement>` element of a POM contains `<dependency>` declarations that can be used by other projects. Child projects of such a POM will inherit these declarations automatically. Other projects can import them by using the `import` value of the `<scope>` element (discussed in a moment).

A project that references a <dependencyManagement> element can use the dependencies it declares without specifying their <version> coordinates. If a <version> is subsequently changed in that <dependencyManagement>, it will be picked up by all POMs that reference it.

In the following example, the version of Netty used is defined in the <properties> section of the POM and referenced in <dependencyManagement>.

```
<properties>
    <netty.version>4.0.31</netty.version>
    ...
    ...
</properties>
<dependencyManagement>
    <dependencies>
        <dependency>
            <groupId>io.netty</groupId>
            <artifactId>netty-all</artifactId>
            <version>${netty.version}</version>
        </dependency>
    </dependencies>
    ...
</dependencyManagement>
```

The dependency <scope> element has a special `import` value for this use: it imports the contents of the <dependencyManagement> element of an external POM (not declared as <parent>) into the <dependencyManagement> element of the current POM.

BUILD LIFECYCLES

A Maven build lifecycle is a well-defined process for building and distributing an artifact. There are three built-in build lifecycles: clean, default, and site. We'll discuss only the first two of these, used for cleaning and distributing a project, respectively.

A build lifecycle consists of a series of phases. The following is a partial list of the phases of the default build lifecycle:

- `validate`—Checks whether the project is correct and all necessary information is available
- `process-sources`—Processes the source code; for example, to filter any values
- `compile`—Compiles the source code of the project
- `process-test-resources`—Copies and processes the resources into the test destination directory
- `test-compile`—Compiles the test source code into the test destination directory
- `test`—Tests the compiled source code using a suitable unit testing framework
- `package`—Packages the compiled code in its distributable format, such as a JAR
- `integration-test`—Processes and deploys the package into an environment where integration tests can be run
- `verify`—Runs any checks to verify the package is valid and meets quality criteria

- `install`—Installs the package in the local repository, where it can be referenced as a dependency by other locally built projects
- `deploy`—Uploads the final artifact to a remote repository for sharing with other developers and projects

Executing one of these phases will invoke all preceding phases. For example,

```
mvn package
```

will execute `validate`, `compile`, and `test`, and will then assemble the artifact and place it in the project's target directory.

Executing

```
mvn clean install
```

will first remove all the results created by the previous build. Then it will run all of the default phases up to and including placing the artifact in your local repository file system.

Although our sample projects can be built with these simple commands, any serious work with Maven requires a detailed understanding of the lifecycle phases.[10]

PLUGINS

Although Maven coordinates execution of all the build lifecycle phases, it doesn't implement them directly. Rather, it delegates them to plugins,[11] which are artifacts of type `maven-plugin` (packaged as JAR files). The Apache Maven project provides plugins for all of the tasks defined by the standard build lifecycles; many more are produced by third parties to handle custom tasks of all kinds.

A plugin may have multiple internal steps, or goals, which can also be invoked individually. In a JAR project, for example, the default lifecycle is handled by the maven-jar-plugin, which maps the various phases of the build to its own goals and those of other plugins, as shown in table A.2.

Table A.2 Phases, plugins, and goals

Phase	plugin:goal
`process-resources`	`resources:resources`
`compile`	`compiler:compiler`
`process-test-resources`	`resources:testResources`
`test-compile`	`compiler:testCompile`

[10] "Introduction to the Build Lifecycle," http://maven.apache.org/guides/introduction/introduction-to-the-lifecycle.html.

[11] "Available Plugins," http://maven.apache.org/plugins/index.html.

Table A.2 Phases, plugins, and goals *(continued)*

Phase	plugin:goal
test	surefire:test
package	jar:jar
install	install:install
deploy	deploy:deploy

In our sample projects we use the following third-party plugin to execute our projects from the command line. Note that the declaration of a plugin, which is packaged as a JAR, uses the same GAV coordinates as those of a `<dependency>`.

```
<plugin>
    <groupId>org.codehaus.mojo</groupId>
    <artifactId>exec-maven-plugin</artifactId>
    <version>1.2.1</version>
</plugin>
```

PLUGIN MANAGEMENT

Like `<dependencyManagement>`, `<pluginManagement>` declares information that can be used by other POMs as shown in the next listing. But this is true only for child POMs, as there is no import declaration for plugins. As with dependencies, the `<version>` coordinate is inherited.

Listing A.2 PluginManagement

```
<build>
    <pluginManagement>
        <plugins>
            <plugin>
                <artifactId>maven-compiler-plugin</artifactId>
                <version>3.2</version>
                <configuration>
                    <source>1.7</source>
                    <target>1.7</target>
                </configuration>
            </plugin>
            <plugin>
                <groupId>org.codehaus.mojo</groupId>
                <artifactId>exec-maven-plugin</artifactId>
                <version>1.2.1</version>
            </plugin>
        </plugins>
    </pluginManagement>
</build>
```

Listing A.3 shows how a child of the POM fragment in listing A.2 could use the parent's `<pluginManagement>` configuration, referencing only the plugins it requires for its build. The child can also override any plugin configurations it needs to customize.

About Maven plugins

When declaring plugins produced by the Maven project, the `groupId` (org.apache .maven.plugins) may be omitted, as seen in the declaration of the `maven-compiler-plugin` in listing A.2. Furthermore, `artifactId`s beginning with "maven" are reserved for use by the Maven project. For example, a third party may provide a plugin with an `artifactId` of `exec-maven-plugin` but not `maven-exec-plugin`.

The POM defines a format for plugin configurations to which most plugins adhere.

Refer to Maven's "Guide to Configuring Plug-ins" (http://maven.apache.org/guides/mini/guide-configuring-plugins.html) for more information. This will help you to set up any plugins you want to use in your projects.

Listing A.3 Plugin inheritance

```
<build>
    <plugins>
        <plugin>
            <artifactId>maven-compiler-plugin</artifactId>
        </plugin>
        <plugin>
            <groupId>org.codehaus.mojo</groupId>
            <artifactId>exec-maven-plugin</artifactId>
        </plugin>
    </plugins>
</build>
```

PROFILES

A profile (defined within `<profiles>`) is a customized set of POM elements that can be enabled (activated) automatically or manually to alter the behavior of the POM. For example, you can define a profile that will set build parameters depending on the JDK version, OS, or target deployment environment (such as development, test, or production).

A profile is referenced explicitly with the command-line `-P` flag. The following example would activate a profile that customizes the POM for JDK 1.6.

```
mvn -P jdk16 clean install
```

REPOSITORIES

A Maven artifact repository[12] may be *remote* or *local*.

- A remote repository is a service from which Maven downloads dependencies referenced in POM files. If you have upload permission, then these dependencies

[12] See http://maven.apache.org/guides/introduction/introduction-to-repositories.html.

may include artifacts produced by your own projects. A vast number of open source Maven projects (including Netty) post their artifacts to publicly accessible Maven repositories.

- A local repository is a local directory that contains artifacts downloaded from remote repositories as well as artifacts you have built and installed on your local machine. It's normally placed under your home directory:

```
C:\Users\maw\.m2\repository
```

The physical directory structure of a Maven repository uses the GAV coordinates much as the Java compiler uses package names. For example, after Maven has downloaded the following dependency,

```
<dependency>
    <groupId>io.netty</groupId>
    <artifactId>netty-all</artifactId>
    <version>4.0.31.Final</version>
</dependency>
```

you'll find the following in your local repository:

```
.m2\repository
|---\io
    |---\netty
        |---\netty-all
            |---\4.0.31.Final
                    netty-all-4.0.31.Final.jar
                    netty-all-4.0.31.Final.jar.sha1
                    netty-all-4.0.31.Final.pom
                    netty-all-4.0.31.Final.pom.sha1
                    _maven.repositories
```

SNAPSHOTS AND RELEASES

Remote repositories generally define separate areas for artifacts that are under development and those that are stable or production releases. These are referred to as Snapshot and Release repositories, respectively.

An artifact with a `<version>` value ending in -SNAPSHOT will be treated as one that has not yet been released. Such an artifact can be uploaded to the repository repeatedly with the same `<version>` value. Each time it will be assigned a unique timestamp. When it is retrieved by a project, the latest instance will be downloaded.

An artifact `<version>` without a -SNAPSHOT suffix is treated as a release version. Usually, the repository policy allows a specific release version to be uploaded only once.

When you build a project that has a SNAPSHOT dependency, Maven will check to see whether there is a copy in the local repository. If there is not, it will attempt to retrieve it from the designated remote repository, in which case it will receive the artifact with the latest timestamp. If the artifact does exist locally and the current build is the first of the day, by default Maven will attempt to update the local copy.

This behavior can be configured using settings in Maven's configuration file (settings.xml) or with command-line flags.

A.2 POM examples

In this section we'll present POM examples to illustrate the topics discussed in the previous section.

A.2.1 A project POM

The following listing shows a POM that creates a JAR file for a simple Netty project.

Listing A.4 Standalone pom.xml

```
<?xml version="1.0" encoding="ISO-8859-15"?>
<project xmlns="http://maven.apache.org/POM/4.0.0"
    xmlns:xsi="http://www.w3.org/2001/XMLSchema-instance"
    xsi:schemaLocation="http://maven.apache.org/POM/4.0.0
    http://maven.apache.org/maven-v4_0_0.xsd">

    <modelVersion>4.0.0</modelVersion>

    <groupId>com.example</groupId>
    <artifactId>myproject</artifactId>
    <version>1.0-SNAPSHOT</version>

    <packaging>jar</packaging>

    <name>My Jar Project</name>

    <dependencies>
        <dependency>
            <groupId>io.netty</groupId>
            <artifactId>netty-all</artifactId>
            <version>4.0.31.Final</version>
        </dependency>
    </dependencies>

    <build>
        <plugins>
            <plugin>
                <groupId>org.apache.maven.plugins</groupId>
                <artifactId>maven-compiler-plugin</artifactId>
                <version>3.2</version>
                <configuration>
                    <source>1.7</source>
                    <target>1.7</target>
                </configuration>
            </plugin>
        </plugins>
    </build>
</project>
```

The project's GAV coordinates

The artifact produced by this project will be a JAR file (the default).

This POM declares only the Netty JAR as a dependency; a typical Maven project will have many dependencies.

The <build> section declares the plugins that will execute the build tasks. We have customized only the compiler plugin; for others we accept the defaults.

The artifact created by this POM will be a JAR file containing the classes compiled from the project's Java source code. The Netty JAR declared as a dependency will be added to the CLASSPATH during compilation.

The following are the basic Maven commands you would use with this POM:

- To create the JAR file in the project's build directory ("target"):

```
mvn package
```

- To store the JAR file in the local repository:

```
mvn install
```

- To post the JAR file to the global repository (if one has been defined):

```
mvn deploy
```

A.2.2 POM inheritance and aggregation

As we mentioned earlier, a POM can be used in several ways. Here we'll discuss its uses as a parent or aggregator.

POM INHERITANCE

A POM file may contain information to be inherited (and possibly overridden) by child projects.

POM AGGREGATION

An aggregator POM builds one or more subprojects that reside in directories below that of the POM. The subprojects, or `<modules>`, are identified by their directory names:

```
<modules>
    <module>Server</module>
    <module>Client</module>
</modules>
```

When building subprojects, Maven creates a *reactor* that calculates any dependencies existing among them to determine the order in which they have to be built. Note that an aggregator POM may or may not be the parent of the projects it declares as modules. (Each subproject may declare a different POM as its `<parent>`.)

The POM for the Echo client/server project in chapter 2 is both a parent and an aggregator.[13] The chapter2 directory, under the sample code root directory, has the contents shown in the next listing.

[13] It is also a child of the nia-samples-parent POM above it, whose `<dependencyManagement>` it inherits and passes to its own child projects.

Listing A.5 chapter2 directory tree

```
chapter2
    |---pom.xml                               <-- The parent/
    |---\Client                               <-- aggregator POM
        |---pom.xml
        |---\src                                  Client
            |---\main                             module
                |---\java
                    |---\nia
                        |---\chapter2
                            |---\echoclient
                                EchoClient.java
                                EchoClientHandler.java
    |---\Server                                        <-- Server
        |---pom.xml                                        module
        |---\src
            |---\main
                |---\java
                    |---\nia
                        |---\chapter2
                            |---\echoserver
                                EchoServer.java
                                EchoServerHandler.java
```

The packaging type of the root-level POM, shown in listing A.6, is `<pom>`, which signifies that it doesn't itself produce an artifact. Rather, it provides configuration information to projects that declare it as `<parent>`, such as the Client and Server projects. It's also an aggregator, which means you can build its `<modules>` by running `mvn install` in the chapter2 directory.

Listing A.6 Parent and aggregator POM: echo-parent

```
<project>
    <modelVersion>4.0.0</modelVersion>

    <parent>
        <groupId>nia</groupId>
        <artifactId>nia-samples-parent</artifactId>
        <version>1.0-SNAPSHOT</version>
    </parent>

    <artifactId>chapter2</artifactId>
    <packaging>pom</packaging>
    <name>2. Echo Client and Server</name>

    <modules>
        <module>Client</module>
        <module>Server</module>
    </modules>

    <properties>
        <echo-server.hostname>localhost</echo-server.hostname>
        <echo-server.port>9999</echo-server.port>
    </properties>
```

<parent> declares the samples-parent POM as the parent of this POM.

A <property> value can be overridden on the command line by using a Java system property (-D). Properties are inherited by child projects.

<modules> declares the directories under the parent POM that contain Maven projects to be built by this POM.

```
    <dependencies>
        <dependency>
            <groupId>io.netty</groupId>
            <artifactId>netty-all</artifactId>
        </dependency>
    </dependencies>

    <build>
        <plugins>
            <plugin>
                <artifactId>maven-compiler-plugin</artifactId>
            </plugin>
            <plugin>
                <artifactId>maven-failsafe-plugin</artifactId>
            </plugin>
            <plugin>
                <artifactId>maven-surefire-plugin</artifactId>
            </plugin>
            <plugin>
                <groupId>org.codehaus.mojo</groupId>
                <artifactId>exec-maven-plugin</artifactId>
            </plugin>
        </plugins>
    </build>
</project>
```

The parent's <dependencies> element is inherited by child projects.

The parent's <plugins> element is inherited by child projects.

Thanks to Maven's support for inheritance, the Server and Client POMs don't have very much work to do. The following listing shows the Server POM. (The Client POM is virtually identical.)

Listing A.7 Echo-server POM

```
<project>
    <parent>
        <groupId>nia</groupId>
        <artifactId>chapter2</artifactId>
        <version>1.0-SNAPSHOT</version>
    </parent>

    <artifactId>echo-server</artifactId>

    <build>
        <plugins>
            <plugin>
                <groupId>org.codehaus.mojo</groupId>
                <artifactId>exec-maven-plugin</artifactId>
                <executions>
                    <execution>
                        <id>run-server</id>
                        <goals>
                            <goal>java</goal>
                        </goals>
                    </execution>
                </executions>
                <configuration>
```

<parent> declares the parent POM.

<artifactId> must be declared as it is unique to the subproject. <groupId> and <version>, if not defined, are inherited from the parent POM.

The exec-maven-plugin executes arbitrary commands from the Maven command line; here we use it to run the Echo server.

```
                    <mainClass>nia.echo.EchoServer</mainClass>
                    <arguments>
                        <argument>${echo-server.port}</argument>
                    </arguments>
                </configuration>
            </plugin>
        </plugins>
    </build>
</project>
```

The exec-maven-plugin executes arbitrary commands from the Maven command line; here we use it to run the Echo server.

This POM is very small because it inherits so much information from its parent and grandparent POMs (and there is even a great-grandparent POM, the Maven Super-POM). Note, for example, the use of the `${echo-server.port}` property, inherited from the parent POM.

The POM executed by Maven after all inherited information is assembled and all active profiles are applied is referred to as the "effective POM." To see it, run the following Maven command in the same directory as any POM file:

```
mvn help:effective-pom
```

A.3 Maven command-line

The syntax of the `mvn` command is as follows:

```
mvn [options] [<goal(s)>] [<phase(s)>]
```

For details on its usage, as well as more information on many of the topics we have discussed in this appendix, Sonatype's "Maven: The Complete Reference" is a good resource.[14]

Table A.3 shows the `mvn` command-line options, which can be displayed by executing

```
mvn --help
```

Table A.3 mvn command-line arguments

Option	Description
`-am,--also-make`	If project list is specified, also build projects required by the list
`-amd,--also-make-dependents`	If project list is specified, also build projects that depend on projects on the list
`-B,--batch-mode`	Run in non-interactive (batch) mode
`-b,--builder <arg>`	The id of the build strategy to use
`-C,--strict-checksums`	Fail the build if checksums don't match

[14] See http://books.sonatype.com/mvnref-book/pdf/mvnref-pdf.pdf.

Table A.3 mvn command-line arguments *(continued)*

Option	Description
-c,--lax-checksums	Warn if checksums don't match
-cpu,--check-plugin-updates	Ineffective, only kept for backward compatibility
-D,--define <arg>	Define a system property
-e,--errors	Produce execution error messages
-emp,--encrypt-master-password <arg>	Encrypt master security password
-ep,--encrypt-password <arg>	Encrypt server password
-f,--file <arg>	Force the use of an alternate POM file (or directory with pom.xml)
-fae,--fail-at-end	Only fail the build afterwards; allow all non-impacted builds to continue
-ff,--fail-fast	Stop at first failure in reactorized builds
-fn,--fail-never	NEVER fail the build, regardless of project result
-gs,--global-settings <arg>	Alternate path for the global settings file
-h,--help	Display help information
-l,--log-file <arg>	Log file to where all build output will go
-llr,--legacy-local-repository	Use Maven 2 Legacy Local Repository behavior; that is, no use of _remote.repositories. Can also be activated by using -Dmaven.legacyLocalRepo=true.
-N,--non-recursive	Do not recurse into subprojects
-npr,--no-plugin-registry	Ineffective, only kept for backward compatibility
-npu,--no-plugin-updates	Ineffective, only kept for backward compatibility
-nsu,--no-snapshot-updates	Suppress SNAPSHOT updates
-o,--offline	Work offline
-P,--activate-profiles <arg>	Comma-delimited list of profiles to activate
-pl,--projects <arg>	Comma-delimited list of specified reactor projects to build instead of all projects. A project can be specified by [groupId]:artifactId or by its relative path.
-q,--quiet	Quiet output - only show errors
-rf,--resume-from <arg>	Resume reactor from specified project
-s,--settings <arg>	Alternate path for the user settings file

Table A.3 mvn command-line arguments

Option	Description
`-T,--threads <arg>`	Thread count, for instance 2.0C where C is core multiplied
`-t,--toolchains <arg>`	Alternate path for the user toolchains file
`-U,--update-snapshots`	Forces a check for missing releases and updated snapshots on remote repositories
`-up,--update-plugins`	Ineffective, only kept for backward compatibility
`-V,--show-version`	Display version information WITHOUT stopping build
`-v,--version`	Display version information
`-X,--debug`	Produce execution debug output

A.4 Summary

In this appendix we presented an introduction to Apache Maven, covering its basic concepts and principal use cases. We illustrated these by drawing on examples from the book's sample projects.

Our goals are to help you to better understand how the projects are built and to provide a starting point for independent development.

index

Symbols

A

B

C

D

O

P

Q

R

S

T

U

W

Z